WIDOWS
AND
WIDOWHOOD

OTHER BOOKS BY JAMES A. PETERSON

Married Love in the Middle Years

Love in the Later Years (with Barbara Payne)

WIDOWS
AND
WIDOWHOOD

A Creative Approach to Being Alone

James A. Peterson
and
Michael P. Briley

ASSOCIATION PRESS | NEW YORK

WIDOWS AND WIDOWHOOD

Copyright © 1977 by James A. Peterson and Michael P. Briley

Published by Association Press, 291 Broadway, New York, N.Y. 10007

International Standard Book Number: 0-8096-1897-4

Library of Congress Catalog Card Number: 76-44250

Library of Congress Cataloging in Publication Data

Peterson, James Alfred.
Widows and widowhood.

Bibliography: p. 237
Includes index.
1. Widows—United States.   I. Briley, Michael,   II. Title.
HQ1058.5.U5P47   301.42'86   76-44250
ISBN 0-8096-1897-4

Printed in the United States of America
Designed by The Etheredges

CONTENTS

PREFACE   *ix*

Chapter One
THE SIGN ON THE MANTEL   *1*

Chapter Two
THE NUMBING ALONENESS   *11*

Chapter Three
WORKING THROUGH THE SEPARATION   *31*

Chapter Four
THE NEW YOU   *50*

Chapter Five
FINDING A NEW WORLD   *63*

Chapter Six
THE BEST TIME OF THE YEAR   *83*

Chapter Seven
A NEW WORLD OF PEOPLE   *109*

Chapter Eight
YOU AND YOUR FAMILY   *126*

Chapter Nine
THE GROWTH OF THE SPIRIT   *151*

Chapter Ten
TO SLEEP ALONE *OR* . . .   *168*

Chapter Eleven
NOT BY BREAD ALONE, *BUT* . . .   *184*

Chapter Twelve
LIFE CAN BE FULFILLING   *212*

NOTES   *229*

BIBLIOGRAPHY   *237*

INDEX   *239*

PREFACE

A special U.S. Bureau of the Census report states that in this country, as of March 1971, there were almost ten million widows over the age of 55. Had the Census Bureau included those below that age the total would certainly have exceeded ten million. These women have the lowest income of any segment of our population, and the minority women among them have an even lower standard of living. There is no national organization of widows. Organizations such as the church or others having to do with the aging have few programs for them. They constitute a population as large as the total that lives in California, but they are a forgotten group. A great many of them are utterly alone, isolated, shut off from the main stream of social life.

This book addresses itself to the economic, social and psychological problems of this neglected group. Our sources of information come from research, from interviews, and from case studies. A goodly portion of the growing literature on death and dying, on grief work, and on consumer education is relevant to our purpose and is included as part of a comprehensive look at ways in which the widow can enrich her life and refurbish her spirit. Much of the ancient wisdom of humanity is relevant and some parts of the book find their sources in poetry and the Bible. The senior author has spent thirty-five years dealing with psychological and interactional problems of widows and some insights come from that experience.

The authors are aware of their dependence upon pioneers in this field whose contributions have created the foundation for this work. Those who should have special mention are Helena Lopata, Eric Lindemann, Carol Barrett, Felix Baredo, Lynn Caine, Barbara Payne, and James Mathieu. All have added sensitivity to our responses. The list is not long because this is a neglected field for both research and therapy.

While this book is directed to widows, it is true that widowers and anyone else suffering separation trauma will find much that is relevant. The purpose of the book is not only to marshal relevant information but also to use those resources in helping widows to construct their futures.

Writing any book requires a great deal of concentration, during which time significant others are often required to have great patience and understanding. Therefore, we are especially grateful to our wives who gave us that time and, beyond that, much critical insight.

WIDOWS

AND

WIDOWHOOD

CHAPTER ONE

THE SIGN ON
THE MANTEL

Jean is an attractive, youngish woman of forty-seven, auburn-haired and chic. Her engaging conversation is punctuated with tears and laughter, wisdom and whimsy, knowledge and wonder. She exudes a fullness of life. Emblazoned on a large-lettered sign on her living-room mantel is the single word "JOY." What of this sign? Is it somehow unlikely that such a message would be displayed by a woman who has suffered—more perhaps than most women—the soul-wrenching cataclysmic pain of widowhood? Not at all. This greeting to her friends means precisely what it says . . . and more. It is a sign of profound readjustment, renewed self-confidence, heightened self-awareness and hope. It attests that personal growth may result from working through deep grief. Such progress is a tribute to humankind. It is proof that we are wonderfully resilient and curiously strong creatures.

The JOY sign can be seen as a milestone of widowhood for Jean. She and her late husband had been deeply in love, with each the center of the other's life. "This was the most mature relationship I have ever known about," she says. "Frank was a well-put together guy: moral, ethical, strong emotionally. He had a lot of quality. He was the only man I've ever loved, and he'll always be a part of me." Every morning when they awakened, she recalls, the first words they exchanged were "I love you."

Considering the depth of the marriage bond, her ongoing recovery is dramatic. Jean's coming to life again as a single person can be an inspiration to others who suffer the pain of widowhood. That is what the JOY sign is all about. Yet Jean and millions of other women like her know it is not easy. They have learned from experience that touching the depths of despond and helplessness —elicited by true grieving—is a necessary step toward building a new and different life. Recovery will come, but it is not a quick or simple process, as Jean's bereavement attests.

She remembers very clearly at least part of that fateful Friday night five years ago. She was knitting a sweater for Frank, putting the finishing touches on it. They were planning to leave the next day for a long-awaited vacation in Mexico. He was two hours late getting home, and she was beginning to be concerned. It was unlike him to be late without calling.

Then the telephone rang.

"This is the university medical center," a crisply efficient female voice said. "Mrs. Lewis?"

"Yes."

"Are you alone?"

"No, my daughter is here. What's wrong?"

"It's your husband. He apparently has had a heart attack. Can you come over?"

"Is he all right? What's his condition?"

"Please just get here as soon as you can."

"Is he grave?"

"Yes."

At that point, she knew he was dead. Dazed, she got her teenage daughter into the car. When they arrived at the hospital, Jean was informed that Frank had died. She wanted to see him. That was impossible, she was told, because the body already was on its way to the morgue.

From then on, her recollections of that night are cloudy and obscure. She recalls that "all hell broke loose." She does remember that she raged and shrieked at her daughter. She pulled a telephone out of the wall. She collapsed.

Even though she was in a state of semishock those first few days after Frank's death, she was able to cope with the funeral arrangements, which in themselves meant taking on added difficulties. She was thrown into conflict with her in-laws about the instructions Frank had left regarding his death. He had wished to have his body cremated. This was counter to his family's religious beliefs, and they were pressuring Jean to allow the body to be buried. She finally told the relatives that she was going to comply with her husband's wishes and that if they didn't let her alone she would have a private funeral, excluding them. The rites were then conducted according to Frank's wishes.

Jean says that her two daughters, aged twenty-one and eighteen respectively, were most helpful to her, particularly in the early days of her bereavement. She was dependent on them for the comfort and support they could provide. Two or three days after Frank's death, she said to her older daughter, "I'll bet you're afraid you'll be stuck with me for the rest of your life." Her daughter was silent, for she, too, was anguished. "I need you now," Jean remembers telling her, "but you can leave in about six months, I'll be all right then."

"During those first few months, I felt my grief very deeply," Jean recalls. "It was very hard on my daughters. Sometimes they were frightened during my periods of deep grieving because I was 'out of it.' I cried and cried. There were times when I moaned very deeply. That would have frightened anyone. The pain was almost intolerable. I couldn't laugh or smile."

Some friends, too, were very supportive, she remembers. "Particularly a couple of women friends of long standing who were capable of being compassionate even at my worst times." She consulted a psychiatrist who was a family friend and who knew the intensity of her bereavement. "He told me the grief process would take a very long time. This was solace. It helped sustain me because it showed me there were other persons who really understood."

Some others, however, were not so perceptive or comforting. Says Jean: "About three months after Frank died, I began to have periods when I was furious at him for dying. I'd say to myself, 'What right did he have to die? He said he'd never leave me. But he did leave me, and at a critical point in my life—just as I was approaching middle age. God, I'd love to talk to him and tell him how angry I am for what he has done to me.' When I'd share these feelings with other people, they'd become upset about my anger and my grief. They'd ask, 'Why do you say that? It's not even logical.' The point is, if you want to help people grieve you must let them cry and be angry and be illogical. But people don't want to come to grips with death. In our society, there seems to be no room for sincere, honest expression of emotion."

A few months after Frank's death, Jean returned to work. "I was teaching a class at the time, and I broke down and cried in front of the group on more than one occasion. I worked about five months and found that I just couldn't function. The added stresses of the job were just too much for me at the time. I had all sorts of fantasies. I had to escape. I even thought of running away to a commune to live another kind of life."

Friends and associates advised her against quitting her job. "But I knew it was right, and it was," Jean says. Unemployed for the next six months, she bought a trailer on a lot overlooking a beach in Mexico and often went there alone, learning to find peace in the solitude. She traveled to Europe with a couple who had been friends of her and her late husband. She found enjoyment in the trip. She renewed her interest in sewing and became active in folk dancing, a new pastime for her. The only reason she returned to work at all was financial need.

About a year after Frank's death, it occurred to Jean that she might remarry some day. She started dating an eligible bachelor she met through her cousin. The relationship lasted several months, but it didn't work out, and she now knows why. In her mind, she was seeking to re-create the life she had led with Frank. But neither this man nor others she dated could measure up. Later, she went with another man for a longer time. Eventually, he proposed to her. "I thought to myself that there are not many guys around. He's a good man, maybe it will work." But this time, the man himself began to realize that Jean had not finished her grief and had not cut her deep emotional ties with Frank, with whom she was still in love. She was relieved when he ended the relationship. At this point, Jean is in no hurry to remarry. She feels, in fact, that she might not remarry, after all.

If the ancient dictum of "know thyself" is indeed among the noblest and most essential of human aspirations, then Jean's confrontation with her profound loss is exemplary. Today, she can look back and describe her widowhood—the crises and mysteries and pains of it, and the resources with which she began and then sustained her recovery. Her telling of the hurts and the healing is beautifully articulate.

"Death is incomprehensible to me. I don't understand it. My grief was at its most intense during the first year, and weathering that was the hardest. But I can tell you, the grief period is not limited to one year. It's an ongoing process. Each subsequent loss in life, such as the separation from my daughter when she went away to school, can retrigger lapses into grief. Loss does not go away. Even now, I'm not quite capable of handling highly stressful situations that arise in my work.

"But grieving is made easier by the presence of persons you love. Yet it's hard on them. When I was driving with my daughter not long ago, we saw an old lady at a bus stop, poorly dressed, very much alone, pathetic. I said to my daughter, 'Will I be alone like that when I'm old?' She answered, 'I've always been there before when you needed me, haven't I?'"

"First and foremost, it was the children who helped me. Nothing they could ever do would alienate me from them."

Regardless of how crushing her grief became, she never became suicidal. Despite everything, she thinks she probably has been more capable of coping than many other widows because of her resources—including her devoted daughters and supportive friends, her education and the previous personal development which that implies, and her professional experience as a social worker that assures the opportunity for rewarding work. "Widowhood and its problems must be approached with the strengths and resources of each individual," she says.

Now Jean is at the point where she can enjoy herself when

alone and when she is with others. She can spend a pleasant week end by herself at home, sewing and reading and engaging in other activities without becoming depressed. She also finds happiness in inviting guests into the home that she shared with Frank for so many years. Pleasure for her can mean going to the opera or the theater alone, as well as spending an evening in the homes of married friends. She cherishes her ability to laugh again, to maintain a close relationship with her daughters, and to enjoy old friends and make new ones.

"I feel I'm coming into a new phase now, taking one day at a time. Now—today—is beautiful." Thus, her message to the world, the sign in the window that reads JOY.

There is much that we can learn from Jean and her ongoing recovery from bereavement. For example, she understands the nature of grieving and realizes the necessity for it. She is able to recognize and accept help from those who would give it. She understands the need to reach out to family and friends. She is aware of her own strengths and has been able to muster them. She has been able to make decisions that are right for her even against the well-intentioned advice of others.

Is Jean a typical widow? The answer must decidedly be No. There is no such person as a typical widow, any more than there is a "typical" wife or, for that matter, any typical person. When Jean said that widowhood must be approached with the strengths and resources of the individual, she spoke with wisdom. Each widow who copes successfully does so somewhat differently. Yet among those who become widows, there are some common denominators, common reactions, and common needs to be satisfied. In forthcoming pages, we will speak more of Jean and present other case histories. In so doing, we will identify many common needs and problems of widowhood and see the various ways they can be met to ensure recovery.

As a widow, this book is addressed to you, to make a new and rewarding life. It is a book for women—and men—who have lost their life companions; for the young and old alike who have been bereaved. There are many losses in life, and perhaps the greatest of these is to lose the one who walked with us, holding our hand, and who held us close when we most needed it. The sense of loss is monumental. It leaves us with such emptiness and loneliness that often there seems no hope that the dawn will ever come again. Still, as we have just seen in the case of Jean—and undoubtedly in the lives of friends and acquaintances who have been widowed—there is hope.

There are moments when the widow feels essentially alone in her agony, but she really is not. The experience is most common. In fact, the statistics are striking. There are some 12 million widows and widowers in the United States today—10 million widows and 2 million widowers. This disproportion results of course from the difference in life expectancy. On the average, women live about 7½ years longer than men. About 75,000 men become widowers before age 34, while some 135,000 women are widowed in these early years. After that, the disparity becomes higher and higher. It has been found that after age 55, there are some 1.7 million widowers compared to 8 million widows. A half-century ago, the ratio of widowers to widows was 1 to 2; today, it has grown to 1 to 4. It has been estimated that 3 out of 4 women now married in the United States will eventually become widows. Not only are there more widows than ever before but their numbers continue to grow each year. That this population explosion of widows is occurring is of particular concern for several reasons:

First, it comes at a time in our history when great social change is a way of life. Technology and other forces of the twentieth century literally are revolutionizing our life-styles. For most of us, the pace of life is faster and more frantic than our forebears could have dreamed. There are generation gaps, credibility gaps, social upheavals, and a questioning of the old values. Alvin Toffler has summed up the maelstrom succinctly with the descriptive catchall title of his best-selling book, *Future Shock*. All of us must cope with change if we are to maintain our physical and mental health and continue our personal growth. It is this "brave new world" of sorts that forms the environment for the person who is widowed today. In addition to the already considerable stresses that we have come to expect, the widow is thrust into another sort of "future shock." Suddenly, she is stripped of her longtime role and status as wife, and she must learn to cope alone.

A second specific aspect of the modern widow's dilemma is the changed structure of the family in American society. It is rare these days that upon the death of her mate a woman takes immediate and automatic refuge in the extended family. This is so, partially at least, because families—for better or worse—have become "nuclearized"—that is, today's family usually consists of mother, father, and children. Gone are the days when three or four generations—brothers and sisters and even cousins—lived under the same roof or at least in close proximity. Today, the greater or extended family often is farflung across the land because, increasingly, we are a mobile people. The net result is that today's widow tends to be on her own more than in the past.

Third, with the dawning of women's liberation, the very roles, expectations, and identities of women are being questioned and redefined. Becoming a widow today is fraught with more uncertainties, perhaps, than ever before.

Yet the astonishing and tragic fact is that society has paid little attention to the plight of its growing number of widows. There is no justification for this less-than-benign neglect. We need not belabor ourselves here with its causes, except to mention some factors that we will discuss later in more depth. One reason for the neglect of widows can likely be traced to the pervasive taboos in our culture about the nature of death. Society is uncomfortable in the presence of death. Instead of facing it as an ultimate fact of life, our culture tends to ignore or even deny it. Many of us are uneasy in the presence of tears and grieving. It is almost a natural reaction for people to tell a bereaved to "buck up," "be strong," "don't cry." But this does not speak of the widow's need to cry and to grieve. There is little consolation for most widows in such cheery little exhortations.

Further, there exists only a rudimentary "psychology of grief." That is, there has not yet been sufficient research to develop a comprehensive body of knowledge to help people grieve effectively. We have amassed, and are continuing to develop, exhaustive data and techniques of child psychology, for example.

But as we all know, grief and loss are as common in our society as child-rearing.

Yet happily there is an awakening to the problems of death, dying, loss, grief. In recent years, some distinguished researchers have turned their interests and their talents to these subjects. A few are specializing in the various aspects of widowhood. When this research is translated into terms that speak to the needs and problems of everyday life, there is much benefit to be realized by widows.

There are multiple problems of widows that we will explore together in these pages, but the overwhelming one is bereavement, the loss and loneliness that engulfs us when a mate departs. There are no arms to hold us and no voice that comes from the empty chair beside us. This period of intense sorrow is essential to recovery. It cannot be foreshortened. We call going through the valley of the shadow *grief work*. In one sense, it is a tribute to the worth of the departed. If we had not been so close, the sundering would not be so painful. It is a tribute to what we had. But grieving also can paralyze us and frighten us. Depression is intermingled with sorrow. The death of a mate ends a significant role for the survivor. It changes the life-style and imposes new obligations that lonely people find difficult, if not impossible, to manage. We will attempt to consider all these problems and review the helps that are available from within one's self and from external sources.

Recovery and a full, rich life now and in the future are dependent on many ingredients, not the least of which is physical well-being. But the vast majority of Americans do not pay much attention to simple pathways to good health. Researchers in exercise, nutrition, and health rules have much to offer. But woman or man does not live by bread or vitamins or exercise alone. There are components of life that are purely mental or emotional. So our mental health is critically important. Maintaining some sort of work life or strong avocational involvement ensures interest in life. Development of mental outreaches, such as those that education and cultural pursuits afford, is rewarding. The loss of a mate can be a maturing experience in that one must build a new life. That new life can have many advantages, and it is important for each person to recognize and capitalize on them. For instance, there is a new freedom from some obligations and a freedom to go places and do things. Indeed, there is freedom to laugh and smile again, and these are more important for mental health than many might realize.

CHAPTER TWO

THE NUMBING

ALONENESS

Every day of our lives, we stitch the design of our psychological shroud. What we are on the last day of our lives is the totality of all that has happened to us and every response we have made. There is at that moment a splendid uniqueness. No single stamp of heredity explains the varied and singular personalities of human beings. Our reactions to the catastrophic loss of a mate are likewise varied and singular. They depend on our psychological and spiritual resources, on the quality of the relationship that has been broken, and on the quality of supports around us. There are some recurrent human themes in the process of adjusting to a final separation, and while these explain some of our reactions, we must be careful not to try to fit these themes tightly around any single human being. Sometimes grief elicits the highest achievement of human dignity. No one can remember the profound pride and triumph of Coretta King as she marched head high behind the simple casket of her husband without wonder at the resources she exhibited. Her later commitment to her husband's work shows how magnificently Mrs. King turned tragedy into triumph. At that same time, we attended a family funeral where the widow could not bear her pain and later committed suicide. There is the heroic widow, the "merry" widow, the depressed widow. In this chapter, we will discover those common reactions that will help all widows identify their feelings and adjust to them. We will look at contrasts. But always we hope to remember that every man and woman is an island with distinctive emotional shorelines. Many reading this book will say, "Yes, I am like that . . . yet there is something else." To deal with the "something else" is critical. We hope to help.

THE DEVASTATED PERSON

We say *the devastated person* advisedly because much of what we describe applies not just to the widow or the widower but to all those persons who are subjected to final separation, whether by death or legal action. When there has been an open and destructive conflict, divorce involves other emotional problems. But particularly in those cases when one mate has been unaware of fundamental friction, and is suddenly confronted with a demand for divorce, the impact can be as devastating as the death of a spouse. In general, a divorced person recoups sooner, remarries sooner, and reorganizes himself or herself more quickly, but this is not always the case. The material in this section applies to all final separations that result in profound sadness and disorganization. Phyllis has given us permission to share her story because she thinks it may help others.

Phyllis was forty-six when her husband's employer called to tell her that John (her husband) had suffered a major heart attack and had died immediately. They had had one of those good marriages that are characterized as vital and fun. In their marriage, their relationship came first, and John often maneuvered his day so that they could have extra time together. They were a childless couple, but the quality of their sharing was such that they did not miss children very much. Phyllis had worked hard the first fifteen years of their marriage, and because of her employment, they were able to achieve almost all of their goals: a house on a hill, travel over the world, sharing in such recreational pursuits as golf and fishing. They laughed a lot, accumulated a great many friends, and thought the world was "their oyster."

John worked hard, ate well—sometimes too well—but had no indication except for some tiredness that he was not as healthy as he was when they were first married. Phyllis and John had it made and thoughts of heart attacks or even illness never crossed their minds. The call from the boss was unbelievable, and Phyllis' first reaction was denial. She thought there must be some mistake. She could not and would not accept it. But when the boss knocked on the door and she was confronted with the need to make decisions, to select a mortician, a day for a funeral, the finality of his death had to be faced.

Phyllis described her first week after that as one of mental numbness and a kind of physical paralysis. She lost all sense of initiative and balance. She had to be prodded to discuss the final rites and immediate financial arrangements. She felt great waves of sadness sweep over her so strong that even tears did not relieve the oppression. Half of the time she said, "It can't be." And the other half, she kept asking, "Why, why?" She was in shock. Although her doctor was kind and administered drugs, the shock overwhelmed her. She stumbled through those days, and they are still unreal in her memory. She tried to listen and respond, but it was her husband's best friend from work that carried the burden.

When the funeral was over, that friend and her brother sat down with her to discuss her future. She resented the conference. She accused them of being indifferent to John, but they were patient, and some tentative plans were made. She would go with her brother for a week so that he and his wife could talk more with her. When she got on the airplane, she began to be aware of some threads in the tangled mass of her reaction.

She was now able to look at the extent of her loss. Her first reaction was anger. She shouted that her husband was good and constructive; God was cruel to take him. She would reach out in her troubled sleep to touch her husband's hand and wake up in terror, remembering that he would never be there again. At times, she would give way totally to deep, body-wracking sobbing. More and more, she tried to make some sense of her husband's death and then self-recrimination began. She had asked too much from him. She had not been aware of his tiredness. She cried out that "If I had only . . ." and blamed herself. After this period of first anger and then guilt, there came anxiety. She wondered what she would do, how she would manage alone, what possible joy life might have. It was then that she could begin to talk with her relatives about alternative courses of action. But it was not an even time, and she often regressed to bitterness and self-pity. But she was beginning the long road to recovery. After that week, she felt she could go home and hold consultations with her lawyer, accountant, and friends to try to gather up the torn threads of her life.

Phyllis made it, but only after a long and painful travail. She says now that everyone was kind and helpful, but it might have helped if there had been someone to walk with her through this valley who had traveled there before.

Phyllis demonstrates that type of person who is content to live in the present and gives little thought to the tomorrow. Both she and her husband had found life so good that they never wished to look for possible clouds in the future. She shows what happens when a very good marriage is suddenly broken.

In Phyllis' experience, there appear some of the typical sequences of grief. At first, there is only disbelief, denial, and paralysis. Those first hours can only be described as being struck by psychological lightning. Numbness and then terror strike so terribly that rational thought is not possible. There are so many strange decisions to be made about housing relatives, meeting planes, feeding large groups, planning the funeral, picking out a grave or crematorium, paying bills that the numbness is interspersed with attempts to function intelligently. In this nightmare, it is not easy to make wise decisions, and those who have arranged most of these details much earlier are far better off. No one functions well under an anesthetic whether it be ether or intense grief. But in one sense, the need to go through all these activities, numb or not, is something of a distraction—one does not have to face the loss all at once.

But when the funeral is over and one must decide where the next days will be spent, the enormity of being alone strikes. Now there is no familiar voice making suggestions or pointing the way.

There is no gentle hand touching the shoulder in reassurance. There is no quick joke to relieve the tension. Where the voice had sounded, there is only stillness, in the comfortable chair where he had sat when decisions were made, there is emptiness. We may even turn to that chair, hoping that he will be there and will help, but the chair is empty, and we know he will never sit there again, except in our memories. This second crisis period is longer and more painful. When relatives, friends, the boss, and the minister have gone, a whole lifetime of emotions have to be faced and integrated into a new role.

During this period, emotions come pouring out like a senseless tidal wave on a dark night, but we can identify some of them. On emerging from the first numbness, there is often a wave of protest against the irrational nature of life. Anyone or anything may be the target of that anger. We curse the ambulance that did not arrive on time, or the doctor who did not do what he should have done. How often we have listened to excoriations of the doctor who should have performed the miracle that would have saved the loved one. And, of course, the employer is often the target. He worked the employee too hard, he did not reward him sufficiently, he should have noticed the symptoms. God, too, is often blamed. He took our loved one even though he had lived a good and constructive life. If He is just and if He is a God of love, why this tragedy? These are not quiet investigations of a life philosophy; they are javelins of anger hurled almost indiscriminately.

Of course, a familiar theme is anger directed at the lost loved one. It is as though we feel he had caused the cancer or the heart attack. He wanted to die; he wanted to hurt us. He left us alone and lonely. If he had really cared for us, he would not have smoked, or drunk, or worked so hard. More than one friend has stood at a casket with a widow whom he knew loved her husband deeply and with understanding, and heard her condemn him to hell because he chose to die.

We now have nothing left; all our dreams and plans are shattered, and he did it. How strange in the tumultuous hours of grief to hear a person say of her beloved: "I hate you—you have deserted me." On the surface, of course, this sounds like hatred, but it is not. It is desperation and utter loss. It will pass, and with time, those emotions will be forgotten.

But often the anger, first directed at the physician or the boss or the deceased, turns inward, and the grieving person assumes all responsibility. She now cries out in mortification that it was her doing that the beloved has passed away. She was not sensitive to his being tired. She drove him too hard. "It was *my* responsibility to look after him, and I was too self-centered to know what he was going through. Once he told me he had pain after dinner, and I laughed it off as "gas." I should have known. Why didn't I watch his diet and his habits. I could have made him stop smoking. I said I loved him, but I failed him. Oh, if I could have him back, I'd behave differently. I didn't even kiss him goodbye on the morning he died. I asked him for money, instead. I am responsible, and I hate myself. If only I had not insisted on going to San Diego last week end. . . ." The "if onlys" may become obsessive, and for hour after hour, the widow excoriates herself because she is angry and blames herself for the loss.

This anger often turns to guilt and guilt to deep depression. We feel enormous loneliness and grief, but it is exacerbated by guilt. Our emotions are raw from sorrow, and there are often a great many physical symptoms. Sometimes we imagine that we, too, are having a heart attack. Sometimes the psychological numbness extends to physical, and our hysterical selves make a cheek or arm truly numb. Very often, we cannot sleep, elimination is disturbed, our stomachs react violently. We have backaches and headaches. In some cases, such physiological symptoms are welcomed because they are part of the price we really ought to pay because of the pain we caused the other. It helps us to suffer because he suffered. Sometimes, to compensate in our dreams for our anger and guilt or simply because our life situation is so desperate, we have nightmares in which we are dying.

There is yet one other psychological reaction we must mention because it is fairly common. In our sense of loss, we may envy others: our sister who still has her husband or our neighbor who cannot know how we feel. Their marriages are intact, and they still go on doing day by day what we wanted. A little tartness may creep into our voices as we listen to their sympathetic words. We may feel it is easy for them to comfort us because they have not suffered. We may even say to ourselves, "You'll learn how it really is." Their fulfillment only seems to add to our discomfort, and we are frankly jealous. We may even resent their grief because John was our husband and "you were really far away from him." All this is natural, but it is not always easy for others to understand.

At the climax of these tumultuous feelings, life seems pointless, for a few so pointless that they commit suicide. But most persons live through it. There seems no place to turn, no direction that is not painful, and we are overwhelmed with melancholy. It is at this point of total devastation that nature intervenes. We begin to sob, to cry in utter abandon, a process whose positive function is well-recognized.

> And of course to cry is good. Tears help to wash away the anguish of the spirit. It was a very harsh man who said that if you weep, you weep alone. He meant that somehow to weep was weakness. It is not. To weep is as natural as to laugh and just as important for good mental health. The Good Book recommends that we drink the whole cup of life. That means that we evade nothing, neither love nor tears, gladness or sadness. This is one reason why widowed people can help others newly widowed, because they have learned it is good to feel all the grief and to sob it all out. They are not upset by display of emotions because they have also gone into the valley of the shadows.
>
> There is another side to intense grief that should not be overlooked. No one cries very much unless something of real worth is lost. In a sense grief and despair are the measures of loss. They are testimonials to the value of that which is gone. In all of life nothing weighs so in the balance of goodness as a mate who is beloved. For the man or woman who has more and more deeply entwined their lives with another, who found each reunion after a day of separation a glad thing, for them to grieve is to celebrate the jewels of remembrance, sad but glistening with the beauty of the past.[1]

At this stage, we may say that we are lost, but this is not true. The first stage of numbness protects us, and the second stage enables us to deal with necessary emotional chaos. The third stage is the one where we measure our losses and begin to move toward a more realistic appraisal of the future. We know now that we shall never again be in the arms of our beloved, feel his passion or his dearness. We know that he can never again console or inspire us. We are overwhelmed with loneliness, with longing. We may be physically weak or hurting. We may wonder at our ability to manage on our own. We may feel alienated from those who are so much better off, not deprived, so secure in their warmth. The anger, guilt, and fear are still with us, but we have to cope, and psychologically, we are almost ready.

During this stage, we look somewhat drearily at the decisions confronting us. Shall we continue to live in that house with all its memories? If we move, where to? How, as a person who has not worked these many years, will we cope financially? It is true that the house is clear and that John left a good insurance policy and a small pension. But, in times of inflation, will it be enough, and how do I manage? To whom do I turn for counsel? If I need to work, do I have to return to school and sharpen my skills? How do I maintain my friendships? After all, most of them were business friends of John's. I am sure I'll be a fifth wheel. The decisions seem mountainous. As a matter of fact, at this stage they are. No one ought to make decisions that will basically determine the next twenty years until the emotional backwash of loss is over and one can consider the future without undue pressures from the past. Too hasty decisions may be regretted for the rest of a lifetime. One may decide to move close to the children, only to have them accept a new job a thousand miles away. One may sell the house under pressure, only to feel a year later that it was a poor economic move and a worse emotional one.

All of these critical areas of choice will be considered later. It is sufficient here to indicate that there is no rule in heaven or on earth that says we must settle everything at once. Time itself soothes many feelings and clarifies many obscurities. If there is an anxiety about settling things, one ought to go away or retreat into healing. Those things that seem overwhelming will not always be so. Patience at this period is critical. If there is one rule for adjustment at this early point, it is that the grieving person should try to accept the present, delay any major financial or geographical changes, and trust that a few months of inactivity will be profoundly good. The rest of this book will throw light on constructive ways of looking at those decisions. Our first advice is not to make any early decisions.

THE MERRY AND THE NOT-SO-MERRY WIDOW

As we have suggested, there are many different life experiences that predispose the bereaved person to differing responses. Still, in our experience, the stereotype of "the merry widow" is not realistic. We simply have not encountered many widows who laugh and dance their way through bereavement. When we have been able to talk in depth with some of those who seem joyous after the loss of their mates, we have discovered that the joyousness is a façade covering up other feelings and sometimes denying them because they hurt too much. In one case where the widow demonstrated a great brightness and happiness, we discovered she totally lacked the ability to relate to any human being. She had nothing to grieve about.

In the majority of divorce cases, there has been a process of alienation that has already conditioned both the husband and the wife to seek relief through the courts. As a result, the occasion of the final decree can call for a celebration. Death is never an occasion for joyous celebration, but for some it may be welcomed as providing release from an impossible relationship. Still, there are many things that will be missed—even the battles! If we accept the testimony of three nationally significant studies, we are aware that after twenty years of marriage a great many couples have exhausted their patience and concern for each other. Pineo and Cuber and Harroff suggest that in our society time is "corrosive" to tenderness, that middle-age marriages are "disenchanted," and that apathy and devitalization characterize the union.[2] If this is true, one would expect that an entirely different sort of grief process would follow the death of one or the other. The case of Hank illustrates such a situation very well.

Hank said he was 56 years of age when he called to ask for an appointment. He complained on the phone of insomnia, guilt and depression. His wife, Mary, had been killed in an automobile accident three months before. When he appeared in the office his depression was obvious. He was slipping in appearance and motivation. He had not shaved, his clothes needed pressing and he had a slight tremor which we later traced to over-indulgence in alcohol.

Hank told a straightforward story. He and Mary had been married quite early while still in school as the result of a "fantastic sexual attraction." They could never be together but they ended up in bed, which was sometimes a meadow, sometimes the back seat of a car, and sometimes his home when his parents were out. Hank said he could not bear to think of losing Mary so he married her too early and they had a "hell" of a time making it because he wanted to finish school but she got pregnant and he blamed her for that. In fact he blamed her for the next thirty years for the fact that he did not climb fast enough in his profession, for having four children that cost money so he could not buy a large boat (he had a small motor boat but it was not enough). As the result their marriage settled down to acrimonious exchanges where almost all of their conversation was an exercise in hurting the other. The children did not escape from this family scene. One was in the reform school, two had simply left and one of them was "lost," the last one having decided to live apart and was openly contemptuous of both mother and father.

Mary became something of an alcoholic and because he had an alcoholic father Hank could not tolerate this. He shoved her in and out of the hospital, with appropriate denunciations. In the meantime he had a long affair with his secretary who, likewise embroiled in an unhappy marriage, was perfectly willing to take from life whatever excitement and joy she could find. Mary questioned him about this but was not sure until she caught them in a nightclub drinking. Mary made a scene and left. She had drunk a great deal and went off the road and killed herself.

Hank had earlier asked for a divorce but Mary delighted in keeping the marriage together to torture him. He had tried to be decent to her but he could not tolerate her drinking, partially, he realized because he was at least partially responsible for it and he could not face his guilt.

Even though Hank had asked for and prayed for a separation from her, he could not now feel good about what had happened. He was prostrated by the death of another human being. His friends somewhat callously wanted him to have the life now "he deserved," but he was paralyzed. All of the things he thought he would do when she died he could not do. His secretary had expected that he would marry her but his relations with her took a negative turn when Mary died. In one sense he thought that he blamed his secretary; in another he felt that he did not deserve a better life. He was utterly miserable and not "merry" at all.

This case may seem overly dramatic to make our point, but it is accurate, and we can learn from it. If one is dearly in love with one's mate, loss by death is devastating. But if one has a long and bitter conflict with one's mate and that mate dies, the guilt reactions may be overwhelming. This is what happened to Hank. Hank's reaction overemphasized his complicity in Mary's death. He had a difficult time coming to terms with that complicity.

While we suggested in the last section that every person is unique and an island, let us now modify that statement and say that in terms of marital interactions no man is an island. All that he does, feels, or says affects another human being. He may be seeking his own salvation so desperately that he is completely oblivious to how his struggle affects another, but one day, he becomes sadly aware that he is part of his mate's destiny. Hank knew that he was part of a family in which Mary could not survive. He had made some attempts at divorce, but by then, Mary was so dependent that she could not envision going it alone. He had not enlisted a psychiatrist or marriage counselor to help. He had only blamed Mary for the unhappiness in his own life.

Consequently, after Mary's death, he had to face his part in her destruction. In detailing their history, he said that he was "drawn to Mary because she was hot, and I got burned." But sexual fires burn very furiously for most adolescents and then are integrated into the more subtle and sharing aspects of marriage. Hank's life was complicated by the fact that he was truly an egocentric person and judged Mary and everyone else by the way they helped him meet his economic, sexual, and psychological needs. When Mary had problems, it was because she was "not strong" as he was, and when his children had difficulties, it was Mary's fault. This game of projecting blame, or "injustice collecting," is an old one for marriage counselors. Unless the game is broken up, the marriage deteriorates as this one did.

Hank's relationship to his secretary is interesting because a year prior to Mary's death he had promised her that he would sooner or later divorce Mary and marry her. But Mary's death evoked such guilt in him that he could not avoid partially blaming the secretary for what happened to Mary. That may have been utterly unfair, but it happened. The secretary had risked her marriage in order to cultivate her relationship with Hank, and she was devastated by his turn around in attitude. Fortunately, she was willing to come for counseling and gained some understanding of Hank's "strange" reaction.

Hank's task was to learn how to live with his guilt. For the first time in his life, he became somewhat socialized in his awareness of his responsibility to another human being. He learned to accept his own frailties and imperfections. Although he was becoming aware of the insensitive interactions of human beings when he first called, it took Hank a long time to know that we all tend to exploit others by projecting blame. It was a long session in the schoolroom of human compassion, but Hank grew. He grew through psychological suffering because as he gained courage he had to face the consequences to his family of his own somewhat sociopathic behavior. But he grew. He grew enough so that he was able to salvage his relationship to three of his children and to his secretary. She, too, had never looked beyond her own satisfactions, and when she saw her complicity in her unhappy relationship with her husband, she was determined to work toward solving their problem. But he was bitter and revengeful and would not work to salvage his marriage. In the end, she divorced him, with no guarantee that she would work it out with Hank. They tried and now have a final relationship that is much different than either had had with their first spouses.

In commenting on this case, we have to say that despite an unhappy marriage Mary's death brought no release for Hank, only pain. But he had the courage to face that pain and understand Mary and himself. We cite this case because there is no certainty that release from a failed relationship frees any person for a better experience. Helen's case was different, and we present it because Helen was in truth a "merry" widow, but in a modern sense.

Helen was forty when we first met her in a social situation. Helen's husband had died two months before, but one would not suspect it listening to Helen discuss the latest rock-and-roll records, the new drama at the Circle Theater, or the world situation. Helen and her husband had early joined the new life-style members. They belonged to the new sophisticated "set" that took life where it was and as it came. She was no Vienna wife capitalizing on release from an impossible marriage to an older man. She and her husband were what she called "existentialists"; they lived for today and counted on tomorrow.

When we spoke about her husband's death, she spoke with whimsical remembrance of some of their brighter moments, but soon drifted off to discuss her latest achievements in the theater. One suspected that she had not been genuinely attracted to her husband and that neither he nor anyone else would for long interfere with her hedonistic pleasures. For exploration purposes, I asked her about a mourning process, and she seemed perplexed and finally said: "You must be kidding."

Helen's world of dramatic experiences and self-aggrandizement did not permit her to abandon her search for stimulation and thrills when her husband died. Life, she said, was too short to waste over futile concerns with what might have been.

We followed Helen because we wondered about her adjustment. There was none. A year later, she was married to an older man who traveled a good deal and who was known for his wealth and for being a bon vivant. He found this merry widow sufficiently responsive to ask her to marry him. That was five years ago, and they are still touring and dancing and laughing.

Our readers should not feel that we are depreciating Helen. She is a modern soul, obsessed with doing her thing and living each day as though it were her last. In this sense, she *is* an existentialist, albeit a superficial one. She accepts the arrows of outrageous fortune as though there was nothing outrageous about them. She is witty and resourceful and merry. Helen's full life history is not yet available to enable us to know with any certainty whether or not she will be better off as she ages than were Phyllis and Jean. At this point in time she is not burdened with any guilt and not trammeled with thoughts of tomorrow. Men may come and men may go, but Helen goes on forever. And, at least to all appearances, that seems to be enough.

This is not true of another kind of "merry" widow. There are those who have a different life philosophy from Helen's. They have a conscience and a respect for their husbands, but they had their own lives as well. They had jobs or avocations that were as rewarding and important as their marriages. They are in a sense the products of women's liberation because they are schooled in the importance of self. They have the need to weep, but also the support of the fact that they have significant roles in life to pursue. Judy was such a person. Judy wept, but not with such deep pain as did Phyllis. Her life was too full. Her questions about her husband's death were not in the area of anger or guilt, but in the area of her future security. Judy was an interesting encounter because in a sense she revealed the reactions of the modern woman. She was able to be exceptionally candid about her reactions.

Judy was forty-one. Her single child was leaving high school, and she regarded him with a kind of tender detachment. Her husband's death left her with some problems. She thought she would have to support her son during his years of college, but her house was almost clear, and she had a good position. Her husband had given the boy masculine identification, and she would give him what support he needed to prepare for life.

Judy said, without much rancor or anger, that her husband was aware of his pace. They had talked it over, and she knew long before he died that she would outlive him. His fatal heart attack had come when they were in the midst of plans for a sabbatical to tour the world. She really cared for him because they had had a good kind of intellectual stimulation and sexually rewarding life.

Judy was not sure whether or not she would marry again. She noted that her single friends were free of many obligations she had had when married. But she wondered now about her adjustment to friends who were married and how she would arrange her affectional life. Ben had been a "hell of a lover," and she knew she would compare any other man with him. At this point, she cried some and said she really missed him, but she was promised a good promotion, and she was counting on her increased responsibilities to carry her through.

There was one man she felt close to who had helped her in the past, and she knew he would be calling at the door of her bedroom. But she was also very friendly with his wife, and she really did not want to interfere with their marriage because she thought it a promising relationship. She would tell him she was fond of him but that he ought to work harder at his marriage. She knew there were other men around if she needed them.

In talking to Judy, we felt that life has prepared her with a defense against the contingency of losing her husband. She had a very rewarding and responsible job. She was not bound by any religious or cultural inhibitions, so her obvious sexual needs would be met. One felt that she had been genuinely fond of her husband, and any future relationship would have to measure up to the good things in that union. On the other hand, she had an independence and security that cushioned her against any frivolous or purely romantic involvement. We suspect that Judy will marry again but only to a superb human being. We really have few concerns about Judy because, contrary to Helen, she is thoughtful, goal-oriented, considerate, and compassionate. She would not marry a man if she felt that she might hurt or exploit him. She is the "new" woman.

What is the essential difference between the reactions of Phyllis and Judy? Both loved their husbands, and both suffered a sense of loss. It is probably in the multiplicity of roles and rewards. Phyllis put all of her bets on her husband, but Judy scattered hers across the board. We have only now begun to analyze the impact of women's liberation, and we are not yet sure of the balance. In this case, where we are considering adjustment to loss, we think Judy, having compensations, has a less severe adjustment. This is a purely impressionistic conclusion drawn from relatively few case analyses. We have yet to test, on a large scale, the inner security of the liberated woman against that of one who invests everything in her marriage. Our conclusions may be in error. Judy may finally be as bereft and as helpless in her readjustment as Phyllis, but we do not think so.

THE INSOLVENT WIDOW

The title of this section is a misnomer. Many of the persons whom we would subsume under this title have a wealth of resources, but they are afraid they do not. They are not literally insolvent, only fearful that they are or will be penniless. Many of them are depression era children whose parents' poverty had impressed them. Their major motivation in marriage was to find security, and many of them ruined their marital relationships by making this economic security their primary goal. We recall with some ambivalent feelings a wife we counseled in San Francisco. She lived in the Berkeley hills in a $100,000 mansion. We had gone to see her at her request because her husband was in the hospital with what appeared to be terminal cancer.

> Grace greeted us with great despair. When we were seated in an alcove in her beautiful home, where we could overlook the bay, she poured out her story. She was fifty-three years old. Her husband had bought this magnificent mansion at her request. She loved it. But what would happen when he died? How could she pay the taxes? How could she afford the upkeep? They had paid $2,400 a year to a gardener. Who would garden?
>
> A number of years ago, they had taken out an annuity policy, but it was not paid up. Where would she get the money to finish paying before maturity? She was not well herself, that was obvious, and she could not go to work. What would happen to her?
>
> They had made a down payment on a villa in the Mediterranean, and she was sure that project was now irretrievably lost. Why had they not invested more wisely? Her husband was a fool to do all these things.
>
> On inquiry, Grace admitted all "of these things" were at her insistence, but her husband should have known better; after all, he was the man. Now she would be left in a mess. He had not really taken care of her.

The interview progressed unevenly because Grace got up to pace, wringing her hands, bemoaning the fate that was ahead of her. It was startling and disconcerting that not a single word of concern was ever expressed for her husband. We suspected early that this was a marriage designed to meet Grace's needs as a depression child. Having been deprived, she wanted everything. But now her source of everything was jeopardized, and she blamed her golden goose for that.

We have met a good many widows and widowers whose main motive in marriage created similar problems. They could not help their economic drives. We have always suspected that Marx exaggerated economic drives, but in these cases, he was far too accurate. Often when we hear sobs and anxious cries from widows, they resolve into economic complaints. In some cases, this motivation stems from early deprivation or family distress that was blamed on poverty. In other cases, the poverty was in the parents' marital relationship, and the widow had compensated by turning to the accumulation of material things. As money was all that was left in her life, when the source died she had no resources to face the future.

Grace's case ended strangely. Surgery arrested her husband's cancer and he recovered. But during his illness, he had to face squarely his wife's utter materialism. When she came to see him, her concern was always about her future and not about him. As soon as it was obvious that he would recover completely, he divorced her. We saw her again after the divorce, and her grief was just as great as it was when she had faced the possibility of his death. He had been most generous in his settlement, but her fears of inflation were so great that she was almost completely unstable. She was referred to a psychiatrist because she needed extensive professional help in order to find some balance in her life.

Economic sustenance is an important part of life, but when it dominates the reasons for, or the relationships in, the marriage, it is destructive. In facing or adjusting to death, it is devastating.

ROLE LOSSES

Psychological losses hit us first. But after a time it is the losses in personal relationships that seem more permanent and are sometimes harder to accept. We play a significant part in the life of our mate, our children, parents, employer, and friends. Psychologists have come to speak of these roles as the roles we play with others in life. All of them are seriously affected by the death of a mate. This loss of our mate is a primary loss. The use of our energy, the utilization of time, the determination of priorities—all of these depend on that subtle but all-pervasive influence of his or her expectations. For years, we have prepared meals, watched television, gone on vacations, planned week ends with one predominant influence: our mate. We have thought of ourselves always in relationship with him or her no matter what we did. In time, a new career of role expectations and role fulfillments must be carved out, and this is not an easy task.

Relationships with friends are equally pervasive. Many of our friendships depend on our being part of a couple. We were a team and as such contributed to other couples. Now we are alone, and our role in relationship to other couples has to change. One does not fit as two did. Friends may try to find suitable and nonthreatening partners for the bridge game, but it is not the same. The old familiarity and comfortableness of the couple are gone, and the widow knows that while she may have the love of her friends her role is difficult, and in a sense, she is less than half of what she was before.

Our role in relation to the business world shifts radically. Before widowhood, the husband always gave assurance that bills would be paid, regardless of who actually wrote the checks. Even in companionship marriages, where financial decisions are made by consensus, his knowledge and strength were critical. Now those decisions are entirely made by one. This is not only difficult but the whole relationship with the business and financial world changes. A widow does not have the ongoing earnings of her husband, nor does she have the status of a married woman. Decisions to buy, that which previously had been almost automatic, now occasion worry and concern. This major shift of role is critical because a wise adjustment is essential to future solvency.

Our roles in relation to our children change too. Previously, they had counted on the fact that Mother and Father sustained each other. Now they may feel threatened that Mother will demand a redefinition of role that will burden them. She may want to live with them. She may expect financial support. She may become dependent and expect constant attention. She may go to pieces. When one is widowed, children hold many and anxious conversations.

There are many definitions of personality, but one of them says that it is the sum total of the roles we play. This may not be all there is to personality, but roles constitute a major part. When there are so many alterations in role, our basic selves are first mutilated and later radically altered. We need to describe some of these role disruptions in greater detail and then think of creative ways of reconstituting our roles and our personalities.

Are there some general features about the experiences of Grace, Phyllis, Hank, Helen, and Judy that give us clues to the problems they are going through? We think a few things need to be summarized.

The first is a recapitulation of our first caution. Every person is an individual. Hank, Phyllis, Grace, Helen, and Judy are different. Their needs and the depth of their sorrow differ. Humans are unique, and we should not generalize about the kind of travail they experience. Some have sorrow and others, like Hank, have guilt. Some have anger and others have anxiety. If we would criticize the efforts of others to deal with separation, it would only be that some have squeezed all sadness into a neatly packaged form and all human reaction into a formula. This is unfortunate because reactions are diverse and unique. If we listen closely, we hear these individual themes and needs. So we are reluctant to package grief work or methods of helping the lonely person. If we are to develop helping agencies or groups for the millions who are and will be bereft, we hope that a large segment of the training will be directed toward listening for uniqueness. We live in a segmented world to which we bring very complex and diverse backgrounds and reactions. It is not possible to fit people to programs. It is possible to fit our own responses to what we hear. We shall discuss that processing in the next several chapters.

A second insight that applies to all of our cases has to do with a sense of timeliness. It is popular to say that the grief work ought to be concluded at least by the first anniversary of the death of the mate or of the divorce. But this is an arbitrary date. We know of a man whose sorrow lasted in full bloom for over two years, and we began to suspect that he was a permanent prisoner of remorse and sadness. Then, even as he built a shrine to his wife, another woman of great appeal appeared, and in three months, he had closed the shrine and remarried. He found great joy in his new relationship.

Tempo is everything. Some individuals need more time to adjust to anything. The important aspect of timing is not to make decisions impetuously or out of a fear but to wait until one's feelings are settled and there is some stability in looking toward the future. Are there clues to readiness to plan ahead? Certainly there are no clear signposts, but we would suggest that decisions about moving, investing, remarrying, or getting a new job wait until the grief work is over and we can turn with a relatively open mind to the future. Timing will be different for Phyllis and for Judy.

This chapter has detailed different emotional reactions to loss. That is but the beginning, and we shall move on to discuss how the various levels of bereavement may be handled. The resources available for help in doing grief work and the management of the grief process are equally important. It may help some to note, as we have in this chapter, the sequences and differences in grief. It helps more to look at efficient and humane ways of handling grief. This we will do in the next chapter.

CHAPTER THREE

WORKING THROUGH
THE SEPARATION

The role losses and psychological deprivations caused by the loss of a mate are monumental. It is one thing to monitor the sorrow and the loss, but it is quite another to stop the flow of tears und find other directions. Many widows may applaud the accuracy of feelings that we have described, but this does not alter their agony or suspend their sorrow. What have we learned to say to the widow to help her through those various phases of grief work? Work she must, and grief must be phased out in favor of more constructive pathways. Roles are lost and new ones must be developed. There are, of course, some therapeutic gains in being able to pinpoint what troubles us and in becoming aware that others have wept as we have wept and have overcome the same losses. In this and subsequent chapters, we shall look sharply at some of the healing processes that are involved in recovery from bereavement. To do this, we need to look at some of the studies that have given us new insights in studying the various types of reactions that others have carefully analyzed. These studies will help us to focus more carefully on some of our own problems, to objectify them, and then to move onward. To them, we shall add insights from individual case studies that lend substance to these more statistical approaches. Case studies help us understand the process of grief; statistical studies tell us how universal those reactions are, and both help us in helping those in need.

LINDEMANN'S CLASSIC STUDY

The first study we shall look at briefly is the classic one by Eric Lindemann.[1] In a series of psychiatric interviews, Dr. Lindemann studied 101 persons who had lost relatives or close friends in a tragic nightclub fire in Boston some years ago. In doing this, he found five major changes that are characteristic of grief. They are: (1) *The syndrome of physical (somatic) distress.* Choking, sighing, shortness of breath, exhaustion, and digestive disturbances. (2) *Preoccupation with the image of the deceased,* along with a feeling of distance from other people. (3) *Feeling of guilt.* The sorrowing persons assess blame upon themselves for the death. (4) *Hostile reactions,* irritability, anger, and some apprehension that this might lead to insanity. (5) *Loss of pattern of conduct.* Because a companion who shared life is gone a sense of normal activity is lost.

In working through these grief reactions, there are three significant goals that need to be achieved: (*a*) freedom from bondage to the deceased, (*b*) readjustment to social environment, and (*c*) formation of new relationships. A great hindrance to successful grief work is avoidance of the pain of facing the loss, along with failure to express the deep emotions necessary to express that loss. In these cases, a psychiatrist shared the grief work, but it is a safe conclusion that an intimate and understanding person will be helpful in normal grief.

THE COLUMBIA STUDY

This study was made at Columbia University by Schoenberg, Carr, Peretz, and Kutscher in 1970.[2] They asked for the help of

133 professional consultants, such as ministers, psychologists, and psychiatrists, to help them understand typical and important aspects of grief. They asked two sets of questions: the first set concerned characteristic behavior patterns, and the second discussed the recommendations of these therapists.

Ninety-nine percent of the consultants predicted that death of a mate would be followed by depression, loss of weight, sleeplessness, and despair. Ninety percent predicted that the bereaved would have dreams about the deceased. Seventy-four percent thought that the widowed would fantasize or have illusions about the presence of the dead person. Seventy-five percent expected the widow to have angry thoughts directed toward the deceased. If it was the wife who had died, over 75 percent of the consultants thought that the widower would experience impotence, and more felt that he would show diminished sexual desires. Seventy-three percent thought that the bereaved would seek advice; about 25 percent would consult a physician, and another 25 percent would talk with the clergyman.

In terms of what they thought would be helpful behaviors to move toward recovery from depression and despair, 91 percent thought that talking with someone who had had a similar experience would be very useful. Ninety percent felt that if the person had been working, the continuation of the work pattern would be wise, but perhaps a change of job might be indicated. Eighty-five percent would recommend eventual remarriage.

The authors of this study used these reports and drew upon their own experiences in making further recommendations. They felt that dealing with practical affairs during the first hours of grief is essential. The clergyman, friend, or therapist who has some access to the sorrowful person will do well to help him talk about "an initial course of action" in order to share advice about what to do, to help the verbalization process, and to give comforting words. They felt that dealing with practical decisions stirs up guilt reactions, loneliness fears, regrets, and feelings of abandonment that surface and can be faced. This recommendation concurs with their consultants, who urged a freedom of expression in which negative and self-destructive thoughts would be ventilated and eventually eliminated.

It is good to talk. If we can find an understanding friend, particularly if we can find a friend who has gone down the valley of the shadows, nothing helps so much as to let our emotions pour out in a veritable flood. We should not be ashamed of our anger, our guilt, or our sorrow because these are universal reactions and, as we have seen in this study, almost everyone must cope with such emotions. They may not be rational, but they are human. One cannot tell grief to go away or anger to dissolve. Sadness does not depart because we will it. It is better to express these emotions than to try to deny them or push them away.

If emotion is bottled up, it will remain with us, always tainting both our memories and our future wisdom. Phyllis, in retrospect, was right when she said it would have helped to have a companion in her sorrow. We know many widows who have been so ashamed of their anger at their mates that they have compensated for that anger by praising their mates and making their lives a monument to their late husbands. But this compensation doesn't work. It stands in the way of discovering new roles and almost destroys the possibility of loving another person.

Unrestrained and honest emotional expression relieves the pressures, helps achieve a balanced insight, and hastens our psychological healing. Research has taught us that an intimate friend can be the difference between growing and failing mental health. We also know that we need those intimates most during crises periods, when they might help us find some tunnel through which to move and, finally, the light at the end of the tunnel. After an interval of time, we find that, through bathing ourselves in talk, depression is washed away.

The different ways that individuals handle grief are illustrated in the following case vignettes:

> Henrietta was known as a "cool" girl. She went through all of her adolescence without much conflict with her parents and through her problems of dating with aplomb. She never seemed to be ruffled. Her mother was proud of her because she had taught her always to "keep a stiff upper lip." For her mother, the great virtue was to appear to be "in control." Even as a little girl, Henrietta was punished if she cried over a cut or even over a lost pet. As she

became older, Henrietta learned that this outward control over feelings served her in good stead because if something bothered her it was simply repressed. When her husband died at the age of forty-eight, a great many people were amazed at her control. She greeted everyone affably at the funeral and held her head high all through the ceremonies. Her mother was proud of her. Some people thought it strange and others were not surprised when she had a complete breakdown a year later and attempted suicide.

Henrietta's good friend, Michelle, also lost her husband when he was fifty. But she reacted differently.

Michelle was always an emotional creature. She laughed heartily, cried vigorously, and loved passionately. She never wanted to leave a party or have the sunset fade. When her husband died, it seemed the end of the world for her. She shook her fist at God and bellowed at the doctors. Then she wept. The tears seemed never to end. At her husband's funeral, she had paroxysms of grief and could not be comforted. Her brother and sister-in-law were so concerned that they elected to spend a week after the funeral with her and finally took her home with them. She was disconsolate and talked about the meaninglessness of life. They let her sob on their shoulders and weep in their arms. But after a time, the cries grew weaker and the tears fell in smaller drops. Before two weeks passed, she was noticing her sister-in-law's problems with three children and began to help. She could listen to music and watch her sunsets. When she went home, no one worried about her because, although sad, her voice had changed, and she was now thinking about the way her husband would have wanted her to continue his interests.

We believe that it is possible to wash depression away with tears and that (although this is not quite all there is to the process) *grief work* is inescapable. If we cannot do it in the weeks and months following a great loss, we will do it one year or five years later, or perhaps a little at a time for the rest of our years.

THE UNIVERSITY OF SOUTHERN CALIFORNIA
STUDY

A study done at the University of Southern California by Dr. Carol J. Barrett in 1972[3] focused on the way three different types of groups helped widows recover their stability. Forty-two widows participated. They ranged in age from thirty-two to seventy-four years. The duration of widowhood was from two months to twenty-two years. Almost half of them had had their husbands die very suddenly, and two-thirds said they had never considered the possibility of being a widow. One-half were at work, full or part time; one-third had retired; and the rest wanted to work but could not find a job. Their average income, even though half of them worked, was about one-half of what it had been before their husbands' death. This study confirms our statement about the drastic change in the economic role of widows.

Dr. Barrett found that of the widows in her study the number-one problem was loneliness . . . and this after many had had years in which to adjust to their new role. The next problems in order of importance were grief and family difficulties. Adjusting to loss and to their new role in family relationships is not easy. Further areas of stress were finances and legal affairs.

The first group was labeled a *self-help group* because the leader never gave direct advice but defined her role as the facilitator of interaction, assisting the group members to help one another. The problems faced by the group came from the members themselves.

In the second, *confidante group*, each widow was paired with another. The leader defined it as her role in this group to facilitate a "helping relationship" for each pair. She did this by using some intimacy techniques and group activities where the couple participated as a pair.

The third group was described as a *woman's consciousness-raising group*. In their discussions, they focused on the ways that sex-roles influenced their adjustment as widows. Discussions of this group ranged around such topics as: "The Stereotypes of Widows," "Sexuality among Widows," "Are You Still a Wife?"

Each of these groups met for two hours a week for eight

weeks. They were matched with a control group. Reactions to widowhoood, psychological functioning, life-styles, and attitudes about other women were studied before the experiment began, during the last sessions of the groups, and in a follow-up study three months later.

The impact of these groups on the widows was significant. Those who participated showed a significant difference in "predicted future health" as compared to the controls. Subjects in all groups showed increases in self-esteem and joy in womanhood. All of the women in the experimental groups thought the programs were helpful, but the women's consciousness-raising participants gave the highest praise to the program. Further, they reported the most positive "life changes." All four groups became less depressed, but the control group recalled more severe problems of loneliness, financial stress, family difficulties, and health problems than did the members of the therapy groups. The confidante group became more active in social roles than did the other groups, and their change in self-esteem was more positive than that of the other two treatment groups. A very interesting and probably most significant result of this experiment was that all three treatment groups arranged for continued contact after the research period ended.

Dr. Barrett concluded from her research that each of these groups had some potential in helping widows adjust and in preventative mental health programs. One final result was so significant that we quote it exactly:

> One of the important findings of the research is that widows continue to suffer from grief as well as the stresses that a male-oriented, youth-oriented and couple-oriented society subjects them to long after the husband's death. Programs which focus on the problems of the recent widow, although essential, are insufficient.

Self-help groups of widows have become institutionalized in a number of other countries. It is puzzling that a similar development has not yet occurred in the United States. In England, almost every community has a group known as CRUSE. This group is made up of widows who long ago learned the value to themselves of sharing their grief burdens. There have been a few such widow groups created as the result of research programs in the United States, but they are still too few. In England, a representative of the widow group makes a call just as soon as the death is announced, but the group waits until after the funeral to invite the widow to join them. Later, CRUSE helps the widow with her emotional, financial, and recreational problems. By contrast, in this country the widow is largely left to walk alone in the garden of her sorrows.

THE ANDRUS GERONTOLOGY CENTER STUDY

This study was done by Dr. James Mathieu at the Andrus Gerontology Study at the University of Southern California.[4] He studied a sample of 189 older persons in Pasadena, California; 183 older persons in Laguna Hills, California; and 115 in the Mountain states. The part of his data that interests us is the follow-up to Barrett's discovery that about two-thirds of her sample had never considered the possibility of widowhood. In light of the greater longevity of women and their high probability of widowhood, this is astonishing. Furthermore, it precludes the possibility of what is termed "anticipatory grief," the possibility of some adjustment to the loss during illness or in the later years. Mathieu found that both urban and rural people share a cultural tradition in which the possibility of death is denied, and families are protected by patients and doctors from knowing about terminal illness.

When Mathieu asked these individuals how often they considered their own deaths, a large percentage of all three samples indicated that they had "Very seldom" or "Never" thought about the possibility. Seventy-two percent of the urban Pasadena sample, 83 percent of the Laguna Hills group, and 64 percent of the mountain-rural sample checked "Very seldom" or "Never." Again, when Mathieu asked the three groups what the doctor should do about providing information on a terminal illness, only 8 percent of the Pasadena group, 13 percent of the Laguna Hills group, and 16 percent of the mountain state sample wanted the doctor to tell the family the truth. On the other hand, about 80 percent of each of the three groups wanted to know themselves. It is interesting that fewer than 25 percent of any of the three samples wanted to be kept alive indefinitely by "heroic" methods. A further interesting discovery was that in no one of the three samples did "love from those around me" offer much comfort when the respondent thought about death. Religion and memories of a full life gave much more comfort.

These conclusions from Barrett and Mathieu leads us to conclude that part of the problem of widows stems from our general cultural pattern of avoiding any confrontation with death or its inevitability. The journey will end for all of us, and a society that denies that fact, so that about two-thirds of widows never once pondered the possibility, inevitably leaves the survivor ill prepared to cope with practical or psychological problems. During a terminal illness, if that information is shared, there is a possibility of "mourning in advance," which helps us cope with the final loss. More significantly, social attitudes that preclude any discussion or planning for death must necessarily contribute to the shock of loss and the depression and despair that follows death.

COPING WITH LOSS

In this country, the widow must generally muster her own supports. The church has never programmed continuous care for her. Psychology has never looked at a total program of rehabilitation for her. Therapists generally are competent to deal with acute depression and suicidal attitudes, but they have not paid attention to helping the widow work through her role losses and loneliness. Communities do not furnish such groups as CRUSE to give any kind of long-term group support to the widow. She is a forgotten legion, and her cries are heard only by the bleak walls of her lonely apartment. The following paragraphs may be regarded as guidelines based on our research and case studies. These guidelines are meant to apply both to community groups and to individual widows.

We can summarize the critical insight that Lindemann, Schoenberg and his associates, Barrett, and Mathieu have shared with us in terms of the subjective or internal necessities that must be faced if grief work is to be effective.

1. *Dealing with the relationship with the deceased*

Lindemann stressed the way in which the grieving person vividly sees the deceased. It is important to embark on a program of dealing constructively with the memories of the deceased. Over time, these can become a mellow, warm strength for the bereaved if the obsessive concentration can be transformed through memory work to an appreciative memory. One has to alter one's emotional response to that person because he is no longer present, he cannot give a response, and past emotions are no longer realistic.

2. *Accepting the pain of bereavement*

Denial of the death of a loved one is one way to avoid facing a final separation, but it is a destructive tactic. As we said before, the greater our pain, the more vitality the relationship possessed. But sooner or later, we have to allow ourselves to suffer the agonies of admitting to ourselves that they are gone. No sedative, no amount of alcohol, no new adventures will help us mitigate that pain. We have to cry and sob and suffer. When we allow ourselves full emotional freedom to probe the depths of despair, we experience relief.

3. *Working through our feelings*

Many of our feelings are strange and frightening. We do not wish to be angry with the departed, with the doctor, or at ourselves, but these negative feelings hit us very hard. We are ashamed and frightened. Likewise, they often make us wonder if we can manage these surges of emotions, these ups and downs, and survive without losing our sanity. All of these myriads of strange, alienating, and threatening feelings are quite normal and should be regarded as such. These, too, will pass.

4. *Expressing our feelings*

We must, of course, accept our feelings as normal, but it helps greatly to express them. It may be that we have a good friend who is understanding enough to listen quietly while we cry, rant, rave, or ponder. If we have, we are fortunate. Perhaps it will be a psychiatrist like Lindemann, a minister who is a good friend, or a social worker. But we may do as well by keeping a diary as Lynn Caine did. It may be that we have an intimate who lives far away, and we can share our tortuous path with that person through a letter. This has helped a great many persons. Some individuals who are accustomed to using a tape recorder might do well to pour out their anguish on tape to be sent to another or simply recorded for the future. Whatever the mechanism, it is important that we deal honestly with our feelings and that we express them.

All of these suggestions are ways of opening ourselves to ourselves, of getting in touch with feelings we might otherwise suppress or deny. We may do it through meditation, journals, diaries, letters, or conversation, but whatever mode we adopt, it is healthy to go down into the deep wells of our being and dwell there long enough to understand our feelings. We remember well Darlene's statement about this:

> I was never a very introspective person, and when Ben died, I was not ready to allow myself to feel. I knew I had feelings, but it was uncomfortable to let them surface. I twisted and turned and ran rather than really get in touch with myself. But one day when I was exhausted, about half-way to sleep, I began to catch some of my most innermost reactions. I was surprised at both my anger and my tenderness toward Ben. I survived that insight, and it rather felt good because I knew that this was me. So I began to practice catching my feelings like that . . . often in a kind of semiconscious state. After a while, I could consciously begin to really feel, and now I'm a different person.

Darlene's life changed after that, and later, she told us that a new relationship with another man was entirely different than that with Ben. Her grief work over him enabled her to become a feeling person.

It is possible to test how we are doing in our grief work, how well we are doing with these different emotions. If we become physically much stronger, if we have zest for new relationships, if we have overcome feelings of guilt and hostility, and if we are making new relationships, we have handled the emotional setbacks due to grief, and our grief work is well done. But if we continue to have psychosomatic reactions, such as sighing, intense hostility, and guilt, we have not finished yet.

B. THE NEED FOR INTIMACY

Every study of mental health and every study of widows stresses loneliness as the root of long-term depression and mental illness. But one can be in a crowd and be exceptionally lonely if the concerns of the crowd do not touch the needs of the individual. Lowenthal's study of mental illness in older persons proves that an "intimate" is the best barrier to depression and despair.[5] Barretts' group of paired confidantes made significant contributions. The first guideline seems to be the necessity of reaching out for a friend who is compassionate and patient and kind.

We have said that a bereaved person is often angry or filled with guilt and with feelings of abandonment. These are all destructive emotions, and they must be expressed and ventilated. Yet Barrett reports that her widows seemed to be living under the spell of old sorrows, lending support to the observation that for many widows of ten to twenty years' standing this grief work was never done. It helps, of course, in times of great duress to speak of these things to a minister or to a psychiatrist, but one does not have a long-term, constant, and close relationship with such professionals. One may call friends at midnight or spend hour after hour talking with them. They know the need for reiteration of the same thing because it took them a long time to cleanse their own souls of sadness.

A poet has said that "when thoughts of the last bitter hour come like a blight upon thy spirit, get thee out into nature," and for many nature is healing. But it is far more healing to get close to a friend and talk and talk and talk.

Where do we find such a friend? We suppose that one generally finds such a friend in the circle of those we have known. Fortunate is the person who has developed such an intimate relationship over the years. They have a priceless asset. When Marge's husband died suddenly of a heart attack, we went to see her. Seated beside her was Helen, a friend of thirty years, just holding her hand and listening. She continued to listen for a year because only two years before she had lost her mate. Not everyone is so fortunate as to have a friend like Marge had in Helen, however.

Of course, there is some possibility that your community has a widow consultation service. There are a few in the nation. A visit to that agency would provide both group participation and individual contacts. To check on that possibility, we studied the Los Angeles phone directories, and there was not a single reference to widows. There were lots of groups dealing with drugs, alcoholics, pregnant girls, and divorcees, but not a single reference for widows. We turned then to the classified personals in the *Los Angeles Times*. Again, there were many places where individuals might call to get married and for help with divorce or with drugs. There were ads for water bags and water beds under the "W's" but nothing for the widow.

But this does not mean that there are not a great many resources close at hand. It only means that one must make some effort to discover them. If one does not have the good and great fortune to have a close friend, one must discover such a person. Go over the list of your acquaintances, and it is rare that you will not find one who in the last few years has not suffered sorrow. Call her up and tell her frankly that you would like to talk with her. It may take several calls until you discover another person to whom you can relate. If this list proves unpromising, call your priest, minister, or rabbi and tell him you need a friend who is understanding. He can often put you quickly in touch with the right person. A conversation with the director of a senior citizens center or a retirement apartment may lead to helpful persons.

Above all, do not feel that you are imposing yourself on these people. Most widows are lonely, and they welcome the opportunity to meet a new friend. Furthermore, all of us need to be useful. To help another human being is the acme of service. In a more profound sense, in listening to you that person will be rehearsing their own inner conflicts, and although they are relatively well, this is useful, too. If our studies are accurate, the greatest need for most widows is for human contact. You should never feel that reaching out to such people is a burden to them. Far from it, such an act helps them grow, too.

C. THE NEED FOR GROUPS

We have suggested that when death or divorce breaks up a marriage one must redefine one's groups. Past groups of married persons will help, but you will have new needs. Actually, there are two different kinds of groups that are essential: the first for healing and the second for the new life. We will discuss such groups in a later chapter.

We hope that you are fortunate enough to live in a community that has a widows' group. However, if you cannot readily find such a group, call your Community Welfare Bureau. The usefulness of a number of experimental groups has been well-publicized, so more and more communities are taking steps to develop such a resource.

If you cannot find a widows' group, there are still a great many other therapeutic groups that will serve almost as well. Group therapy has proved to be a quite efficacious way of bringing people together to help each other. There are groups in every large city and in most small communities. Many churches have them, and they particularly welcome widows as members. Many psychologists, family counselors, and psychiatrists have organized private groups that are well structured.

It would be very surprising if you entered such a group and did not encounter others with your same life situation. Death is a universal visitor, and it leaves all of us with intense needs.

You may hesitate at first to join such a group. You may feel that you do not want to bare your private agonies to strangers. But there is no pressure to do that. You can participate to the degree you wish and reveal only what seems comfortable. On the other hand, the group does not remain a collection of strangers for very long. You will find yourself concerned with them and helpful to them and they to you. They will give you support as other human beings and advise where you need it. Many lifelong friendships emerge from this kind of group.

D. THE WIDOW AS A WOMAN

As one reviews Barrett's study, one must be singularly appreciative of her acumen in using her third group, which was a woman's consciousness-raising group. She felt that part of the problem of the widow was rooted in the peculiar status given to women in general, particularly to older women. Her hunch in structuring this group was that women who could be rescued from the stereotypes associated with widowhood still needed some help in escaping from those proscriptions that apply to women in contrast to men. The interesting conclusion of her study was that of all three groups those who focused on changes of their self-concept resulted in the most life-style changes.

Widows and older divorced women may not be able to articulate their feelings about their relative status in society, but some of their peers have said it well. Susan Sontag, in one of her more insightful moments, reminded us that "For the normal changes that age inscribes on every human face, women are much more heavily penalized than men." And again, "Most of the physical qualities regarded as attractive in women deteriorate much earlier in life than those defined as 'male.' Indeed, they perish fairly soon in the normal sequence of body transformation," and "Every wrinkle, every line, every grey hair is a defeat." Sontag is saying that there is a double standard of aging. Oldness in a man is not decried; but it is defeating for a woman. She asks that women "let themselves age naturally and without embarrassment, actively protesting and disobeying the conventions that stem from this society's double standard about aging."

This honesty about age and aging would certainly help widows' self-esteem, but it does nothing to alter the demographic fact that there are five older single women for every older single man. Sontag does well to give women an option in terms of their self-view, but she has not told us how this may be used to escape from loneliness and to find companionship in the distorted age group-ings we will face. To accept one's age and one's status as a widow is a first step to contentment. It may go a far way in escaping from thinking only of oneself as an "ex-wife." But we must go from there and explore possible heterosexual avenues of fulfillment if the single female is to be assured of satisfaction in life.

That Barrett's consciousness-raising group was judged by her total sample as being the most helpful of all the therapeutic groups must tell us that the status accorded to women, and to widowed women, is a powerful decrement. But some widows seem predestined not only to accept society's low evaluation but also to perpetuate it. Barrett called attention to the fact that widows "suffer from grief as well as stresses that a male-oriented, youth-oriented and couple-oriented society subjects them to long after the husband's death." This means that widows have to es-cape from the limits of thinking of themselves only as ex-wives and to begin thinking of themselves as persons who individually have much to learn, much to experience, and much to share. She will learn to think of herself as more than an ex-mate and to play a role with focus on the development of herself. It is possible that this role will be the most rewarding she has ever experienced.

The table on page 47, which is taken from a study by Baredo,[6] indicates that all groups suffered from psychological and physical distress. It is apparent that a larger percentage of widows than marrieds suffered from many of these symptoms, and on eight of the twelve listed items widows experienced troublesome reactions more frequently than widowers. This confirms our earlier state-ment about the multiple problems of widowhood.

If such psychological problems are severe, if one's spirits dip so low that one asks oneself whether it would not be better to join the dead mate, or easier on loved ones if we were gone, it is time to seek expert help. If the depression is so deep and continues for such a long time that we settle into a routine of nothingness, it

TABLE 1
PERCENTAGE OF RESPONDENTS REPORTING
PSYCHOSOMATIC SYMPTOMS "A FEW TIMES" OR "OFTEN"

SYMPTOMS REPORTED	TOTAL (496)	MARRIED (271)	WIDOWERS (44)	WIDOWS (181)
Nervousness	47.8	45.7	45.5	51.4
Trouble getting or staying asleep	45.3	42.8	40.9	50.0
Upset stomach	41.3	36.9	38.5	48.3
Spells of dizziness	36.4	31.0	43.1	42.7
Headaches	31.9	28.5	29.5	37.6
Heart beating fast	28.1	22.8	18.6	38.2
Shortness of breath	22.5	20.2	18.1	27.1
Nightmares	16.3	16.1	18.2	16.3
Trembling hands	11.7	9.5	13.6	14.7
Cold sweats	10.2	9.1	11.4	10.1
Hands feeling damp or sweaty	8.8	10.9	9.0	5.6
Fainting spells	5.3	4.5	2.3	7.4

indicates that we need professional help. If sleeplessness, loss of weight, or any other symptom goes on and on, we should steer our course to a psychiatrist or psychologist because, at least for a while, the burden is more than we can bear and we are blind to light at the end of the tunnel.

E. THE WIDER VIEW

We have suggested that part of the depression and despair that come to the widow in America has its roots in our strange denial of death. La Rochefoucauld summed up our attitude when he said: "One cannot look directly at the sun or death." But we have learned that we can look at the eclipse, through smoked glass, and new attitudes toward death will enable us to open our eyes to this last significant event in our lives.

There are many significant courses and books dealing with

death, and altering our dread and denial can help us in facing the death of a loved one. A list of the best of these books is contained in the bibliography at the end of this book.

One institute, the Andrus Gerontology Center at the University of Southern California, has gone beyond most of the death-and-dying literature to propose that every person be helped to think clearly about how he should die, how his remains should be handled, how his heritage should be shared, and how he should be memorialized. This effort is under the title of the Journey's End Foundation Fund. It has already produced a movie and a book, both entitled *Journey's End.* If a widow has been traumatized because of lack of planning on the part of her husband, she ought not to leave her own family and friends in such shape. The Journey's End Foundation will help her look at the logical steps to take to put her own affairs in order.

The widow herself can play two parts in trying to change that part of our culture that destined her for difficulty when death came. She can advocate and help form widow's groups in her community. And through the years, she can become helpful to that corps of persons who offer consolation and help to those who are recently widowed. She will find in time that such sharing helps alleviate her own pain and helps develop new and significant roles to compensate for her own losses. In doing so, she will overcome the double standard.

CONCLUSION

This chapter has stressed the need for (1) early activity and decision-making; (2) confrontation of our innermost feelings with either an intimate friend or in an intimate group setting; (3) consultation at times with a professional, whether a member of the clergy or a psychiatrist; (4) a look at the stereotypes we hold about ourselves because we are female; and (5) helping other bereaved individuals either by changing society's myths about death or by personal intervention when others are in need.

Most widows probably never question the legitimacy of their anger against their departed mates or their guilt about their complicity in that death. Both emotions are universal and universally distorted by the pain of separation. If they are not put into good perspective, they will plague us until death. Many widows come close to a breaking point in their pain, and some do commit suicide because they do not call in professional help in critical moments. Sadly, if they had only asked for help, they might have had thirty years of a better life than they had ever known. Many widows retreat into a gloomy half-life because they have accepted an obsolete definition of a single, older woman's place in society. They have never listened to Susan Sontag or Marjorie Kuhn or any of their peers who are leading the way for an escape from yesterday and into individual achievements.

A good many universities are now instituting training for retired men in what is called "second careers." But widows are a much more viable audience. They have much to contribute and a longer life in which to do it. Society must begin to help them reconstitute their objectives and self-esteem so that they can become the resource they ought to be, in their "second careers."

Until society does offer those opportunities, widows can seek out both groups and individuals who can help them escape from the prison of self-pity, guilt, anger, and depression and move forward to razing the walls of containment and building the as yet unpenciled walls of new temples of humanity.

CHAPTER FOUR

THE NEW
YOU

"Once before I wrote that my grief was done, and then it suddenly returned. . . . But now it will not return again. Something within me is waking from a long sleep, and I want to live and move again. Some zest is returning to me, some immense gratefulness for those who love me, some strong wish to love them also. I am full of thanks for life. I have not told myself to be thankful, I just am so. . . ."[1]

With these simple, moving words, writer Alan Paton closes *For You Departed*, a poignant memoir of his wife of forty years. The message is full of meaning for those recovering from bereavement. In it, he senses that his grief work finally is over. He has cut the ties with his late wife, but she still is remembered and beloved. He is experiencing a reawakening to life as a different person. He relates the mystery of his newly developing identity, his new being as a single person.

Cutting the ties to the deceased is an essential function of grief work. Make no mistake. If the ties are not cut, the grief process has not been completed. This is attested to by human experience through the ages and by social scientists' studies. Dr. Erich Lindemann, whose classic research into grief and bereavement we mentioned earlier, described this aspect of the grief process as "emancipation from the bondage to the deceased."

This might seem to be a harsh, jarring, virtually incomprehensible idea, particularly during the initial phases of mourning and grief. But it must occur, as virtually anyone who has successfully recovered from bereavement will tell you.

Cutting the ties to the deceased does *not* mean dishonoring, rejecting, or forgetting him or her. In a sense, he or she always will be a part of your being. Recall that Jean says, even as she affirms that the ties to her late husband are being cut, "He'll always be a part of me." It is so. Psychologist David K. Switzer in fact calls "the resurrection of the deceased within the self of the bereaved" a need in the healing of grief.[2] All of us are products of our past in the sense that we have been more or less permanently influenced by others. That is, the personalities and values of those who have been particularly close to us are enshrined in our own being.

What does "cutting the ties" or "emancipation from the bondage to the deceased" mean? It is a gradual realization within yourself that you have become a different person than you were during your married years and indeed different than you were during the deep, dark phases of grieving. Somehow you are aware that life goes on and that you are here and alive. It dawns that you now are a single person. You are an "I" and no longer part of a "we." It starts a gradual sort of rebirth into a life of different circumstances. To be sure, there are strange, bewildering, mysterious feelings in addition to the hurts and sorrows that linger. As Paton writes, ". . . Something within me is waking from a long sleep and I want to live and move again. . . ."[3]

. For purposes of discussion only, release from the deep emotional ties to the deceased might be seen as a milestone or "stage" of bereavement. However, delineating such set "stages" of widowhood has great pitfalls, and you should be aware of them. First, there is no set timing for the various aspects of grief work and recovery, despite widely held assumptions to the contrary. For some, the grief work might require a few months; for others, longer. Second, the various steps toward recovery often overlap. One does not simply release oneself from the bondage to the deceased on Tuesday and on Wednesday begin a readjustment to the environment and two months from then start to form new relationships.

Helena Z. Lopata, a distinguished researcher on widowhood, has found that the events of grieving and recovery "are not likely to happen in such a neatly structured sequence."[4] Therefore, those who are grieving and recovering should not expect to be making progress on some specific timetable or in some logical, prescribed sequence. Human emotions—in all their depth and complexity—are not necessarily logical, nor are they sequential. Do not attempt to overstructure your recovery. Do not be discouraged when you seem unable to measure up to tacit or implied or expressed expectations of others. Do not allow yourself to be pushed by others—regardless of their good intentions—from "stage" to "stage." Others can be understanding and supportive, it is true. And surely you need this. But bereavement is an intensely individual, private experience. In a sense, you are alone in your grief work, and you alone know the pace and experience of recovery.

BEING A WIDOW

If, for purposes of discussion, we can say that release from the emotional ties with the deceased is a "stage" or milestone of widowhood, what then? Are you thrown into some emotional vacuum when you are emancipated from this bondage? No. The answer in simple, general terms is that you become a different person. At this point, there is dawning within you a new *identity*. The identity is "widow." Interestingly enough, as we shall see, it is a *temporary* one.

Studies by Lopata provide a helpful perspective on this phase of bereavement and recovery. In a research paper, she has written: ". . . Modern American society has been phasing out the *status role* of 'widow,' with its all-pervasive identity and its main function of maintaining the distinctions between a woman so labeled, and a wife, a single girl, and a divorcee. . . ."

She continues:

> For an increasing proportion of American widows this movement from the role of wife into the pervasive role of widow and settling down in it for the rest of her life is not possible or desirable. Usually, "widowhood" seems to be a temporary stage of identity reconstruction. . . .

And she concludes that:

> . . . The process of identity reconstruction is, in the long run, necessary and inevitable, if the woman built her identity and sentiments upon being a wife, the wife of that particular man, and a member of a team. Few women can remain stationary in their identities by living in memory alone. . . .[5]

Lopata points out that this temporary phase of "widow" has several problems, including disorganized emotions and the sudden, almost stunning challenges and obligations she must face alone. But this period also has its "cushioning effects"—such as help and attentiveness from others—that tend to deflect and modify the impact of the death.

A NEW IDENTITY

Moving out of the temporary phase of "widow" is not always easy, according to Lopata, because of two major complicating factors. One is the pervasive "stages of widowhood" theory and its consequent problems, which we outlined previously. The second, which she says causes problems for many women, is that "they have no place to go" in terms of identity. This is so, she contends, because "American society is still socializing women to be wives and mothers and not to have alternative identities at any stage of the life cycle. . . ."[6]

One must be aware of the problems of this phase in order to be better able to resolve them. But this is not to suggest that we should dwell on problems and complications, for the picture is certainly not all that bleak. Regardless of the complexity and gravity of human difficulties, there abides within us a marvelous set of capacities to deal with them. Far from being merely a nice thought or a rather simpleminded platitude, this is proven fact. Research documents it. Listen to the good news reported by Lopata on the basis of her research observations:

> However traumatic the problem of not having any place to go in terms of identities and goals for the rest of life, and however long it lasts, most widows usually work out of this stage. Some reconstruct their lives and identities dramatically, entering a completely new lifestyle than the one shared with the husband in the past. They re-train themselves into new or dormant skills and enter jobs or volunteer for social roles requiring commitment and insuring the feeling of competence in a new social world that responds to them individually, not as former wives or widows. Such a woman sees herself individualistically as Mary Smith, although the memory of having been Mrs. John Smith still forms part of her identity package, even when no one interacts with her in the role of wife. Those women who no longer have small children learn to live alone, often for the first time in their lives, and with feelings of loneliness (but) which are accompanied by satisfaction with independence. . . .[7]

"Identity reconstruction" is a graphic term. The two words pack a lot of meaning. And they mean what they say. The process is one of profound change—of identity—of self. It implies activity, not passivity. But how does one go about it? The first step is knowledge. Knowledge of self. If you are to solve a problem, you must first know what it is. If you are to meet a challenge effectively, you must first understand it. Likewise, effective reconstruction of your identity requires that you first cultivate the art of self-knowledge.

The concept of self-knowledge—knowing who you are—has preoccupied the great thinkers and writers of history and is explored increasingly by the social scientists of today. Invariably, self-knowledge emerges as a great imperative. It is a necessary underlying goal of anyone who will find meaning in life, grow as a person, and strive toward realization of the vast human potentialities that reside within all of us. Socrates said simply, "Man, know thyself." Lao-Tze held that "He who knows others is clever; he who knows himself is enlightened." Shakespeare wrote, ". . . of all knowledge, the wise and good seek most to know themselves." Modern day psychotherapists urge the benefits of "being in touch with one's self."

By no means are these platitudes that one should simply accept vaguely in the abstract. They are exhortations to action. They have special meaning to you, a widow who has suffered a great loss and is working through bereavement to recovery. This is so because, as we've seen, in being bereaved you are undergoing what popular terminology describes as an "identity crisis." That is to say, your identity is in the process of profound change from wife to widow and then to what it will be in the future.

But "identity crisis," real as it is at this point in your life, is not as ominous as it might sound. Undoubtedly, you have experienced—and indeed have grown from—identity crises in your past life. As a child, working through the maelstrom of adolescence into adulthood, you experienced an identity crisis. The things of a child were put away, and the independence and responsibilities of adulthood became realities of life. When you were married, you passed almost instantaneously from single, independent, young adulthood into an entire new spectrum of roles, obligations, dreams, hopes, and growth. If you became a parent, you were confronted with major changes in your identity. You experienced an identity crisis.

However, the identity crisis consequent to bereavement and grief probably is the most marked and profound one that you are likely to have encountered. This is so because of the deep loss that you have suffered. A life pattern of many years' standing suddenly is ripped away. In most cases, it is impossible to prepare for it. Complicating this is the fact that—unlike others we have mentioned—the identity crisis of bereavement does not serve up prescribed, expected new roles and responsibilities. There is nothing that *automatically* fills the void. You must make of the future what you will. Yet ironically, you might be quite well prepared, almost "programmed," to handle this more severe identity crisis. This is so because you have grieved deeply.

This might sound strange. And for some, indeed it is not the case. But careful reflection can lead you to see the general truth of what we say. Dr. Lindemann points out that the bereaved ". . . has to accept the pain of the bereavement. He has to review his relationships with the deceased and has to become acquainted with the alterations in his own modes of emotional reaction. . . ."[8] Think of it for a moment. To do these things, to perform grief work effectively, you must be turned inward. Sorting out such profound emotional concerns requires that you, the bereaved, direct your thoughts inward. Like many other activities in life that are relatively constant, one becomes better at self-examination with practice. Assuming that you have done your grief work, you already have cultivated this habit. Thus, you have a heightened ability of self-examination. This brings self-knowledge, which in turn is crucial to handling the identity crisis effectively. It is as if nature has provided you with the ability to handle the identity crisis by forging it within you in the white heat of prior grief.

Are we prescribing some formal, structured program by which to psychoanalyze yourself? The answer is no. Is this self-examination of which we speak a sort of exaggerated self-consciousness that has us walking around turned so inward that we do not smell the flowers, admire the view, or, most importantly, relate fully and lovingly with others? Absolutely not.

Theodore Isaac Rubin, the prolific psychiatrist, has written of the folly of such schemes:

> Many people sit and think and think and think about themselves, and their thinking branches this way and that way, and they continue to think about themselves and really cannot stop except with very strong distraction. This kind of 'obsessive ruminating' is not at all connected to self-analysis, opening up, extending self, or growth. . . .
>
> This kind of self-thinking is very often a subtle and sometimes a rather blatant form of self-torture. . . . It is often used to prevent honest and valid feelings about one's self from entering

awareness because they do not fit prescribed and acceptable standards. . . .[9]

So Rubin helps us describe what identity discovery—self-knowledge—through self-examination is *not*. Yet elsewhere he writes: "Another way of referring to self is by use of the word 'identity,' that is, who you are. It is all important to have a feeling for who you are because it is your identity, yourself, which is the single most powerful instrument you will ever have with which to relate to [others]. . . ."[10] And, we might add, to live creatively and to grow. Thus again, there emerges the importance of "knowing yourself," "being in touch with yourself," whatever phrase you want to use.

In his sensitively written collection of short essays, *The Pain of Being Human*,* priest-psychologist Eugene Kennedy spells out in a warm, down-to-earth way what constructive self-examination should be:

> . . . If a man wants to understand himself he must take the soundings of his own depths. He does this, not by asking what he thinks nor even what he believes, but by asking what he feels. A man's emotional life is not some independent subsystem that operates according to random rules. His emotions tell him, as nothing else does, the kind of person he is. His feelings are an integral part of himself. They provide an accurate indication of his reactions and his values in the face of the experience of life. Beneath his feelings, the feedback mechanism of his personality, lies the real man or woman.
>
> The person who can begin to hear what his feelings are telling him gets at the roots of his being. "What are the things that get me mad?" "What are the things I am touchy about?" "When is it that I am so shy?" "What are the things I would make sacrifices for?" "What are the things that embarrass me?" "What are the things I feel sure about?" The answers to these kinds of questions yield a profile of ourselves that is truthful even if it is sometimes difficult to look at. . . . The truth alone frees us to be ourselves. We are very uncomfortable in life until we are ourselves. . . .

Kennedy continues:

> When a man begins to hear what his feelings are telling him, he begins to understand himself. He can, with a little reflection, and sometimes with a little help from another person, get to the bottom of his feelings and thus to the bottom of himself. . . .

And expands on this thought:

> . . . Unless a man identifies his emotions correctly, he has neither self-knowledge nor self-control. He is, instead, whether he knows it or not, controlled by his emotions. Although he may hide this from himself by denying or disguising his feelings, he does not thereby alter their influence on him. Sooner or later, in direct or indirect fashion, what is really going on inside himself will break through. Suppression of our inner dynamism never really works with great effectiveness. . . .[11]

"Listening to the fascinating messages about our identity which our feelings constantly whisper to us. . . ."[12] Ah—there is the stuff of growth, eloquently put. And it is what we are suggesting to you as you confront the identity crisis of bereavement. The experience of listening to one's feelings in a noncritical, tolerant way is one of the most potentially rewarding opportunities in life. It is available to most of us, rich or poor, young or old, man or woman. Yet how rarely it is practiced effectively in our "other-directed" society!

INNER- AND OTHER-DIRECTED LIVES

Indeed, many of us in this complex, modern world live almost exclusively other-directed lives. That is, society thrusts on us a plethora of expectations, and more often than not, we tend to move through life measuring up to a host of spoken or unspoken criteria. The external forces directing our lives are many. They include governments, employers, organizations to which we belong, friends, family, competition, quests for "status," and a host of other social expectations and mores. The external directions become internalized within us, and we become conditioned to respond almost automatically. Many of us live by assumptions that go unexamined and unchallenged. Seldom do most of us evaluate these external influences in light of our own impulses and feelings. This is unfortunate to say the least. Because in order to grow, to make a good effort at realizing the potential within ourselves, we must become inner-directed, at least in part. This is not to say that we should become withdrawn or introverted. Far from it. The compelling truth is that inner-directedness enables us to go out of ourselves more fully and vibrantly. In other words, inner-directedness amounts to marshaling more of who we are and bringing a fuller self to living our lives. And inner-directedness begins with constructive self-examination, "listening to the fascinating messages about our identity which our feelings constantly whisper to us."

Within each of you, there is a rich data bank of the things that makes you uniquely individual. Contained therein is precious information that is applicable to every area of your life. By searching your heart and soul, you can discover what it is that makes you comfortable or uncomfortable, fulfilled or frustrated, relaxed and at peace or anxious and apprehensive. If you are in touch with your feelings, you eventually can arrive at conclusions and decisions that are right for you in such areas as relationships with family and friends, work, recreation, creative pursuits, religious and philosophical commitments, living arrangements, and financial affairs. This is not to say that you will be ruled by your feelings or emotions. Just the opposite. Instead, you will have freedom from such domination because the rich amalgam of your inner self—your feeling-values—will inform and deepen that other part of you that has to do with logic, reason, and conscience. The overall combination begets intelligent, creative, self-determination in your future life as a single person.

Constructive searching into self results in the gradual painting of a highly individualized, personal, unique self-portrait. In it, you will detect all that is implied in the word *human*. There will be feelings that absolutely defy any rule of logic. There will be inconsistencies. There will be conflicts and crosscurrents. Learn to chuckle at some of your foibles; in turn, you will become more understanding of them in others. Try to be tolerant about your self-revelations.

For surely, you will also discover personal attributes, qualities, talents, values, convictions, and strengths of which you can be justly proud. You might well become conscious of personal resources and capabilities of which you have not been fully aware. Think this over. Recall some of those times in your past life when you seemed to rise above yourself in making a difficult decision, in being a source of strength to others in a crisis, or in marshaling all that was in you to forge ahead in the face of adversity. Think of the remarkable strength you already have evoked to be working through the desolation of bereavement. If you can do this, you will have taken a giant step toward arriving at a new level of self-esteem.

ACHIEVING SELF-ESTEEM

Self-esteem is a prerequisite for growth, for realizing your human potentialities, for relating to others in the fullest. As you learn to like and love yourself more, you can like and love others more fully. Remember one of the great commandments of Scripture in all its psychological wisdom: "Love thy neighbor as *thyself*." As you become aware of that vast reservoir of talents and that emotional power within you and affirm it in self-esteem, you begin to have some of the confidence and assurance that are underlying necessities for full, creative, rewarding experiences in all areas of life. The cycle runs thus: Self-examination produces self-knowledge, which can beget self-esteem, which is necessary for self-confidence, which is demanded if we are to use our God-given talents and thus live creatively.

In the course of your self-examination, take an inventory of your abilities and interests. Consider reactivating pursuits of the past that were rewarding. Make plans to follow up long-suppressed interests that you never had time for previously. Combine together your interests with your skills in activities that utilize both in a challenging way. Bear in mind, there are compensations to widowhood, such as time and freedom from past responsibilities, that enable you to pursue fulfilling personal interests.

Be aware that the opportunity for self-knowledge through self-examination should not be approached only as a temporary measure to help you through the immediate days and then be discarded. To the contrary, look on this listening to yourself, your feelings, your values, your identity, as the beginning of an aid that will serve you well through every day of the rest of your life. The worthiest goal is not to achieve some plateau and remain static. It is to change and grow.

The more you practice this constructive self-examination, the better you will become at it. Do not expect miracles at first. Your deep self will not be served up to you via instant replay as in a televised football game. Do not force the issue. Do not be a perfectionist, expecting instant crystal clarity with perfect harmony and perfect organization. Above all, do not be harshly demanding and ultracritical of the person you come to know. Patiently practice the habit of self-examination, and it will build. Gradually, you will have increasing self-knowledge in more profound ways than you ever realized was possible.

And what does all this mean in terms of *your* identity—that catchall term that denotes who you are? That question is for you to answer. Because every person is unique, each answer will be unique. One widow says that as the result of her self-search she decided she didn't want her identity to be "widow." She wanted it to be social worker-teacher. So she entered graduate school and earned her doctorate, which she incidentally feels is a restoration of personal status lost in bereavement. Now she is creatively pursuing her new identity on the faculty of a major university. The answer to who *you* are might not come so explicitly or simply or succinctly. For example, your identity might be grandparent-artist-businesswoman. The combinations and possibilities are virtually limitless. Whatever it might be, your underlying identity can and should be based on self-determined, creative, open, *single person* in touch with myself capable of enjoying the moment and hopeful for the future."

We have alluded briefly to another helpful measure for you

in these days of identity reconstruction, one that can be used most profitably in conjunction with your continuing self-examination. It is self-affirmation. As you discover your attributes, declare them to yourself. And as you develop goals for the future, tell yourself you can achieve them because you are a remarkably able person, capable of functioning and performing at increasing levels. It is helpful to jot down a list of these for review every day. Do it twice—just after awakening and just before retiring. Recite them aloud to yourself. One such affirmation might be, "I like myself, and others like me too because of my personal qualities of openness, friendliness, awareness, and warmth." Another might be, "I have the free, unfettered spirit to make the most of my creative abilities in everything that I undertake to do." Another might be, "I am successful at (activity) because I have the self-assurance and discipline to make the most of my talents (in this area)." As you jot down these daily affirmations, it is important that they be as above, in the present tense, as if they already are a full-blown reality in your life. Keep the various items on the list, and repeat them daily for as long as you feel is appropriate. The list should be changed as you change. You will discard some and add others, depending on your progress. This daily "dialog" with yourself, in self-assured terms—coupled with increasing knowledge through self-examination—can be most helpful in your journey through identity reconstruction. And again, it can be an invaluable measure in all the days of the future.

One of the saddest truths of life must be that so many persons go through their entire lives using only a small fraction of their talents and capabilities. So few call on the emotional power within them to live to the fullest. So few venture into continuing self-search and self-affirmation. But you need not be among them. During the bewildering days of post-widowhood identity reconstruction, you can develop a formula for living that will serve you inestimably throughout the rest of your life. Then you can say, as Paton does so eloquently: ". . . Some zest is returning to me. . . . I am full of thanks for life. I have not told myself to be thankful, I just am so. . . ."[13]

CHAPTER FIVE

FINDING
A NEW WORLD

Columbus found a world, and had no chart,
Save one that faith deciphered in the skies;
To trust the soul's invincible surmise
Was all his science and his only art.
—GEORGE SANTAYANA[1]

How many uncharted courses there are! How well you know this as you work toward recovery. You have journeyed through the stormiest of uncharted waters. Now the sea is calmer. The confusion and deep sorrows of bereavement begin to subside, haltingly and temporarily at first, then more and more. You may feel that the journey is nearing its destination.

There is yet another voyage on which you must embark. Like Columbus, you must find a new world. While maintaining your inner consciousness, you must turn outward again. To be sure, your voyage may be no easier than that of the explorer. There will be false starts. There is no turning back. Despite loneliness and lapses into discouragement, you can reach your destination. You can prevail. Although there are no charts for this high adventure, you will find that trust in your "soul's invincible surmise" will be all the basic science and art that you need.

Although Columbus had no chart, he was well prepared for

his great adventure. Historians tell us he had extensive maritime experience as a trading ship captain and had sailed many previous voyages. In that sense, you are like Columbus. You already are somewhat prepared for your voyage into a new world if you have taken journeys into yourself as we described in the previous chapter. The self-awareness you have gained can give you the freedom necessary to navigate your own best course and to be the captain of your own ship.

WHAT IS FREEDOM?

Freedom is surely one of the most meaningful words in our language, for it designates a host of revered values. Freedom of speech. Freedom of worship. Freedom to travel and to live where one wishes. Free enterprise. Freedom is enshrined in marble, in bronze, in the parchment of the Constitution, and, even more significantly, in the consciousness of our people. On the level of our day-to-day lives, freedom is a no less significant value. We tend to be uncomfortable when we are backed into a corner. Those with balanced, integrated personalities live and breathe personal freedom. Our most cherished dreams must be clothed in freedom if we are to make them come true. The value of a person's freedom is pointed up most emphatically in the results of losing it or having it taken away. From their clinical experience, psychologists report that when freedom is lost, a pattern of anger, frustration, hatred, resentment, and self-pity result. Freedom figures largely in our mental health.

Freedom and independence are listed as compensations of widowhood by Chicago-area widows studied by Helena Lopata. Despite tragedy and sadness and grief, half the respondents agreed with the statement, "I like living alone." Despite the loneliness involved in losing their husbands, half the women found release from housewifely duties to be a major compensation of widowhood. One widow, even then still grieving, listed several compensations of widowhood related to freedom and independence. "You don't have to cook if you don't want to; your time is your own; you can come and go as you want. . . ." Lopata indicates that widows' feelings of independence don't necessarily mean that they had been unhappy with their marriages. "Many were unhappy," she writes, "but an undetermined number of others simply closed that stage of life and adjusted to living alone without necessarily redefining their past as too restrictive or lacking in compensations."[2]

There is far more to freedom, though, than a release from duties and obligations or having more discretionary time. Freedom is written in larger and in more profound terms than that. We speak here of inner freedom, that deep foundation that supports all that we are and can be. It is a point to ponder as you start to build a new life.

In his book, *Man's Search for Himself*, the psychotherapist and writer, Dr. Rollo May, addresses the nature and implications of inner freedom. It is, he says, the human's capacity to take a hand in his own development, his capacity to mold himself. In this quality, we are unique among all creatures. To the extent that we have it and pursue it and grow in it, we become more of what it is to be human. May expands on the description by saying that "freedom means openness, a readiness to grow; it means being flexible, ready to change for the sake of greater human values."[3]

May points out that deep inner freedom must be achieved, not once and for all, but every day of our lives. He thinks that a basic step toward achieving freedom is to affirm fully the self and to accept responsibility for living our lives, realizing our potentials. This in turn implies making our own decisions and choices. So responsibility takes on a new meaning. I *accept* responsibility. It is not simply mine because it has been thrust on me from an outside source. Discipline becomes *self-discipline*.

Thus, our quest for freedom goes hand in hand with the development of self-awareness. May underscores this in noting that if we had no knowledge of ourselves we would be "pushed along by instinct or the automatic march of history, like bees or mastodons." Amplifying, he points out that the less a person is aware of himself, the more he is likely to be controlled by inhibitions, repressions, childhood conditions. ". . . The more he is pushed by forces over which he has no control. . . ."[4] The old Latin proverb, *veritas vos liberabit*, the "truth will make you free," applies most vividly when expanded to, "the truth *about yourself* will make you free."

There are rich examples of how inner freedom is cultivated and achieved when widows start to make discoveries about their feelings and gain new self-awareness. Remember the desolation of Jean, the widow we met in the first chapter. Still grieving for her husband, she returned to work. It was difficult for her to function, and it became more so over the course of a few months. She began to realize that the stresses of her job were too great. When she was considering resignation, friends and associates vigorously advised against it. They advanced all sorts of logical and compelling reasons why she should remain. But as we recall, she said later that "I knew it was right, and it was." *Her own* decision has stood the test of time. Even amidst the desolation of her grief, she was beginning to search her inner self and to get in touch with her own feelings. And that was what fostered the inner freedom she needed. Jean affirmed herself, took the responsibility for her own existence in the present and in the future, and was able to make her own decision even though it ran counter to the conventional "wisdom" that surrounded her.

The process does not always occur so simply or quickly, as the case of Carol attests.

When her husband died, leaving her with one teenager and two younger children to rear, she cried little. She buried the hurts deep within herself, for there was no time—or so she thought—to confront them. With little concern about herself, she proceeded to assume the heavy responsibilities of single parent and bread-winner. "I was busy, worked hard, and did what had to be done," she recalled later.

For years, she made an adequate living and saw to it that the children had good care during the days and all the motherly attention she could give them evenings and weekends. Periodi-cally, she experienced moments of depression, but isn't that normal? After all, it hadn't interfered with my work, she rea-soned. Friends commented on how strong and capable Carol was, and how well she "adjusted."

But gradually, as her children grew older and had less need of her attention, Carol became aware of an emptiness in her life.

She began to experience a numbness, an inability to feel much of anything except a vague sense of depression, which worsened. Carol had always prided herself on her efficiency, but now depression was beginning to interfere with that. A sense of purposelessness set in. She could not laugh or cry.

Fortunately, Carol sought help from an understanding psychotherapist who helped her to realize that she was suffering a delayed grief reaction. In the course of many sessions with this counselor, she began to search her inner self and her feelings. As she did this, she was able to work through the healing process that she had denied herself years earlier. She began to care enough to take charge of her own life and to develop some personal goals. Now virtually a new person, one who is alive and growing, she is pursuing an advanced degree in preparation for a professional career. She is functioning again, but most importantly, this time as a self-aware, whole person.

Unfortunately, Carol's experience is common. During the years that she kept her true self and true feelings buried, she was unable to take control of her own life and her own destiny. From all outward appearances, she functioned well under the circumstances. But she simply responded to responsibilities instead of accepting them on her own terms. She was carried along by the momentum of life, rather than determining her own direction and pace. She did not gain real inner freedom and all the promise and joy that it implies until she confronted the profound realities of her inner being.

Failing to adjust to crises like bereavement is only one way a person can neglect the inner self and thus fail to achieve inner freedom. Modern man, May points out, largely has surrendered inward psychological and spiritual freedom to the routine of work and social expectations. With this comes a partial abdication of one's humanness. Such culturally ordained goals as money and status are pursued furiously, even though in the process one's real talents and dreams and personal values might be ignored and ultimately sacrificed. Many who are outwardly "successful" are desolate and alone in their pyrrhic victories. Others, never questioning, seem to be pushed along by social and economic forces that they assume have unalterable control.

This is not to say that in our complex modern society there are no external factors that have some control over what we do or how we live our lives. Of course there are. But as May points out, "[T]hrough his power to survey his life, man can transcend the immediate events which determine him. . . . he can still in his freedom choose how he will relate to these facts."[5]

The early days of Alice's bereavement illustrate this truth:

> Soon after her husband died, Alice realized she had next to nothing in the bank. Her small income was insufficient for her needs. "I felt lucky at first to find a file clerk's job with an insurance company. The salary was not large, but it did provide some security. I was in a haze the first few months. As I gradually sorted out my feelings, the daily routine—which seemed to help at first—became more and more of a grind. It got to the point that I hated to get up in the morning to go to work. The work really was unchallenging drudgery leading nowhere. But I needed to keep that job—or so I thought. I wallowed in self-pity. What a rotten lot I had! I didn't like myself very much. Yet I was afraid of what would happen if I didn't have the financial security. Maybe the arguments going on within myself spurred me on to thinking more clearly. Whatever, it dawned on me that the only thing *I had to do* was earn a certain income. *I didn't have to stick* at a frustrating, unrewarding job. I made up my mind to do whatever was necessary to get into work that would interest me and challenge my abilities. It took some time, but I made it. The waiting and the preparations weren't so bad because I had the satisfaction of knowing that I was taking charge of my situation. That all sounds so simple, doesn't it? The hell of it is, you can't always see things so clearly. When you realize you're free to better yourself, it's as if a light has been turned on in your life. . . ."

So it goes for many widows who begin to achieve freedom and reap its benefits. They discard the enslaving "Oh, but . . ." and "I can't . . ." syndromes.

We are not suggesting that inner freedom provides immunity from all problems or dispiriting feelings. It does not bring a magic eradication of the thousand and one fears and anxieties and frustrations and loneliness and uncertainties that creep into every life. There is no Camelot. But inner freedom does awaken dormant power residing within ourselves. Inner freedom does equip us with the ability to confront difficulties creatively and with a certain emotional poise and self-assurance.

You achieve freedom by learning it, by experiencing it, and by exercising it. You learn you have some control over your life by making this small choice and that single decision. You learn freedom by telling Aunt Mildred kindly but firmly that you have plans other than moving in with her and Cousin Alice. You thank your brother George for his caring and his kind advice, but you really don't want to sell the house, even though, yes, the market is good now, and it is a lot of space for a person to rattle around in alone. You learn freedom by deciding to return to college as a fifty-year-old junior to complete degree work that was inter-rupted by marriage thirty years ago.

What happens when one who has been widowed—or anyone else facing a crisis for that matter—strives for inner freedom and begins to achieve it? First, there is a new and enhanced aware-ness, not only of self but indeed of life, and she will *live* it. The awareness begins to focus on one's self, not as an island, but as part of the world. Newly found freedom simultaneously brings a renewal of faith, perhaps in the religious sense, but assuredly in one's self. She learns to become more comfortable with herself. New self-esteem and new self-confidence develop. The virtues that so naturally accompany faith—hope and love—can become real again. This is no rosy glow of shallow optimism. It is a real affirmation of life and the joy that can characterize it. For, now, the person realizes that she has freedom to be. Freedom to do or not to do . . . freedom to respond or not to respond on her own terms . . . freedom to set goals and to work toward them . . . freedom to become committed and to release herself from bur-dens that would stultify her growth. She has freedom to be spontaneous—to laugh again and, indeed, to cry. Freedom to love again. She has freedom that brings growing courage to be con-cerned with nothing but the truth about herself and the world. She revels in the joyful assurance that as she starts life anew she is taking charge of her life in constructive self-determination.

WHAT IS MENTAL HEALTH?

You learn freedom and discover its sweetness and piquancy. You sense that freedom is good for your outlook, your mental health. But beyond freedom, what? A touch of lubricant will free up a wheel on an axle, but will it turn, necessarily, just because it is unfrozen? All right. Take one step farther in your thinking, one step beyond freedom. Enter the realm of what psychotherpaist Carl Rogers called "becoming a person." Go beyond self-determination to what humanistic psychologist Abraham Maslow called self-actualization. These ideas are much the same, and they mean personal growth in the broadest, richest sense. Herein is the stuff of mental health.

BECOMING A PERSON

Rogers has written eloquently of the personal growth processes he has observed in his patients. These manifest themselves in the person beginning to drop masks, false fronts, or roles with which he or she has faced life. There is an experiencing of feeling "all the way to the limit." That part of the self that has been hidden within emerges in consciousness. "Thus, to an increasing degree, he becomes himself—not a facade of conformity to others, nor a cynical denial of all feeling, nor a front of intellectual rationality, but a living, breathing, feeling, fluctuating process—in short, he becomes a person."[6]

The person who emerges, Rogers wrote, is one in whom defensiveness and rigidity have been replaced with an increasing openness to experience. There is a heightened awareness of personal feelings and attitudes and a broadened awareness of the world of external realities. Along with this comes a new trust in himself, his organism, his emotional reactions and tendencies. There emerges a tendency to look more into one's self than to others for standards or approval in making evaluations, choices, decisions. And finally, there is what Rogers calls a "willingness to be a process." That means the newly emerging person is content to see himself or herself as a fluid, changing being, one in the process of becoming, instead of a fixed, static, finished product.

These hallmarks of personal growth are major benefits of good psychotherapy. They are achievable for many widows without formal therapy, and they can be stimulated by many potential catalysts in one's day-to-day life. Eve, a middle-aged widow, recalls a particular conversation she had a few years ago with her son, who was then home on vacation from college:

> He told me, "You changed so much after Dad died. You're uptight—like you're playing a role of what the ideal person, the ideal parent should be. It's as if you have to measure up to some standard. You're a wonderful lady, Mom, but you're trying too hard, demanding too much of yourself. Loosen up. Be yourself. I learned long ago that neither you—nor Dad for that matter— were perfect. You're human and I love you for what you are. I'm not a kid anymore, and you have your own life to lead."
>
> Out of the mouths of babes! I didn't say anything at the time, although I had listened carefully to what Bill had to say. That and other things—talking with my friends and reading— maybe just living day to day started me thinking. I guess you could say I learned some things about myself and learned to be myself all over again, little by little. I've learned to enjoy the present time more, and I'm not as insecure as I used to be about the future. I look forward to it because I have more faith in myself. . . .

In her own words, Eve has described events and characteristics of her personal growth process. They illustrate the sort of human dawning that Rogers means in the phrase, "becoming a person."

SELF-ACTUALIZATION

An additional perspective is reported by Maslow. He described self-actualization as "full use and exploitation of talents, capacities, potentialities. . . . Such people seem to be fulfilling themselves and to be doing the best that they are capable of doing, reminding us of Nietzsche's exhortation, 'Become what thou art!' They are people who have developed or are developing to the full stature of which they are capable. . . ."

Maslow identified and selected for study some extraordinary men and women who were self-actualized persons. They were found to share a pattern of characteristics that draws a picture of excellent psychological health. For example, they perceive reality more efficiently and are more comfortable with it than are others. They are able to accept themselves and others and the world they live in for what they are, shortcomings, warts and all. They tend to be spontaneous, especially in their thoughts and impulses, and to some extent in their behavior. They are strongly focused on some problem or cause outside themselves. Most of them like solitude and privacy, and are able to remain detached, "above the battle," unruffled and undisturbed by events or conditions that bother others deeply. They are autonomous in the sense that they are less dependent than others on the outside world for satisfactions and personal development. They have continuing freshness of appreciation—that is, they retain awe, wonder and joy for repeated experiences that become stale for others. In short, they are not jaded. Commonly, they have "mystical experiences" of intense feelings in which there is a temporary loss of placement in time and space. These self-actualized persons have strong generalized feelings of identification with human beings and a sympathy and affection for them. Not inconsistent with this, their circle of friends tends to be rather smaller than that of others. The self-actualized persons have especially deep ties with a few people. They delight in loving. They are very democratic in their associations and friendships. Their notions of right and wrong may not always be conventional in nature, but they are strongly ethical and rarely are confused about right and wrong in their personal dealings. They have a sense of humor. And they are highly creative.[7]

Who can these people be, you might ask. Are they a breed apart? Are they some genre of demigod? Are they by nature different from all other human beings? No. They are blood and bone and muscle and brain as we all are. They laugh and cry and have anxieties and imperfections and virtues. They have not erased all the problems of life because they have attained a fuller humanness than most people. Nor are they finished products. Even though they have attained a high level of living, they still are in the state of becoming. Maslow indicates that this upward growth trend is by no means an otherworldly phenomenon. It is a human process arising out of the basic *human* nature that we all share. So it is a very optimistic, hopeful view of the human condition. These self-actualized persons might be a sort of elite in terms of what *they* have been able to make of themselves, but do not be frightened by them. Do not feel insecure in yourself with a negative feeling of "I couldn't." Self-actualization is not an "all or nothing." Most of us can make positive moves in that direction and thus become self-actualizing in our own daily lives.

Nora found a pathway to self-actualization in beginning a career as a writer. She is articulate in describing her experiences:

> For years, I'd had in the back of my mind that I would like to write, but I had little time for it during my married life. After the worst of my grief was done, I started to realize that at age fifty my life was far from over. What would I make of the rest of my years? I realized too, from a few past experiences, that I had some talent for writing. I was full of doubt at first, but thought it might be worth a try, anyway. I'm glad I did because I'm now selling articles to magazines and enjoying the work more than anything I've ever done. It has taken time and hard work. Whoever said that being a good writer involves ten percent inspiration and ninety percent perspiration surely was right. I might or might not ever write a best-seller, but I do have the feeling that I'm developing myself and my abilities with every day that I work at it. It's not just the writing itself, either. Learning to write well demands that you develop certain personal characteristics such as an open attitude, inquisitiveness, sensitivity, judgment, and the ability to see life with some clarity. I've grown in these, too. It might sound like an ego trip—as the kids say—to tell you that I'm growing in ways I'd never imagined, but it's true. . . .

Developing one's potential in a particular pursuit often brings with it a more general pattern of personal growth, as Nora herself attests. Such self-actualization is not restricted, however, to those with special literary or artistic talents.

Maslow (in *The Farther Reaches of Human Nature*, a collection of his later papers published posthumously) discussed in a down-to-earth manner the everyday pathways to ongoing self-actualization. "It is not true," he wrote, "that on Thursday at four o'clock the trumpet blows and one steps into the pantheon forever and altogether. Self-actualization is a matter of degree, of little accessions accumulated one by one. . . ."[8]

Self-actualizers go about it in these little ways:

• They become absorbed in their experiences of the world and their activities in it, without the sort of self-consciousness that adolescents have. They forget their poses, achieve full concentration, and go about it "whole hog."

• They muster the courage to make the growth choice instead of the fear choice that might be safer and in tune with public opinion. Every time they make a growth choice, one that is true to the self and its potential, they take a step in self-actualization.

• They retain the "self" of self-actualization by shutting out the noises of the world and all its cues and assumptions and really listening to themselves. They taste wine, for instance, without looking at the label or noting the price tag, deciding whether it tastes good to them, whether they like it. They listen to music attentively without regard to what this or that critic says and decide whether *they* themselves find it pleasant, whether *they* are thrilled by it.

• They have the courage to be honest even if that means being different. They don't play games. They take responsibility.

• They work hard at developing their individual potentialities and talents.

• They shun a cynical outlook and are able to see themselves and others and life in their sacredness and symbolic meanings.

These small, gradual pathways to self-actualization are roads that we can take, but they are not always easy. Sometimes they require considerable courage. Sometimes self-actualizers feel lonely in their quest, surrounded as they may be by persons who live on a more superficial level and must be defensive about it. Maslow pointed out that "where everyone is blind, the sighted person is suspect."

Lillian's recollections illustrate this point:

. . . My kids vigorously advised against it when I told them I was planning to move permanently up to our cottage at the lake. I've always loved that place. It's the best move I've ever made because being close to nature is very important to me. I'm away from the city's overcrowding and smog and noise. It's a place where I can be on my own and have solitude; yet I have friends in the area who live there all year 'round. I read and paint and enjoy my life as much as or more than I ever have. I guess you could say I've set down some roots here, even to the point of getting active in local politics. My life there is full of promise because it's me; it really is. . . .

Moving away is not necessarily the answer to most widows' probems, but Lillian is a very independent woman who realized that her change of location would, and indeed did, stimulate her own growth. She saw it more clearly than did her children, and she had the courage to carry through with her plan. In so doing, and in thus making a new life in a new place, she demonstrated several of the small pathways of self-actualization that Maslow has described. It is revealing also to note that Lillian is a widow who suffered more than most at the loss of her husband. He had died two years before she made her decision to move.

In a sense, it is ironic that particularly bereft widows who have suffered and grieved deeply may be particularly well prepared for the difficulties one encounters along the road of self-actualizing growth. Maslow acknowledged this bittersweet aspect when he suggested that if grief and turmoil are sometimes necessary for growth, then not allowing people to go through their pain may be overprotection. "This, in turn, implies a certain lack of respect for the integrity and the intrinsic nature and the future development of the individual."[9]

In some ways, the self-actualizer must, by his or her growth impetus, march to a different drummer. But self-actualization does not require a radical change of life-style or holding one's self apart in isolation from other persons. Personal growth does not mean doing far-out, outrageous things or failing to consider the feelings of others. If self-actualizers have a sort of selfishness, along with this they exude a selflessness that is healthy for their own being and for the social fabric at large. Growing persons have values, which necessarily means they are turning away from nonvalues such as hypocrisy, meanness, and pettiness. They radiate a largeness of soul.

BEING, BECOMING, AND DOING

Ingrained in the American consciousness is a pride in our historical status of being movers and shakers. We are doers. One who is engaged in a continual, frenetic pace of activity is thought of somehow as being more virtuous, more worthwhile than those who are comparatively less busy. Those who seek their own counsel, those who meditate are somewhat suspect. We are quick to call such persons "introverts," which elicits all manner of negative connotations, even though these individuals may not be withdrawn at all. Perhaps much of this attitude stems from the work ethic, which continues to influence our cultural consciousness significantly.

It is not surprising, therefore, that many popular notions equate psychological health with doing. Busy-ness is not only virtuous but it's healthy as well. "An idle mind is the devil's workshop." "A busy ship is a happy ship," "The devil finds work for idle hands." And on and on. Accordingly, many self-help books preach the value of keeping busy as the keystone of mental health.

Some devote themselves largely to listing all sorts of pursuits, including volunteer work, hobbies, jobs that are good for a person. We don't quarrel with the suggestion that meaningful, fulfilling activity of one's choice is an important, reinforcing aspect of what we call psychological health. By now, however, you're aware that we are taking a somewhat different approach. Although we will discuss some constructive pursuits later in this book, we are more concerned with being and becoming than we are with individual activities. To us, the basic *how* is more important than the *what*. So we will emphasize the creative attitude rather than specific, creative things to do.

WHAT IS CREATIVITY?

Contrary to widespread assumptions, creativity is not the exclusive possession of an elite. It is not an attribute that belongs only to those relatively few specially gifted men and women who can combine form and color and perspective into a truly unique painting, those who can compose a moving symphony, or those who have a special talent for writing out a deeply human story. Creativity can be cultivated and increased and enhanced in all of us. It is an attitude that enriches our total lives.

Psychoanalyst Erich Fromm broadly defined creativity as a character trait that involves "the ability to see or to be aware and respond."[10] This is not as commonplace as it might sound. It means the capacity to *fully experience* persons and things about us for what they are, in all their rich essences, without distortion.

Maslow, observing the creative attitude in subjects he studied, reported that "self-actualizing creativeness stresses first the personality rather than its achievements . . . it stresses qualities of character such as boldness, courage, freedom, spontaneity, perspicuity, integration, self-acceptance. . . . It is emitted like sunshine; it spreads all over the place . . ."[11] Emphasizing that creativity is not restricted to specially gifted persons, artists, and geniuses, he observed that "a first-rate soup can be more creative than a second-rate painting, and that generally, cooking or parenthood or making a home could be creative, whereas poetry need not be. . . ."[12]

If it's possible for you and me and our friends and associates to cultivate the creative attitude, the next question is how? In a paper presented at a creativity symposium some years ago, Fromm discussed some of the conditions of the creative attitude.[13]

First, it requires a sort of childlike wonder. "Children still have the capacity to be puzzled. Their whole effort is one of attempting to orient themselves to a new world, to grasp the ever-new things which they learn to experience. They are puzzled, surprised, capable of wondering, and that is what makes their reaction a creative one." But most people, he wrote, tend to lose these traits as they approach adulthood. "They feel they ought to know everything and hence that it is a sign of ignorance to be surprised at or puzzled by anything. The world loses its characteristic of being full of wonder and is taken for granted."

Another condition of the creative attitude is the ability to concentrate, which seems to be relatively rare in Western culture. We always seem to be busy, but with little concentration on the matter at hand. We do two or three things at once, or we give what we're doing little real attention as we think about the next thing to do. Concentration means that there is only the here and now. Instead of living in the past or in the future, concentration means experiencing "in the attitude of full commitment to whatever I do, see, feel at this very moment."

The creative attitude also requires the experience of self, "I" as the originator of my acts and my experiences. That, however, does not mean remaining isolated or unrelated. The person "has to give up holding on to himself as a thing and begin to experience himself only in the process of creative response; paradoxically enough, if he can experience himself in this process, he loses himself. He transcends the boundaries of his own person. . . ."

Another characteristic of the creative attitude is the ability to accept a certain amount of conflict and tension, not just in thinking but also in feeling. Conflict, Fromm pointed out, is a source of wondering. When feelings are "flattened out," one might function like a smooth-running machine, but one does not live creatively.

"The willingness to be born again every day" is the way Fromm described the willingness to let go of "certainties" and assumptions and illusions that might have accumulated over the years. This requires "the courage to be concerned with nothing but the truth, the truth not only in thought but in one's feelings as well." In turn, such courage is possible only on a foundation of faith and trust in one's self.

PSYCHOLOGICAL HEALTH REVISITED

"My feeling," Maslow wrote in one of his later papers, "is that the concept of creativeness and the concept of the healthy, self-actualizing, fully human person seem to be coming closer and closer together, and may perhaps turn out to be the same thing. . . ."[14]

We share this feeling and agree with the profoundly optimistic view of human potentialities that Maslow, May, Rogers, and Fromm have shared with us. Although they have varying points of emphasis and use different terminologies, taken together, their conclusions can be woven into a tapestry of hope. These modern-day humanists seem to be light-years above and beyond those in psychology who tend to regard the human as a simple bundle of neuroses or as a pawn in a stimulus-response game. It is as if the humanistic psychologists we have quoted—and their patients and people they have studied—are representing all the human family in reaching a helping hand out to you, a bereaved person who needs such aid now more than ever. In this light, take these suggestions to heart:

1. Meditate on the pathways to freedom, becoming a person, self-actualization, growth, creativity that we have discussed in the framework of psychological health. Some thoughts are immediately obvious and meaningful; others are more subtle. Relating them to your own life and putting them into practice can lead to new attitudes and habits that will feel natural and right and joyous as you begin anew in the world. This growth pattern can abide into the future years.

2. Consciously turn anew to the world. This is an acknowledgment of the healing process and an affirmation of yourself in new terms. Thrill to the realization that you are captain of your own ship, and a good one at that. Nothing need be as it is or was. Change is the name of the quest.

3. Deepen your experiences of the world by becoming a truly sensuous person. Too many persons today seem to have consciously or unconsciously restricted their perceptions by failing to attend to what their senses bring to them. You may have spent many afternoons by the seashore, but have you fully experienced the symphony of sounds and smells borne by the afternoon breeze and the panoramic view of life around you? Deep encounters with nature can be cleansing, spiritual experiences. Savor the shades of food flavors. Close your eyes and listen fully to the moods and nuances of an orchestra. Vivid perception be-

gins with the senses but soon transcends them as you delight, for instance, in the incredible sweetness of a child's face. Experience the warmth that close friends and family members radiate, even amidst their shortcomings. Experience their vulnerability, their richness, their dignity.

4. Accentuate the positive about yourself and your capabilities whenever you can. We all have reveries—little conversations with ourselves—somewhere between our conscious and unconscious minds. Motivational researchers have found that persons who are able to give themselves pep talks, bits of encouragement, and assurance are successful in reaching their goals. If you should find yourself "talking" about nothing but obstacles and problems and discouragement, tell yourself to stop—now!

5. Seek help whenever you need it along the line. We have stressed this in previous chapters dealing with grief, and it is no less important for all the days of your new life. Again, the caring friend in whom you can confide might be the best source or professional counseling may be preferable. Remember, it is no disgrace or admission that you are "sick" if you seek therapy when you feel it might help you. To the contrary, it is a healthy sign. It is the job of psychologists and other counselors to help their clients grow.

A BASIC MESSAGE

The message is this: Despite desolation and suffering, wounds can heal. Although it might be difficult to believe that bereavement has any positive aspects at all, it does indeed, for it brings the necessity to start life anew. This does not mean overnight changes, hasty decisions, or attempts to become a person other than you are; just the opposite. It means becoming more fully what you are, for you bring a wealth of personal history to this crossroads. If you seek and find within yourself, you will be raising your consciousness, and you can clothe yourself in an attitude that discovers opportunities in the world. The result can be a continuing pattern of growth, fulfillment, psychological health. Each move in the direction of growth begets other self-actualizing pathways and makes them more accessible.

There is no doubt of this. It is proven in the lives of those who have walked the long road before you. There are many, some perhaps among your own friends and acquaintances. One famous person who readily comes to mind is the late Eleanor Roosevelt (identified, incidentally, by Maslow as a self-actualizing person). Mrs. Roosevelt was a highly motivated woman throughout her life. But her greatest growth and achievements occurred after she was widowed. When the late Adlai Stevenson simply but movingly eulogized her as a person "who would rather light one little candle than curse the darkness," he spoke eloquently to all of those who make a new life after bereavement.

A widow who articulates the journey through desolation and beyond to hope and growth is Lynn Caine, who wrote *Widow*, a moving, personal book about her own bereavement. Writing in the January 1975 issue of *Vogue* Magazine, she has this to say about her own case history:

Perhaps it seems curious that someone as closely identified with death and grief as I should feel optimistic about 1975.

When Martin died, I realized that I possessed a survival mechanism, an instinct perhaps, that permitted me to endure total pessimism. Gradually I learned that surviving pessimism was not living. Yet for me, as for many, it was a comfortable place to be, a neutral place. Much harder, in a way, was learning to go beyond mere survival to find the courage to build and to grow and especially to build and to grow by myself. Discovering the ways in which I could take small joys and extend them was a beginning. Making an attempt to seek out joy came next. Finally I was able to accept rebirth as an antidote to death and not as an affront to the dead.

Optimism is the belief that things will be good and that implies a desire to make things good. When I wrote *Widow*, I wrote it partly as catharsis, partly with hope of gaining some independence, partly because I felt it would fill a need. I was very surprised at what happened—not at the catharsis, which I expected—but at the independence, which was more than a release from dependence. It was the knowledge that I had some real control over my life. But perhaps most remarkable was the reaction the book received. It had helped many people. I had, in effect, made things good. If I feel optimistic, it is because I have learned that simply being alive is happy and that there is a joy in extending that happiness for myself, for my children, and for others."[15]

Not all widows have the opportunity to be so potent a force for social good as Eleanor Roosevelt, and not all may be so articulate as Lynn Caine in describing their journey beyond bereavement. However, the patterns of continuing renewal that mark the lives of many widows bear testimony enough to their remarkable human potentials and their ability to realize them. And like them, you too can find a world without a chart, save one that faith deciphers in the skies. You can trust your "soul's invincible surmise."

CHAPTER SIX

THE BEST TIME OF

THE YEAR

"Health," Franklin Pierce Adams once mused, "is the thing that makes you feel that now is the best time of the year." What a perceptive way of celebrating that sense of exhilaration and well-being that the physically healthy person experiences! Good health is not only a joy in itself, it makes other joys possible. It conditions all that we are and can be.

The achievements of the medical and health sciences in the last few decades have helped make the second half of the twentieth century the most fascinating and exciting period of history. Research in recent years has eradicated several major diseases, and prospects for many new treatments and cures are bright. Never before in history has medical care been so advanced and so available to so many people. Some scientists indicate that an average one-hundred-year lifespan is probable in the next few decades, a century of life in which the healthy middle years are prolonged . . . rather than just adding more years of old age.

Through the news media, books, and magazines, scientists' accomplishments are reported to the American people. Every day we have more definitive information on the role that personal health practices play in determining whether we will be sick or well. This knowledge gives each of us unprecedented control over our physical being.

Despite all the knowledge of good health and our ability to do something about it, we are strangely and ironically neglectful of good health practices. The disease and death statistics bear this out. We can't do much to alter our heredity, that is, to modify any inherited predisposition to various diseases. But much can be done by way of our health practices to minimize any genetic susceptibilities. And most of those fortunate enough to have no significant, hereditary weaknesses can keep themselves out of the "risk" column by their own efforts.

To determine why so many people neglect their health need not detain us here. It's not that people don't care. It may be a sort of laziness, procrastination, or rationalization. Like Mark Twain, some might feel that "The only way to keep your health is to eat what you don't want, drink what you don't like, and do what you'd rather not." That attitude is more shortsighted than amusing. And it is not even true.

Good health practices—ultimately the best health insurance policy you can adopt—need not be so distasteful and dreary. To the contrary, they can be pleasant and rewarding. Given a positive attitude, the challenge of pursuing good health can be creative and fun. The rewards far outweigh the effort involved. It is our intention to explore the constructive, positive pathways of good physical health as we walk with you through your recovery from bereavement toward a new, promising life as a single person. One's emotional and physical well-being are inseparable. It is essential that our present concern should be the health of you as a whole, integrated person. So come along and reflect with us on the physical aspects of total health.

BEREAVEMENT'S PHYSICAL EFFECTS

Your mate's death has been a deep wound, a severe trauma to your emotional life. We have understood that the treatment for this is working through your grief and rebuilding your identity. Given time and the necessary effort on your part, the wound will heal. But bereavement and its effects are not confined to your emotions. They assault the whole person. Mind and body are not separate entities operating independently. To the contrary, science continues to demonstrate the ways in which our emotional and physical well-being are intertwined. The deep wounds of bereavement have inescapable physical consequences.

If you experienced bodily symptoms of one kind or another almost from the beginning of your bereavement, you are not alone. Scientists have documented many symptoms that are common to the bereaved. In his classic study, Dr. Lindemann reported "remarkably uniform" physical symptoms of acute grieving. These included a feeling of tightness in the throat, choking with shortness of breath, need for sighing, an empty feeling in the abdomen, lack of muscular power, exhaustion, digestive difficulties, and an altering of the senses.[1]

The most common physical disturbance mentioned by British widows studied by Peter Marris was difficulty in sleeping. Some also experienced more serious, acute ailments, including weight loss, rheumatism, asthma, bronchitis, cramping chest pains, recurring ulcers, indigestion, swollen feet, falling hair, skin irritations, headaches, dizziness, and "nerves." In the opinion of Marris' widows or their doctors, such ailments were either caused or aggravated by the shock of their husbands' deaths.[2]

Other studies show that many widows and widowers tend to consult their physicians more frequently than do others and that the widowed often say their general physical health has not been good since the death of their mates.

Is this to say that bereavement automatically portends ill health? Not necessarily. A reasonable perspective is offered by Dr. Colin Murray Parkes in his important work, *Bereavement*. He thinks that the scientific evidence is insufficient to justify a dogmatic claim that bereavement per se causes this or that disease.

However he feels that bereavement can affect physical health and that serious conditions can be precipitated or aggravated by such a major loss.[3]

We are not suggesting that sooner or later you will fall victim to one or the other physical affliction. The intent is to focus your attention on the need to take care of yourself physically, particularly at this time. Even if bereavement does not create problems for you, it can be hazardous to your health. The anxiety of loss can deprive you of that much-needed restorer, a good night's sleep, and so keep you tense during the daytime. Hence, you lose the rest and the relaxation that your body needs to repair itself and function well.

Neglect of health is a serious problem. As one writer put it, this can come from the "laziness of grief,"[4] a sort of apathy or ennui following bereavement. Or such neglect can make you reel. The shock of losing your mate might have swept away many of your routines, including previous good health practices.

Jenny R. had been a model. She cherished her slim figure. Even when she gave up her profession for marriage, she maintained a svelte profile. At forty-six she was often mistaken for a young woman of thirty. She watched her diet, exercised, and relaxed. She had an ideal relationship with her husband, who adored her. And she was careful to monitor carefully all of her good points that he adored. But at forty-six her husband was killed in an automobile accident. It seemed to her then that nothing mattered. She ate too much, drank too much, and never really faced her grief. Consequently, she grew indolent and fat, depressed and immobile. When we talked with her about the radical changes in her health practices, her habits, and her attitude, she responded: "What does it matter?"

There is a way to be health-conscious in a balanced, realistic, prudent way. There is an opposite extreme that befalls some widows. The anxieties and confusions of bereavement can foster an exaggerated, unrealistic overconcern about health that borders on hypochondria. At the first ache or pain, they're off to their doctors, assuming the worst. Some refuse to take their physicians' words that they are not physically ill. Such fall into a cycle in which anxiety breeds anxiety and the result is additional unnecessary wear and tear on both their emotions and their bodies. It is wise to be aware of this danger so that it can be avoided. When a mate dies, it does not mean that one is going to be ill.

BEREAVEMENT AND DRUGS

All the stresses imposed on your mind and body add up to a bewildering morass. The hurts have made you vulnerable. There is a natural need to reach out for help in repairing torn emotions, and the temptation is great to try to ease the pains artificially.

Ours is a drug-conscious culture. This derives from the vast pharmaceutical advances of the last few decades—the era of wonder drugs. Some are indeed that, for they have eradicated or ensured recovery from major diseases. But many people exaggerate the capabilities of drugs. To them, whatever the illness, whatever the problem, the solution can be found in the medicine cabinet. There is a whole spectrum of drugs for both physical and emotional pain. Physicians often prescribe strong sedatives for the newly bereaved. This may be temporarily necessary. But long-term use of barbiturates or other habit-forming drugs is dangerous. Competent doctors know this and take care to prescribe such drugs only when they are absolutely necessary and, then, only for a limited duration.

Another type of drug used to alleviate emotional distress is the tranquilizer. These preparations are so broadly used that over the last several years the top-selling drug in the United States has been a well-known tranquilizer.[5] These mood-altering drugs are very controversial, and there are dangers. Many respected physicians often write refillable prescriptions for tranquilizers, obviously convinced of the benefits to their patients. They, and other health authorities, say that tranquilizers are nontoxic, non-habit-forming, and useful antidotes for potentially destructive anxiety. Of the millions who take tranquilizers, some have used them for years and are grateful for the help they provide over the rough spots.

There is another side to the question. Some who have taken tranquilizers report unpleasant and frightening side effects, including psychological dependency. Critics of tranquilizers within the medical community contend that the drugs are overused and over prescribed. Some complain that these drugs undermine willpower and self-reliance and diminish the desire to face one's problems squarely. A San Francisco psychiatrist gave his frank viewpoint in a newspaper interview:

> The doctor is under a lot of pressure to maintain his practice and satisfy his patient, who may go elsewhere if the doctor doesn't write a prescription. That kind of pressure makes him write prescriptions too frequently. People should seriously ask the doctor or themselves whether they need the drug, whether they need as much of the drug and whether they need it for as long as they are using it.[6]*

The last sentence has good advice for you. Try to maintain a balanced perspective. It might be sound judgment for a doctor to recommend a tranquilizer for a period of time. Discuss it frankly with him. If you do take them, monitor the drug's physical and emotional effects. If it helps erase excessive, threatening anxiety at a particularly trying time, that is one thing. But it is quite another if the drug numbs and masks your emotions, tranquilizing you into a sort of limbo. If that happens, it might prevent you from taking the painful steps of grief work and confronting your true feelings. Obviously, if the drug is interfering with your recovery, it is doing more harm than good and should be avoided. Tranquilizers can be soothing. But they are not a magic potion for recovery from bereavement. There is no panacea for grief in a pill bottle.

When you are reaching out for help, don't reach for alcohol either, for there is no cure-all in the liquor bottle. It is not only impossible to drown life's sorrows but it is dangerous to try. Some widows have become alcoholics. You might be a person who has enjoyed predinner cocktails and moderate social drinking for years. But you will find that in times of deep emotional distress

---

* Daryl Lembke, "Valium: All Is Not Tranquil as Use Grows," *Los Angeles Times* (February 11, 1975). Copyright 1975, Los Angeles Times. Reprinted by permission.

drinking will not provide relief. Alcohol does not alter your moods or emotions. It intensifies them. It is a depressant that deepens depression. When a couple of drinks do not help, the temptation may be to drink more, possibly to the point of intoxication. Excessive drinking is a destroyer of one's physical and emotional health and can lead to addiction.

This is not to say that you should never drink, nor does it imply that if you do alcoholism is automatically likely. For most people, alcohol taken moderately can be enjoyable and safe. It is important to maintain the same prudent perspective and judgment with which you view any drug. Many widows find it wise to abstain from drinking until they are well along the road to recovery. Perhaps one should avoid drinking alone and drink only moderately on social occasions. If you find you are drinking much more now than you did before, curtail or stop it. Monitor the physical and mental effects as honestly as you can. Obviously, alcohol is readily available without prescription, which is the external control a physician has over other potent drugs. The responsibility for "prescribing" alcoholic drinks rests solely with you.

YOUR PARTNER IN GOOD HEALTH

Keeping and enhancing good physical health is not simply a matter of red flags, warning signals, and a massive collection of "don'ts." Mark Twain's sarcastic view need not burden you. The "do's" are even more important. And they are up to you. Ultimately, the person most responsible for "prescribing"—and following through—on that prescription for good health is you.

Of course you don't have to go it alone; that is what doctors are for. A competent personal physician can be a very important person at this time. Hopefully, he will be more than simply an efficient professional who examines you briefly, writes a prescription, and sends you on your way. Ideally, he will be a personal health advisor and counselor, one with whom you can frankly discuss the many health issues that may concern you. It is important to have one principal doctor, a general or family practitioner or an internist, who assures you of continuing care. Such a physician compiles your medical history and gets to know you and your physical and emotional traits. He treats the whole person. You need this holistic approach now more than ever.

What should you ask yourself when you are evaluating or choosing a personal physician? The most immediate question of course is his professional competence, which is indicated in many ways: his credentials, his background, his reputation, and from your own careful observations. His competence is important because you are entrusting yourself to his skills and because you must have confidence in him. If you have doubts, you'd best go elsewhere. Is he willing to talk with you, explain circumstances to your satisfaction, answer your questions? Do you have good rapport with him? What is his availability to you? Does he make provision for another doctor to take his calls during nights and week ends? Is there provision for emergencies? Will he help you find a specialist if you need one and still remain your personal physician?

You have the need for, and the right to, careful, considerate explanations and counsel about your health. But don't put the entire burden on the doctor. To get optimum results, you have to help him help you. One good way is to prepare for the visit in advance. Try to "rehearse" an explanation of your purpose for the visit and any symptoms so that you can inform him as accurately and as briefly as possible. Jot down in advance any questions you might wish to ask. You should have realistic expectations about the doctor-patient relationship. You are not his only patient, but above all, he should be able to talk with you and answer questions. Many physicians have a staggering caseload. This does not mean that you should be rushed through his office like a product on a factory assembly line, but consideration for the demands on your physician can help both of you handle the matters at hand most effectively.

You must follow your physician's instructions and heed his advice faithfully and carefully if you expect him to help you. It bears repeating because so many people go to their doctors and then proceed to ignore their counsel. Work with your doctor, for he is an indispensable partner in your health enterprise. And whenever you are in doubt about any health matter, it is safer and wiser to call your physician than to take a chance.

It is unfortunate when widowhood comes to a woman during menopause. For she must cope with her loss when she may already be beset by the physical and emotional imbalances of life's change. Some are widowed in the latter stages of menopause, when it is thought that the worst is over. But flare-ups might ensue because of the emotional shock of loss. Depression and physical malaise can be compounded. If you are widowed at this time of life, be aware of this, and by all means, discuss it with your physician. He might be able to help you to a great extent, for example, by prescribing a carefully monitored course of hormone therapy.

Everyone should have a complete physical examination at least once a year. This should become your practice. But because bereavement is a severe trauma, it is wise to have a thorough physical as soon as possible after the loss of one's mate. An examination at this time enables your doctor to practice preventative medicine and to help you improve your health practices. Further, it can have the healthy psychological effect of allaying any baseless fears you might have about your physical condition.

POSITIVE GOOD HEALTH, THE STEP BEYOND

There is a great deal more to health than simply being free from disease. There is the realm of positive good health. This means physical self-actualization—rising above the status quo of "not sick" toward becoming literally as well as we can be. In one sense, positive good health is the best insurance against illness because it implies that body systems function at high levels of efficiency . . . strengthening various organs and tissues, building up reserve, and lessening wear and tear on our physical constitution. Positive good health means physical fitness and all the energy, vigor, and sense of physical well-being that underlies a full, rich creative life. A "not sick" person might survive. One with positive good health can *live*.

Sadly, this may be a foreign concept to many, because they

never have had the vibrant experience of positive good health. Many millions may not be sick, but they are overweight, under-exercized, poorly nourished, as well as being long on tension and short on energy. Many people find they are so fatigued and tense after a day's work that an evening of recreation is out of the question. They might make it up a flight of stairs, but even that is like climbing the Matterhorn. They have no acute symptoms, but their muscles are tight and they are more or less constantly beset with aches and pains. They may not be sick, but how do they really feel? It is often "pretty well but . . ." instead of "wonderful," or "never better."[7]

That you need not fall into this unfortunate category will become apparent as we discuss three vital keys to positive good health: *exercise*, *nutrition*, and *relaxation*. Indeed, striving for excellence in these can be as rewarding in the effort as it is in the result. In the early days of your grieving, it can be expected that you will not be disposed, or even able, to think of these important keys. But the veil lifts in time, and attention to them will not only hasten recovery but will also help in your enjoyment of positive good health during all the days of your new life.

EXERCISE, THE REJUVENATOR

Our bodies thrive on use. You have only to look around you to verify this, for the most vigorous and healthy-appearing persons generally are the ones whose life-styles include regular exercise. The scientific evidence that exercise is beneficial to health—in fact, a necessary ingredient in any health program—has become overwhelmingly persuasive. Accordingly, our schools now put more emphasis on physical education than they did years ago. The values of exercise are being expounded by the medical profession, health agencies, and community programs. The accelerating emphasis on physical fitness is well placed, particularly in this age of labor-saving devices and automobiles. In terms of fitness, technology hasn't been all that much of a blessing. A good case can be made that sitting—not baseball—is the national pastime. To a great extent, we sit at work and play, and we sit for hours a day in front of that electronic marvel, the television set. "A hodgepodge," one exasperated doctor noted, "of sagging livers, sinking gall bladders, drooping stomachs, compressed intestines, and squashed pelvic organs. . . ." It's bad enough, as the doctor said, that we're out of shape anatomically. Worse, as a people, we're out of shape physiologically—functionally. That sad truth is reflected not only in low energy levels but in the disease statistics as well.

Many have assumed that exercise is really only for the young. Recent research has shown this to be an old wives' tale. Studies by Dr. Herbert A. deVries of the University of Southern California Andrus Gerontology Center have demonstrated that, if it is carefully planned, exercise can be safe and very effective for those in middle and old age. This applies even to older persons who might have been inactive and sedentary through most of their lives. DeVries found that those who had been least active in their young and middle years benefited the most.

In his recent book, *Vigor Regained,* deVries reports on his research into the effects of exercise by a group of men and women between the ages of fifty and eighty-seven in a California retirement community. He found that exercise can positively rejuvenate older people.[8] Comparison of before-and-after-exercise test results produced dramatic findings. The findings indicated that his three-hour-a-week program of controlled exercise helped men and women in their seventies regain much of the vigor and physical function of their forties.

"Exercise brought about a considerable renewal in the heart function of our older research subjects," deVries writes. "That is, despite a chronological age of 60 or 70, many of our subjects' 'physiological age' had been reduced. Their hearts were beating and pumping like those of 40 and 50-year-olds. . . ."[9] DeVries' program simultaneously provided participants many important health benefits. These included significant increases in oxygen consumption (the best single measure of an individual's vigor), lowered blood pressure, loss of fat, increased muscular strength, along with an improved ability to relax and avoid stress and nervous tension. These scientifically documented improvements represented a renewal of bodily function. Each improvement was a worthwhile health goal in itself. Further, the sum total helped the elderly participants to *feel* years younger as well. The people enthusiastically reported that they were more relaxed, fatigued less easily, and had more energy to do things than they had had in years. Some even credited the exercise with giving them relief from chronic aches and pains. The benefits were not entirely physical either, for many participants said the program had helped their outlook and actually had given them a new lease on life.[10]

Such benefits make exercise an essential pathway to positive good health. We recommend it to you during the days of your recovery from bereavement and for the rest of your life. But to tell someone simply, "You should get some exercise," is very general and imprecise. For exercise is like a potent drug that must be used prudently. The first and most important common-sense rule is that anyone past their youth should consult a physician for a complete physical examination before a vigorous exercise program is begun. A second essential consideration is that exercise should be a progressive pursuit. Improvement in performance comes gradually. Take care to avoid overdoing. Exercise must not be a sometime thing. You cannot expect to realize its benefits by doing it once a month or whenever the spirit moves you. When you stop exercising for a significant period of time, you lose whatever level of fitness you might have achieved.

What sort of exercise is best? Science has found that the rhythmic, dynamic activities, such as walking, jogging, swimming, and bicycling, are excellent. They improve and strengthen the heart, circulatory system, and lungs. How much exercise is enough, and how much is too much? Certainly, an occasional, slow, two-block stroll will not produce much improvement. To register significant gains, you have to challenge your system vigorously. Your heart, lungs, and muscles will respond by working more efficiently and by growing in capacity and strength. The challenge involves gradually increasing your capacity. During vigorous exercise, this means an elevated heart rate, deeper breathing, and perspiration. DeVries found that his subjects did not have to exercise beyond forty to sixty percent of their capacity to register improvements. Working harder than that, he writes, is unnecessary and hazardous, particularly for older people.[11] This all points to the need for putting exercise on a systematic basis. Accordingly, we recommend deVries' program to you, for it includes a self-testing and self-monitoring component based on frequent taking of your pulse before, during, and after exercise. Monitoring this measure of stress, along with the close advice of your own physician, can help make exercise safe and effective for you.

This all may be fine, you might say, but I've never had the motivation to exercise. Or you might say, yes, exercise is a good idea; I'll take it up sometime. . . . Hopefully, you will not allow these reactions to be your final thinking, for you have a great deal to gain from exercise, particularly now. You don't have to become a disciplined athlete with a rigorous, unyielding training schedule to realize the benefits. Recall that deVries' older exercisers registered their remarkable health gains from just *three hours a week*. And exercise is not just hard work and drudgery. Some find that it initially requires conscious dedication to get started and to stick at it, but the work aspect soon fades away, and vigorous activities take on an element of fun and joy. For many, nothing is more refreshing than a regular swim or bicycle ride, set of tennis or long brisk walk. These activities can be substituted for the more formal aspects of an exercise program after you have established your routine. The joys of walking, for instance, are all but forgotten and neglected in our modern day. Put a spring in your stride, breathe deeply, and enjoy the symphony of sights, sounds, and life abounding around you. In this way, the *experience* of exercise can be as rewarding as its physical benefits.

NUTRITION—WE ARE WHAT WE EAT AND WE ARE HOW WE EAT

Science has also learned a great deal about nutrition and its role in health. And like exercise, nutrition is a way of exerting control over our health, for literally, we are what we eat. In another sense, as we shall see, we are *how* we eat.

The most urgent point for you to concentrate on now is getting adequate nutrition. Some tend to encounter difficulty from the instant of bereavement and into the days of grief and readjustment. Among Dr. Lindemann's acutely grieving subjects, several told him food had lost its appeal; that it "tasted like sand." They even had difficulty in swallowing. This diminished appetite and reduced appreciation of flavors may persist for some time.[12] The enjoyment of food lacks its social context when one loses a mate with whom a lifetime of meals has been shared. Mealtime— particularly the dinner hour—is the loneliest part of the day. Who wants to cook for one's self alone, many ask. There may be a temptation to skip meals entirely or to turn to less-than-balanced snacks. Daylong nibbling on candy and other sweets might satisfy a craving or take the edge off your appetite, but it wreaks havoc with your system.

You need to work out your routines so that you get *balanced* nutrition on a *daily* basis. This simple truth is obvious to most people, but it is worthwhile to stress again and again because it is so widely neglected. The reasons for a balanced diet are well-known. It provides the "building blocks" of our bodies and the power by which they are assembled. A balanced diet is fuel not only for survival but for all our energy-demanding activities. It is an excellent health insurance policy against illness, and it enables us to recover quicker and more fully when we do become ill. The term "balanced diet" means exactly that: enough of all the necessary foods. No extremes, no neglect of any important food. Not too much or too little of any one food. What is a balanced diet? Nutritionists say this means *daily* portions from the four basic food groups: Meat and fish, dairy, grain, and fruits and vegetables.

Good nutrition is important for everyone, but particularly so for middle-aged and older persons. As people grow older, there is a normal physical decline, a lessening of reserves and resiliency. Sadly, the elderly as a group tend to be poorly nourished, with many suffering potentially hazardous vitamin and mineral deficiencies. In fact, the two age groups in our society with the poorest eating habits are teenagers and those over sixty-five. The specific foods required to maintain good health do not vary much by age, but the required amount of food does. Older persons need fewer calories than their younger counterparts, but they still need the same balanced diet. So, as one grows older, care must be taken to reduce the quantity but not the quality of the diet. Older people frequently ask about the advisability of taking food supplements or vitamins. While it is literally correct that vitamin supplements are not needed if one has a sufficiently regular, completely balanced diet, it is probably a good idea to take a multiple vitamin capsule daily as insurance against inadvertent deficiencies. Still, there is no substitute in capsule form for a balanced diet of wholesome food.

With well-publicized research showing excess cholesterol to be a real danger, increasing numbers of persons, especially those past their youth, are aware and careful to keep their intake as low as possible. But not so many are wise about eating sugar-rich foods, so an additional comment is appropriate here. So pervasive is our sweet tooth that in the United States per capita sugar consumption has doubled since the turn of the century.[13] Some persons literally are sugar addicts, with an almost insatiable craving that has been built up over the years. If you are approaching that point, it is urgent that you make every effort to kick the habit. If you are not, keep your sugar consumption routinely low. The hard truth is that sugar is generally a principal villain in overweight. In recent years, research studies have implicated heavy sugar consumption in diabetes and other diseases.[14]

It is not the end of the world, either, if you must restrict other foods because of doctor's orders. If, for instance, you tend toward high blood pressure, your physician might restrict or eliminate your salt intake. There are substitutes not only for salt but for other foods, and a whole range of dietetic foods that can make your diet palatable and enjoyable.

Any discussion of nutrition in this day would scarcely be complete without reference to the practical, dollars-and-cents aspect, although we will speak of budgeting and saving money in more detail later. The soaring costs of food make those of moderate means wonder how they can afford good nutrition. The quick answer of course is that they can't afford to be without it. But it is difficult, especially for older persons on fixed incomes, and supermarket prices are going up monthly and even weekly. It is remarkable how far some careful shopping and planning and a creative approach can go to see that you have a balanced diet of good, wholesome, appetizing food.

There is virtually no limit to the potential of your talents in the kitchen. If you have freezer space, prepare a full recipe for four or six, and package what you don't eat into your own individual TV dinners for future use. Investigate and experiment with ideas that are new to you, such as foil cookery, which is relatively easy and has varied possibilities. With some thought and planning, you might be able to do most of your week's cooking in one or two days. Don't assume that doing so for one will be a difficult-to-impossible task on a budget. For instance, you can take a large chicken and a few vegetables you've purchased on sale and some other ingredients—including the creative attitude —and you have the basis of a couple of chicken dinners, a rich broth for soup, several chicken salad sandwiches, or perhaps a casserole main dish. You will be surprised at how little is wasted. Your enterprise will not be wasted, considering the enjoyment of such appetizing meals and the nutritional value they provide.

WEIGHT CONTROL

We have considered the first major aspect of nutrition, that of a balanced diet and its role in attaining and preserving positive good health. The conclusion is clear: "Eat wisely." But the other half of the old saying, "But not too well," is equally important.

Overeating seems to be one of the most serious nutritional problems of affluent societies. The evidence of overeating can be seen in almost any crowd. There's usually a relatively high percentage of overweight persons, ranging from the slightly chubby to the frankly obese. Eating too much of the wrong kinds of foods—the "empty calories"—is an all-too-common form of overeating. One state agency on aging made an unusual point in this regard. It reported that obesity often is a more likely indicator of malnutrition than is the wasted, shrunken, hollow-eyed appearance normally associated with malnutrition.[15]

Overeating—exactly as the word indicates—means taking in more calories than one can burn as energy or store efficiently.

When this happens, the excess turns to fat. Overeating does not necessarily imply gargantuan meals such as football players and lumberjacks eat. It can be a far more subtle form of overindulgence and still lead to the inevitable long-range effect—overweight, or, more precisely, overfat. All the euphemisms aside, overfat is far more than a cosmetic problem; it portends ill health. Overfat can lead to high blood pressure, the precursor of heart attacks and strokes; to coronary heart disease itself; and to a host of other maladies such as diabetes, gout, and gallbladder problems.[16] If you aspire to positive good health, and you should, weight control is a must.

However, knowing these facts is easier than putting an effective weight control program into practice. Because of inherited individual differences, some find the prospect extremely difficult. And research also is determining that persons who were overfed as children—the "fat baby is a healthy baby" misassumption of years ago—find weight control more difficult in their later years. It is unfortunately true that almost everything some people eat seems to turn to fat. They go up and down in weight for years, become discouraged, and give up. Unfortunately, they are as subject to the hazards of overweight as anyone else. It might be unjust, somehow, but these people simply must work harder than others to control their weight.

And there is a whole host of weight control difficulties that can be characterized as psychological in nature. Food can have great emotional overtones. For instance, some persons who are vaguely aware of certain emotional lacks in their lives unconsciously use the symbolic intake of food to compensate. They fail to differentiate between physical and emotional hunger. Some overeat in response to underlying anxiety or emotional distress. Eating becomes a nervous habit or is used as a tranquilizer.[17] Others simply seem to be addicted to food. If you are falling into such traps because of the anxieties of bereavement, you should identify the situation as early as possible and make some changes. Excessive eating is not therapy. It is not substituting one ill for another. It is simply adding another problem.

It is beyond the scope of this book to outline specific weight control programs, but some general observations are worth considering. The first practical suggestion is that you honestly assess your weight problem and resolve to do something about it. Set some goals, determine a program with the help of your physician, and follow through. Dietary control is essential.[18] The extent of this is dictated by your particular weight loss goal and your individual makeup and needs. Remember, the idea is to cut down on the quantity, not the quality, of your diet. Don't do without important foods or neglect a balanced diet in your zeal to lose weight. As a person grows older, fewer calories are needed, but too large a caloric deficit can result in problems, and too rapid a weight loss is hazardous. If you are a person who finds weight control relatively easy, you probably can do well on an informal regime of keeping snacks and desserts to a minimum and by restricting your carbohydrate intake. If you are not, you need to have a more formal program in which you count calories. As you achieve some success and routinely maintain a good weight, formal calorie-counting may no longer be necessary.

Exercise goes hand in hand with caloric-consciousness. Elderly exercisers in Dr. deVries' research program showed the precisely desired effect, as they lost three times more fat than weight. Exercise coupled with dietary restrictions can put you into what physiologists call the negative caloric balance, in which more calories are expended than are taken in, so the fat melts off slowly but surely. This combined effort is the most efficient and healthful approach over the long haul because it adds fitness as it subtracts fatness.[19]

You should be aware that overweight and dieting have generated more than their share of misinformation and quackery. This realization should make you wary of fad diets, gadgets, "sure thing" crash programs, and other schemes, regardless of their momentary popularity. And chemical weight loss, such as pills and injections, should be viewed realistically. Some might be effective and even the treatment of choice in certain cases under a physician's supervision. But it is safe to say that chemicals in themselves cannot give you a long-range, realistic weight maintenance program. That depends on you, your common sense, motivation, and persistence.

Two University of Southern California psychologists, Drs.

Perry London and Albert Marston, have conducted studies observing how people eat. They theorize that there are some basic differences between the eating habits of fat and thin people. Fat people, they said in a newspaper interview, tend not only to eat more but also to eat and chew faster than thin ones. The fat persons enjoy food less than their thin counterparts and usually always clean their plates, while the slender ones do not. The psychologists have concluded that changing eating habits can help people to reduce and to control weight.[20]

Learning to recognize real hunger and to differentiate it from an emotion-induced urge to eat is important of course. Learning to leave the table without being completely full is another good practice. This might be difficult at first, but as it becomes a habit, it can provide a relatively painless way to cut down on excess calories. It is important to know yourself and your characteristics, for what works for one might not work for another and vice versa. Perhaps the conventional arrangement of three square meals a day is not for you. You might get equally good or better nutrition and find it easier to control your weight by having a series of five or six small meals spaced at shorter intervals. Research has shown that this practice—provided the diet remains balanced—can be even better for you physiologically than three heavy meals with longer intermittent periods of fast.[21]

It is worthwhile to note that there are sources of outside help for those who need it. Some find that psychological counseling enhances their ability to control weight, as a sort of side effect. Others find part of an answer in group therapy. Still others report great success from membership in one or the other mutual-help organizations of overweight people. Do not be reluctant to seek outside help if you feel you need it. Far from being an admission of failure or weakness, it might be the wise first step that will mean eventual and continuing success in winning the battle of the bulge.

RELAXATION

Relax. What? Who, me? you might ask. How can I possibly relax with all the problems of widowhood that I've been through?

I've never experienced anything like the soul-wrenching anxieties of losing my husband. And now I have to make a new life for myself. Rebuild my identity. Get to know myself anew. Make my way in the world again among people. Plan for the future. Financial problems. It seems there's more to worry about than ever before. All this on top of the every day stresses of living with which everyone has to cope. How can I expect to relax with all this facing me?

Slow down a minute. The cumulative effect of reciting all these difficulties in rapid succession is causing a churning in your stomach. Your pulse rate is increasing imperceptibly. Although you might not realize it, your blood pressure is slightly elevated. The electrical impulses in your nerves and muscles have quickened and increased so that your nervous system is beginning to resemble a hopelessly snarled telephone exchange. You might discern some signs of this overload by the tightness in your muscles and by an overall, somewhat ill-defined feeling of tenseness. You feel jittery. A tension headache is lurking. You hope that you are not in store for another sleepless night.

The foregoing is an example of how personal emotional anxieties—such as those imposed by bereavement—can cause nervous tension. Aside from such anxieties, there are other causes of nervous tension that affect most of us to one extent or another in our modern-day world: sensory overload from noise pollution, overcrowding, rush-hour traffic, and other environmental influences. A pace of life that is faster than our forebears could have imagined. The vicissitudes of economic survival in an on-again, off-again, inflationary economy. Self-imposed stresses involved in our unrelenting drive to achieve or those begotten by our attempts to "measure up" to a whole host of social and cultural expectations.

Whatever the causes, the results of nervous tension on our health are becoming increasingly clear, according to health scientists. The word hypertension gives us a verbal clue—it literally means a pronounced, acute state of tension. It also is the word used to designate high blood pressure. The role of nervous tension in high blood pressure is well identified, and so are the results of high blood pressure: heart attacks and strokes. There are direct links between nervous tension and heart disease. Many persons who suffer massive heart attacks have a common syndrome involving nervous tension. It is also well known that ulcers can result from nervous tension. Case histories from health scientists' and physicians' files also show that nervous tension can be a causal factor in skin disease, asthma, colitis, and other ailments. The tragic end result of nervous tension for some is the so-called nervous breakdown.

Nervous tension is not always so extreme, the results so tragic. But often it is a key factor in common health problems that either are potentially hazardous or are just such unpleasant discomforts in themselves that daily existence becomes a dreary prospect. These include insomnia, headaches, jitteriness, fatigue, or an overall, generalized feeling of tenseness and tightness that seems impossible to unwind. The compelling proof that such ills are widespread lies in the millions of dollars that Americans spend annually for analgesics, tranquilizers, and sleeping pills. That might be fine for the pharmaceutical manufacturers, but it is not really so good for those suffering with these discomforts. Moreover, they are only treating the symptoms of nervous tension, and even that in a stopgap, transitory way. There is only one really effective remedy for, or alternative to, nervous tension. And that is habitual relaxation. Accordingly, *relaxation* is your *third vital key* to positive good health.

Let's clarify. When we speak of nervous tension, we mean *excess* tension. A certain amount of tension is normal and natural and necessary. It is present in all of our muscle contractions and consequent movements and is involved in all that we do. If all tension were eliminated, we would simply repose on a surface like a glob. But the physical phenomenon of excess tension is abnormal. It is more than our systems need or were designed to handle. Hence, the condition manifests itself in health problems. In tense persons, the nerve cells are overstimulated and are as volatile as an explosive. Even though the victim might not perceive it directly, his or her system is overalert and overworking. The rest that the body needs both in sleep and in waking hours is difficult to achieve.

Regardless of how it originated, it can feed on and perpetu-

ate itself. The discomfort of muscle tension can magnify emotional anxieties that in turn elicit more physical tension, and on
and on. Mind and body become united in an unpleasant overall
sense of ill-being that hinders us emotionally and physically and
makes us uncomfortable.

There are many wrong assumptions about relaxation, the
antidote to nervous tension. Some tend to equate relaxation with
recreation or hobbies or, on the other hand, with a simple lack of
activity. They are not synonymous, for a person can be either
relaxed or extremely tense during such pursuits. Scientifically,
relaxation is a relatively quiescent state of the nervous system, an
absence of excess tension. Some tend to assume that relaxation
brings indolence and laziness, that when we are relaxed, we can't
function creatively or efficiently. Nothing could be farther from
the truth. Relaxation frees us to work more efficiently and think
more clearly, to be alert, energetic, and more effective in all that
we do. Relaxation—not excess tension—is what is normal and
natural.

A personal tragedy such as bereavement can affect individuals differently. For some widows, the anxiety of loss compounds
itself, adding up to a perpetual state of excess tenssion in which
they find it virtually impossible to relax. In some cases, the
extreme effect is a series of acute anxiety attacks.

For the sake of your health and well-being, it is important to
determine whether or not nervous tension is becoming a problem
for you. Are you relatively relaxed? Or do you have a vague sense
of being pushed or driven? Are you more impatient than you had
been previously? Do you find yourself overreacting to minor
frustrations and annoyances? Do your muscles feel tense and
tight? Are your movements clipped and rigid, or are they easy
and fluid? If you have recurring headaches, difficulty in sleeping,
and constant fatigue, and your doctor can rule out any disease or
other physical dysfunction as the cause, there is a good chance
that the unseen, sometimes subtle stalker of good health, excess
tension, is present. The next step—developing and cultivating
relaxation—is up to you.

How do you go about it? How do you learn to relax and
manage to make it a habit? There are many ways, and we will

suggest some. But, given your personal characteristics, individual needs, and relative level of relaxation, the best general answer is whatever works best for you. However, don't work too hard to relax, which is a contradiction in terms. Putting forth more effort than is needed to accomplish a goal is characteristic of tense persons, not relaxed ones. So don't fall into that ironic trap.

And don't go about it with the idea that relaxation only means "resting" or that relaxation is only for certain occasions or prescribed times. Your goal should be to develop increasing relaxation as a habit that is part of your work and play and rest.

Knowing yourself is important in achieving physical relaxation because it is necessary to identify causes of tension in order to either eliminate them or reduce their potency. If you are tense primarily because of emotional anxiety, that is a logical area in which to make some changes. Of course, it is easy to tell a person not to worry, but putting that into practice is not so automatic or easy. We have written a good deal in previous chapters about discovering the realm of your emotions, getting in touch with yourself in the recovery process. Meditating on these points and putting some of the suggestions into practice might help significantly in cultivating relaxation, for coming to terms with one's self can produce peace as surely as it stimulates growth. Remember also that you are free to do or not to do, to be or not to be this or that. Perhaps some anxiety can be prevented simply by refusing to impose certain stresses on yourself or to allow them to be imposed by outside sources. For instance, you don't have to respond to certain expectations of others. You don't have to force yourself into a culturally ordained mold. A sense of your growing personal freedom in this way might go far toward helping you to relax.

Emotional peace is not the only pathway to relaxation. There are well-documented physical means as well. A pioneering researcher in the field, Dr. Edmund Jacobson, studied the effects of excess tension on health and developed what came to be called "progressive relaxation." Patients were taught to recognize excess tension and instructed in techniques of eradicating it through relaxing their various muscle groups. Jacobson and others have written some very helpful books for the layman that provide instruction in the techniques he developed in his research.[22]

Exercise also can be a natural and effective tranquilizer, Dr. deVries found in his research. One of the elderly exercisers' more significant health improvements was a drop in levels of nervous tension. Some subjects registered dramatic improvements and reported a loss of tension-related ills. In a related experiment, deVries focused specifically on the tranquilizer effect of exercise. He found that a brisk, fifteen-minute walk is more effective than a single dose of a well-known tranquilizer in alleviating tension. The average effect of the exercise dose was a "highly significant" reduction of electrical muscle activity ranging from twenty to twenty-five percent for at least an hour and a half after the exercise. DeVries writes that he has conducted several studies on young, middle-aged, and older men and women "in which appropriate exercise has been shown to improve the ability to relax both immediately and over a sustained period. This is another indication to us," he concludes, "of the desirability of controlled exercise—all its side effects are beneficial."[23] This research confirms what many have known for years: That even as relatively mild a form of exercise as a pleasant walk can induce overall relaxation and help one to sleep better.

There are other pathways toward developing the relaxation habit that are satisfactory to many persons, such as the practice of Yoga and the various forms of meditation. Perhaps they are worth exploring. Regular participation in a hobby might be a sort of therapy that promotes relaxation. Or taking a daily nap, perhaps just lying down, closing your eyes, and attempting to shut out anxiety-producing thoughts might be excellent. Prayer helps a great many persons.

We have mentioned that insomnia haunts many widows, with debilitating results. A pattern of sleeplessness takes its toll on our health and thus on the way we feel and function as well. Insomnia is such a problem for many people that they're willing to try anything to get some rest, including prescription and non-prescription drugs that carry negative side effects. The old saw about counting sheep—or anything else—isn't much help for most of us, but persons do develop their own strategies to get to sleep. Many find that a hot bath before retiring is most helpful in falling and staying asleep. There is scientific evidence to confirm its value.[24] Others say that if they can't fall asleep, they get up, instead of staying in bed and "trying" to sleep, and immerse themselves in light activity that eventually leads to drowsiness. Some find that reading at bedtime does the trick. Others say that a glass of hot milk or a cup of cocoa helps. The ability to consciously "turn off the mind" to avoid turning one's worries over repeatedly—which interferes with sleep—seems to differ among individuals.

Whatever your circumstances and the remedies you attempt at bedtime, be aware that you should not look on sleeplessness as a singular, isolated problem. It is not in most cases. It is far more logical to consider your inability to sleep as part of a pattern, an intertwined aspect of your total tension level twenty-four hours a day. If you are suffering from excess tension more or less constantly during your waking hours, it isn't likely that this will change suddenly at bedtime. In most cases of insomnia, underlying excess tension is a factor. Hence, the remedy for insomnia can be completely or in part your remedy for erasing excess tension, in general terms, developing the relaxation habit. So put into long-range practice some of the means for total relaxation, and sleep will come. Such measures as working your way toward emotional peace and exercise can be part of the best and most enduring cure for those sleepless nights.

A FINAL WORD ABOUT YOUR PHYSICAL HEALTH

The old clichés about health are common and numerous. "Health is the most important thing. . . ." "If you have your health, you have everything. . . ." On and on. There is solid truth behind them, and so we have attempted to make some important points about health. But health matters are complex, and most are the subjects of several books in themselves. Because of this and because of the many important concerns of widowhood to be covered in this book, our discussion of health has been limited to some of the major points as they relate to your circumstances of bereavement. But the relatively short treatment of these topics is by no means intended to minimize their significance. Accordingly, we urge you to read further and to learn more about them from reliable sources so that you can become health conscious in an informed, constructive way. The notes to this chapter provide important books on exercise, nutrition, and relaxation.

Anyone who aspires diligently to positive good health will find that the task is not as involved as it might appear initially because the three major keys or pathways—exercise, nutrition-weight control, and relaxation—are not only natural in themselves, but indeed they complement and help one another as well. For instance, relaxation elicits a state of being that makes everything we do more rewarding and efficient, including nutrition and exercise. A properly balanced diet nourishes and helps us to control our weight, while providing fuel for activities such as exercise. Exercise helps weight control while it promotes relaxation. So the keys represent a total and self-sustaining kind of health-program package.

Similarly, improvement in your physical health goes hand-in-hand with the process of emotional recovery. Reassessing your health practices promotes physical and emotional well-being and has the healthy psychological effect of doing something positive for yourself. It means taking the initiative again. And that, as we have stressed, is a characteristic of one who is recovering from bereavement.

But more than recovery is in your mind now. There are the days, weeks, months, and years of your future life ahead. Now is the time for starting over. Your growth potential virtually has no limit. Positive good health is a kind of self-actualization that underlies everything that you can be. As a very important person, you owe it to yourself. Almost every day you should be able to affirm—because you enjoy positive good health—that now is the best time of the year.

CHAPTER SEVEN

A NEW WORLD
OF PEOPLE

Some widows are very perceptive about the events of their lives. Jocelyn told us about her successive emotional problems:

At first, it was just physically and emotionally painful, like great waves of pain . . . and numbness. I was paralyzed. But that kind of agony wore off after several weeks, and then I was mad and depressed. I guess that was the time of really facing the fact that John was gone. It wasn't the first kind of wretching pain, but it was still a kind of paralysis. I remember I didn't want to go anywhere or see anybody or do anything. I don't know if others do that, but I would review my life with John and try to hold on to the good times. I got over most of the depression after a couple of months but not all the sadness. I was lonely; and not just for John, for the life we lived, for the friends we'd shared. I guess then I was realizing how my life had to change. Most of it was gone. I was really alone.

Intense grief and the depression caused by separation can be overcome, but loneliness may last a lifetime. Barrett found that loneliness was the number-one problem of widows and that long-term widows were often as lonely as those newly bereaved.

It may be that loneliness is the problem of a great many other persons besides widows and widowers. Our society is fragmented and tends by its very nature to alienate and isolate individuals. The small community is gone, and relationships in large suburban areas tend to be superficial. Friendship networks involve professional or work groups separated by long distances. This alienating structure of society makes it far more difficult for the lonely person to reestablish social nearness to any individual or to a group.

One of Helena Lopata's many contributions is analyzing in detail the various types of loneliness. She helps us by carefully identifying some specific forms[1]:

1. "A loneliness for the immediate presence of a particular individual who is no longer available for interaction."

This may just involve a desire to "recapture past scenes," or it may be a complete romanticization of the relationship to the deceased that is quite unreal.

2. "A loneliness for a companionate relationship of the depth provided by the deceased, for the sharing of experiences with another human being."

As we have said and respondents say: "You can be lonesome in a crowd." This kind of loneliness stresses the need for a companion with whom to share experiences.

3. "A feeling of loneliness for the presence of another human being within the dwelling unit."

The emphasis here is on the presence of another person, his being and his sounds. There is no one to discuss the television program with or to read a sentence to. There is only silence.

4. "A feeling of loneliness as unhappiness over the absence of another person who shares the work load or carries out tasks which the remaining partner cannot, or does not want to."

The enormous problems of taking care of all the physical aspects of a home, the complexities of taxes, the weight of the garbage pail . . . all these and a hundred more are involved in the loss of a mate.

5. "Loneliness as a homesickness for the style of life or specific activities formerly carried on with the husband."

Here one refers to a companionable evening bowling, a fishing trip, dinners out, a visit to children, and so on. When the husband dies, a great many common and long-experienced activities die too.

6. "Loneliness as an alienation from others in consequence of felt status losses, due to lack of male escort. . . ."

Some have status because of what husbands did in their jobs or what they did in a lodge or church. This is suddenly shut off, and all the couple-oriented activities are gone. One woman said that as a result of this she felt like a "second-class citizen." Parties can be "shattering."

7. "The death of the husband can have repercussions on many interaction scenes with prior associates."

Lopata thinks that this is the "consequence of de-institutionalization of death, mourning and bereavement sequences."[2] And it is possible that a long illness erodes keeping up contacts and contributes to the isolation of the widow. Another point is that grief reactions themselves alienate others so that they tend to withdraw from the widow. Others are fearful of death and withdraw because of the widow's inevitable association with a dead person. Contributing to loneliness and social problems are the widow's fears of being a "fifth wheel" and the very real possibility that some of her married female friends may be jealous of her. Finally, some women have depended on their husbands to arrange for the couple's socialization, and she is naive and unpracticed in promoting interaction.

All of these types of loneliness may dominate any widow, or she may be a victim of only one or several of them. She may, in Lopata's terms:

> . . . miss her husband, find the burden of maintaining her home alone very heavy, modify her life sufficiently to make difficult contact with former friends, and feel strain in their presence,

while lacking skills needed to convert casual or secondary relationships into ones of greater intimacy.

Another scholar who has studied the social problems of widowhood, Dr. Felix Baredo of Washington State University, compared older widows, widows, and married persons in a 1967 study of 495 respondents.[3] In developing this study, he was much concerned with social isolation and developed special means of measuring it. As the following table shows, he found that some 40 percent of widowers and 20 percent of widows are highly isolated as compared to only 10 percent of married persons.[4]

TABLE 2
SOCIAL ISOLATION INDEX RATING BY MARITAL STATUS

SOCIAL ISOLATION INDEX RATING	MARRIED		WIDOWERS		WIDOWS		TOTAL
	NO.	%	NO.	%	NO.	%	
High (0–3)	26	9.6	18	40.9	37	20.4	81
Medium (4–6)	170	62.7	22	50.0	122	67.4	314
Low (7–9)	75	27.7	4	9.1	22	12.2	101
TOTAL	271	100.0	44	100.1	181	100.0	496

Chi square 4df   43.25   P 0.001

Baredo asked his respondents to tell him what activities they enjoyed during one week. It was discovered that reading and radio listening took a great deal of time of all three groups. A careful look at those items involving visiting friends, relatives, or participating in social organizations or volunteering for community service shows the same pattern of relatively greater isolation of the widower than the widow. This confirms Baredo's conclusion that widowers "are the least active, most isolated of all marital groups despite their having the most spare time."

The family is a large, pulsating group of people with thousands of interactions every day. When the children depart for college or marriage, the home becomes very still. There is much less interaction and less communication. But when one mate dies, all is silence. Baredo shows in his data that most widowers and widows live alone. This may be related to loneliness.

TABLE 3
LIVING ARRANGEMENTS BY MARITAL STATUS

LIVING ARRANGEMENTS	NUMBER	MARRIED %	WIDOWERS %	WIDOWS %
Living alone	137	0.4	61.3	60.2
Living with spouse only	224	83.0	——	——
Living with spouse and children	34	12.5	——	——
Living with spouse and other friends or relatives	9	3.0	——	0.6
Living with children but not with spouse	54	——	13.6	26.5
Living with other friends or relatives (not with spouse)	30	0.4	22.8	10.5
Other	7	0.7	2.3	2.2
TOTAL	495	270	44	181

The community has many organizations designed to provide social interaction and to serve some special function of its members. Participation in organizations promotes social interaction and build new social networks. Baredo studied the participation of his samples of married persons, widows, and widowers to see if there were differences in membership and participation. He again found that the widower tends to be more isolated from the community organizations than married persons or widows.

Baredo's major conclusions summarize the problems of isolation very well (using the term "widowhood" to cover both men and women)[5]:

1. The aged married, by and large, occupy a distinctly advantageous position compared with other marital counterparts. They are, for example, in better health and more favorable economic circumstances than the widowed, whether such factors are measured by broad indexes or by specific indicators. A similar conclusion is generally applicable in most of the other areas examined.

2. Widowhood status results in a reduced capacity to main-

tain satisfactory economic circumstances, especially in the case of females residing in rural areas.

3. Widowhood leads to a deterioration in health status, especially in the case of males residing in a rural area.

4. Widowhood leads to a decline in the level of living, especially in the case of males in a small town.

5. Widowhood is accompanied by an overabundance of free time, creating problems of loneliness and isolation, especially in the case of males.

6. Frequency of interaction with kin and friendship groups declines when the spouse dies, especially in the case of the death of the wife.

7. Widowhood is more likely to result in a decline in activity on the part of males.

8. Adaptation to widowhood is more difficult for males than females.

9. Widowhood status creates greater strains for rural residents.

10. Adaptation to widowhood is dependent upon and affected by the variables of age, education and place of residence.

11. Duration of widowhood does not have as great an influence as the age factor.

12. Religion plays an important role in the process of adapting to widowhood, especially in the case of females.

There are some other variables that are important in understanding the isolation of older widows and widowers. Poor health was frequently cited as a reason for the withdrawal of these two groups. Lack of transportation is another major factor. If you do not feel well enough to participate, it is difficult to make the extra effort needed to be part of a group or even to visit friends. But even if you are well enough and transportation is difficult, one may still elect not to respond to opportunities for social life. Whenever we study older persons, whether widowed or not, poor health and lack of transportation appear to be major decrements that inhibit a full life.

A further consideration has to do with finances. In Baredo's sample of widows, nine out of ten had to make ends meet with an income of less than $2,000 per year.[6] They had to rely on public assistance and gifts from their children, but even then, they found it difficult to maintain even a minimum style of life. Widows in general are the most impoverished group of all. This lack of money undoubtedly interferes with social participation. It compounds health problems because there is little money for medical assistance. It reinforces transportation difficulties because there may not be enough left over for taxi or even bus fare. Baredo feels that there are some role differences in recreation that mitigate this situation for widows. Their role prescriptions were primarily that of homemaking, and there is no interruption in this role with the death of a mate, although it changes in complexity. Furthermore, many of the widow's recreational pursuits before her husband died were things such as sewing, knitting, or home crafts. These can continue to be a source of satisfaction regardless of whether she is in relatively good or poor health, and in spite of transportation or financial difficulties. In this sense, the widow has some sources of fulfillment that the widower does not have because his work role—if he is retired—is completely gone, and he may not be able to pursue such "masculine" recreational interests as golf, fishing, or even watching sports events.

If we try to put together some picture of the types and causes of loneliness of both widowers and widows, we have to stress the fact that most of them are, in fact, alone. They live alone, perhaps with no companionship other than that of a pet. There is no human voice in the apartment, home, or hotel room. Many find it difficult to cope with the loss of all the complex network of relationships they had with their mates, even though they have children, friends, or organizations close by. Others are in poor health, lack transportation, or do not have the financial means to begin a life of rich social interaction that would help them adjust to their loneliness. What are the opportunities for widowers and widows to reach out in spite of these inhibitions and to reorganize a social life?

SOCIAL ADJUSTMENT AFTER WIDOWHOOD
A. HOUSING

It is important to stress the critical nature of where one lives, and what that location means to social adjustment. In our study of the new residents of Leisure World, a retirement community, we made important discoveries.[7] We were inquiring why individuals would leave their old homes and move into congregate housing. One of the unexpected findings was that living in the same location for twenty-five years can result in the loss of friends, creating social isolation. During those twenty-five years, friends and neighbors died, moved away, and changed their status. During the same period, many of the significant others in life, such as lawyers, doctors, ministers, bankers, and accountants, moved or died. Our children and our brothers and sisters, living in a mobile world, moved in order to match talents with opportunities. For many, the result of living in one place was greater and greater isolation from those for whom we cared. Beyond that, it gets more difficult to find transportation or the energy to go some distance to participate in our church or to go out to a golf course. You can stay in one location and, as a result of the changes in that location, find yourself a stranger. Many of those persons who moved into Leisure World did so because they felt that by moving into a community of their age peers they could find new friends; be close to church and recreational facilities; and increase their friendship networks, their organizational participation, and meet their recreational needs. They had begun to feel that *location* was a significant factor in their lives.

When a widow faces the question of housing, she has a great many conflicts. There are sentimental bonds of great strength to the old home. Children were reared there, and family festivals, such as Thanksgiving and birthdays, were peak experiences. On the other hand, friends, neighbors, ministers, doctors have departed, and she is increasingly isolated by the mobility and death of others. The old social network is often gone. We want to discuss in another place the economic and energy requirements that complicate this problem, but for now, we are concentrating on the social aspects of housing.

A follow-up study in Leisure World indicated that the residents were indeed rewarded. In two years, they were able to double their number of friends. They were able to maximize their participation in organizations and in recreational activities. We are not offering the result of this study as a panacea for all widows and widowers. Not everyone should move into a retirement community; that living pattern does not fit everyone. But we are suggesting that where you live—in relationship to people, to transportation, to organizations—may be a powerful factor in social adjustment and must be considered when choosing living quarters.

There is a further consideration that is critical in choosing a life-style and a location. We have mentioned the primary needs of men and women for heterosexual contact. The majority of widows living alone in their apartments rarely see a man, except as a clerk in the store. She has no recreational life with men and, few social contacts. But in a retirement community when she joins a club, goes to church, goes to a dance or a community planning meeting, she is bound to have contact with males. We are not suggesting that retirement communities are happy hunting grounds for marriage; although it is true that there are a number of marriages in these communities. What we are suggesting is that such groups make it possible for a great many normal heterosexual contacts that add an important dimension for the widow.

A word of caution is in order. In some retirement communities, widows have been a problem, and no widow in her right mind wants to be regarded as such. But some who came to the community as part of a couple subsequently lost their mate. After that loss, they insisted on being included in events that were designed for couples. They were literally obnoxious in their expectations and soon wore out all of their welcome. People loved them but not when they used that friendship or love offensively. Consider the case of Helene, who came into our lives because the director of a community could not cope:

Helene made a point of visiting all of her friends in the retirement community on Thursday or Friday and not so subtly inquired about their weekend activities. When she discovered they were going to have a party, she would ask who was coming. When it included old friends that she and her husband had had before his death, she would broadly intimate that she had not seen them for a long time and that she would appreciate seeing them. Her hostess would have no alternative but to invite her. But at the party, she, out of desperation, would dominate the conversation, recall past events that included her dead husband, and the party would die. It got so bad that her old friends would pretend they were not at home when Helene knocked. She complained bitterly that she was being isolated.

This case leads us to a consideration of our relationships with past friends.

B. ADJUSTING TO A NEW ROLE IN AN OLD SOCIAL SITUATION

The friendships we have were developed during shared experiences with our mate. Relating to those friends is a specific case of the general problem of the widowed when they begin their new social adjustment. The friends we have before the death of a mate were related to two persons as a couple. When a mate goes, much of the meaning of those relationships is gone. As the widowed begin to reach out for a new social role, it becomes obvious that old affiliations often do not fit.

Most couples associate with couples. Those couples engage in a series of activities that need both a husband and a wife. If it is a dinner party of several couples and the widow is invited, she has to change her role. She may not ask for the attention of married men as freely as before. She is immediately suspect because now she is a single woman. She cannot dance very much with them. She has a new role that is incongruent to the nature of that group. They may love her and want her companionship, but she no longer fits.

Furthermore, her husband carried much of the burden of socializing. He generally had broader contacts in the world, and he knew the business interests and temperaments of his friends. Now she is alien to the group because, by definition, she is a new person.

She may be wrong, but too often she imagines that she is invited because the group is sorry for her. Frequently, when she is striving for a new role, she is too anxious. She may feel like an "intruder" in social affairs when her presence is regarded as not quite appropriate. She may call too often on couples who were past friends. One of the largest components of her successful adjustment to the new role of single person is her cultivation of companions, but to pursue old friends who are still married may be self-defeating.

How then does the widowed or the divorced person reach out? One cardinal rule may be important: You should not attempt to establish new friendships or reactivate old relationships until you have reached some balance in adjusting to the major loss of your mate. These deprivations have been vast. Our need for personal reassurances is so great that too early an effort may mean that we do foolish things. If the widow tries too soon to compensate for those deprivations by "quickie" relationships, they will disappear or be exploitative. When the major grief work is over—and no one can estimate how long this will take—we are ready for the stimulation of new relationships. If we do not wait, we are apt to ask too much from married friends or from our family. Of course, we ought to add that our measures of widows' loneliness lead us to believe that the danger is in the other direction . . . that we do not begin soon enough to construct a new set of social relationships. The rule still applies. We must wait until we have some perspective before we launch into reestablishing past friendships or starting new ones.

There is no cure for loneliness but other people. But you cannot establish satisfactory relationships until you have established some kind of adjustment, quieted your fears somewhat, adjusted to your sorrow, and emerged as a new person who has something to offer. You will find then that the satisfactions you get from others are different from those you had when you were part of a couple.

C. OPPORTUNITIES FOR NEW SOCIAL CONTACTS

When you feel sufficiently at one with yourself to move out into the world and to make new friends, play new roles, and establish new relationships, where do you turn? What opportunities are there? We already have suggested some basic components that are essential to this enterprise. Let us review them. You may wish to change your housing so that the possibility of interaction will be maximized. You may wish to investigate retirement high-rises, communities, or other forms of congregate living. You may wish to find a health base for that enterprise by paying more attention to nutrition, exercise, and relaxation. You will certainly have a need for a sound financial plan that will erase fiscal anxiety and give you certainty as to the economic level on which you are going to operate. You will need to solve problems of transportation so that when the opportunities are before you can get there. All these considerations are basic before you begin your new social role.

If you can find a widow's group such as has been organized in New York, or such as CRUSE in England, or a Widowed Persons Service, you may start by finding new friends among the widows and widowers who are enlisted in that enterprise.

If you have elected to move into a trailer court or a retirement village, you will want to assess the varied activities that are offered and see which offer you (1) rewarding activities and (2) the opportunity to have constant and rewarding experiences with other persons. It may be that the effort is entirely outside of any social contact that you have so far enjoyed. For example, you might join the Sierra Club.[8]

If you are younger and still have children or adolescents at home, there are other groups that are helpful.

You may have heard about Parents Without Partners.[9] You may find companions in your church, lodge, political party, volunteer work, classes at a community college, or at a dance, or a card group. You will soon see some of the 12.5 million widowed persons that walk the lonely paths of this urban country. If you are friendly and compassionate, you will soon find people who want to share their lives. Learn how to play the single person's role a little at a time because it is really a role without definition.

If your children are grown and far away and you miss your role of parent, you may find satisfaction, companionship, and personal reward in associating yourself with one of the volunteer groups that work with schoolchildren, retarded children, adolescent drug victims, delinquents, or any group that asks for warm and responsive persons to help them carry on their remedial work. The personal satisfactions of helping a spastic child learn to dance, a retarded child achieve a new level, or an unloved child some tenderness are beyond description. Adele tells us what happened to her life:

> I was desperately in need of finding some way of being close and useful to someone. I seemed shut out from everyone, and yet I had had great rewards as a mother. Finally, I went out to a retarded children's center . . . and volunteered. Even with my own kids, I seldom felt as useful as I did in helping these limited children grow. I needed them, but they needed me, too. Now I'm almost full time in that center, and my life has a purpose it hasn't had for fifteen years.

The church remains one of the best opportunities for widowers and widows to find a meaningful social group. Looking at the social activities' record compiled by Baredo, one sees that the church has always been more of a resource for widows than for widowers. It still offers both spiritual solace and fellowship to those who participate. There are always, for both men and women, innumerable roles to play in furthering the institution's work with children, youth, young married, and older persons. Widows seem more apt to affiliate with the church and to gain more sustenance from its program than do widowers, but that is history and does not mean that both cannot benefit from the opportunities for service and social life that the church offers. The church does not organize its activities on the basis of couples, so it is particularly hospitable to both widows and widowers. One of the more recent developments in church life is the outreach program, in which the church seems anxious to help provide transportation and other supports necessary to involve widows and widowers in its activities.

The outward thrust of educational programs is encouraging for all single persons. Continuing education in secondary schools and community programs in community colleges are fully pledged to meet the career or developmental needs of bereft individuals. They are in the midst of programs and plans that will enable persons caught in any stage of life to hone old skills or establish new skills so that they can reenter the business world if they wish. They also offer travel or cultural courses in which isolated individuals can enlarge their knowledge and find new horizons of interest. Here is an exciting environment to find other lonely persons who wish for companionship, those whose minds are alert and who would make excellent friends.

There are innumerable opportunities to participate in dynamic groups or organizations, providing your health, transportation facilities, and economics are stabilized to the degree that you are able. Were you and your mate involved in political affairs? Then the party or county or school organization will welcome further help. Did you contribute time as a couple to a lodge or club or hobby organization? They still need all types of participation. Being a widower or widow will not stymie future participation. You ought to inventory past associations, and see if your contacts with them are still viable. They probably are. But this should not preclude investigation of new hobby groups, new interest groups, new educational ventures that will provide unique and compelling rewards. You may have had interests in dancing, or singing, or rock-hunting that were never developed because of the time pressures involved in being a wife or a mother. But now you are free to do whatever you would like to do. It is a time for exploration and growth.

The initiative, however, lies with you: Undoubtedly, many volunteer or community organizations would welcome you, but they are not going to seek you out. They do not know who you are or where you are. If you are fortunate, you may have a friend in one of these groups who will invite you to join him or her in exploring a new situation. However, the initiative generally must come from your own need to associate. This is crucial because there are scores of worthwhile organizations that need precisely what you can offer, and they are eager for your participation. But unless you volunteer, they will not know about you. Far too many widowers and widows sit in their armchairs waiting for someone to invite them somewhere. In our fragmented society, that is a forlorn hope. Try exploring. If at first you don't find what you wish in terms of opportunities, people, or congenial friends, try again: The rewards are great.

DATING

A good many widows know almost by instinct that they will never meet a man like their late husbands. This is true insofar as every human being is unique, and no other will speak to us or caress us as our beloved did. But this truth may lead us to overlook the fact that others have their own uniqueness to offer. We have all the negative signs; Marjorie, among others, taught us. Marjorie gave up on men, and she told us why:

> Well, I'll tell you why I don't date any more. Every man I met was interested in only one thing . . . going to bed. He'd take me to a lovely dinner, we'd have a fine time, and then, at the end of the dinner, he'd say: "You must miss your husband, how would you like to come to my apartment?" Well, I was not about to go to his apartment. So, disappointed, he'd take me home and I'd never see him again. It got so that I just quit accepting invitations.

Ahead of us, we have a whole chapter devoted to the sexual adjustment of the widow, so we'll not dicuss that now. What we are interested in at this time are the general problems of dating. The time comes when the widow is reconstructing her life, and she wants more than the companionship of other women. She begins guardedly to think about another marriage and to welcome the attention of eligible men. The so-called merry widow has no problem at this point. She has been waiting for, or pushing for, this moment, and she is able and willing to give her best attention to making the other person feel comfortable and aware of her charms. But this is not always the case. There are a great many widows who feel insecure or guilty about venturing into new heterosexual relationships after a marriage.

The widow's role is often not an easy one. There may come a desire to remarry, but the possibility of widows finding eligible men diminishes with advancing age. There are some 251,000 widowers each year in contrast to 592,000 widows. Most of the older men in this country are married; most of the older women are not. A widow or divorcée will have a great many opportunities for temporary affairs with men, married or unmarried, who are not satisfied in their love relationships. Some will offer her tenderness and consideration, but others will not. She is troubled by the thought that she may be sitting alone watching television for the next twenty or thirty years when what she really wants is intimacy. This is a very natural need. She must eventually solve this problem alone. But she must develop a system of values for her situation, or she will be badly hurt. Our society has long ignored the emotional needs of the single person.

When we have spoken about the problems of dating with groups of widowers or widows, they often have reacted vehemently. They have said that they can handle the problems we have been discussing but that the real problem is where and how to meet other single persons. Insofar as there are 12 million single persons in our nation, this really ought not to be a problem, but it is. Three suggestions are in order. The first is that often our anxiety about meeting others is so great that we overplay our part. We talk too fast, too often, too long, and turn the other person off. We try too hard to please others because we are anxious. The second suggestion is that we pay more attention to making ourselves attractive. There is some merit in manicuring our manners as well as our fingernails, to watching the depressive tone of our voice as well as the eye shadow we apply. Not that fingernails and eye shadow are not important, too. But they often are overshadowed by negative self-presentations. The third suggestion has already been made. We have as many dynamic contacts with interesting persons as we can find by enlarging our circle of interactions. Divorcees seem to have an advantage over widows in this regard. They remarry sooner and in greater numbers than do widows. We are not entirely sure why, but we suspect it is because they do not burden their new social relationships with so much sorrow or depression as do widows. Furthermore, they have more or less willingly left a mate, while widows involuntarily were forced to surrender their companion.

If we have one suggestion to make, it would be that widowers and widows beginning a new career of dating should talk with others in their age group who have already experienced such adventures. They will thus become aware that persons with their experience and history are not expected to respond as they did during the courtship of their late teens. They will also hear some sage advice as to how to handle embarrassing or unexpected situations.

CONCLUSION

We have suggested that widowhood involves for both men and women not only the creation of new personal roles but the assumption of new social roles. We have explored the widow's responsibility in moving through intense sorrow to the development of a new personal outlook. What we have discussed here is the need for the widowed to achieve emotional independence from their deceased mates, recognizing that they now are new individuals with new status and that there are still many chances for a creative life. When the widowed no longer feel the stigma of being single, they have made a good adjustment and will have the poise and purpose to handle any new problems in their social life.

CHAPTER EIGHT

YOU AND
YOUR FAMILY

"First and foremost, it was the children who helped me. Nothing they could ever do would alienate me from them. . . ." The speaker, you'll recall, is Jean, the widow we met in the first chapter. Jean's recollections of familial closeness and support are in marked contrast to those of Dorothy, who recounts the early days of her bereavement with some bitterness:

> I can't understand how the children I gave birth to and reared have grown up to be so selfish and unfeeling. Here I was, suddenly alone, and after the funeral my daughter rarely took the time even to call. She was so tied up with her club work and social activities, and God knows what, that she seemed impatient and put-out even when I got in touch with her. As for my son, well he did help with the arrangements and immediate problems, but I scarcely saw him after that. I have two sisters, but they live in different parts of the country, so they weren't any companion-

ship to me. If I've survived losing Fred, it wasn't because my family helped me. . . .

Jean virtually elevates her daughters to sainthood status for their crucial support to her during the early days of bereavement and celebrates the ongoing warmth and closeness between her and them. In the other case, there are only angry recriminations and unresolved hurt. Case histories like these—and many variations between these extremes—can be garnered from talking with widows. Such recollections are most revealing and indicative of how some families react to bereavement and the degree to which they offer support to the widows. But in interpreting them, we must be conscious that often they are perceptions formed by the widows under conditions of deep emotional stress and distress. Could it be that Dorothy's son and daughter really were not so uncaring as she indicates? Could it be that what she took for indifference on their part really was a more complex set of emotions colored by their own reactions to the death of their father? Were they confused about what they should do, and was their reaction tempered by the rapid pace and heavy obligations connected with their own families and personal lives? Could it be that Dorothy's expectations of them were greater than they honestly were able to meet? Were her expectations really undefined and confused in her grief? Or were the adult offspring in fact as uncommonly selfish and unresponsive as she indicates? Need it have happened this way?

It becomes immediately clear that there are great differences among families, differences among individual family members, differing mutual expectations, and differing reactions to crisis—all likely to be magnified in times of bereavement.

Just how good and viable a source of support and comfort is the widow's family in time of bereavement? What are their roles in relation to the widow? And vice versa? What can the widow expect in regard to family relationships during the continuing years of her life alone?

Of course, in each case, "family" varies not only in members' attitudes and styles and expectations but in composition as well. For some widows, family might mean living parents, several brothers and sisters, several offspring, and a network of in-laws. For others, there may be only a few and distant living relatives. Some have no family at all. Differences of family situation also are a function of the woman's age at which she was widowed. Some become widows when their children are small and thus have a different family situation than the ones who lose their mates after the children are grown and on their own. We will discuss these different relationships in terms of case histories and the research that has been conducted and offer some suggestions for dealing with this most difficult area.

WIDOWS WITH YOUNG AND ADOLESCENT CHILDREN

Some of the most poignant case histories of widows are those of young women with small children. Marianne's is such a story:

> When her husband was shot and killed in a holdup, Marianne was twenty-eight, the mother of a three-year-old son, and seven months pregnant. "After John's death, I felt I was on display. I held up without shedding a tear during the funeral and for the weeks afterward," she recalls. "But when I got to the hospital to have the baby, I broke down and cried and cried. Other fathers came to see their babies, but I felt I was taking my baby home to nothing. . . . Whom would I share my baby with? In the space of two months, I went through a death and a birth. What more traumatic experiences are there?" Her recollections of the next three years become a blur of mothering—diapers, strollers, washing, cooking, cleaning. "I kept busy and tried to be attentive to the children's needs, but in many ways, I was withdrawn, like a zombie." She remembers very clearly one time shortly after the funeral that her three-year-old ran down the hall screaming in uncontrollable desolation, "I'll never see my daddy again!" She told the sensitive boy the truth, that his father had died, and tried to console him, to keep him busy, to reinforce the idea that life will go on. She did this in the midst of her own desolation, which caused her to awaken often from twilight sleep to confront her loss very much alone. Since that time, she and her family largely have recovered from the loss, but even today, as she explains, "We have some emotional problems. It's difficult when other chil-

dren tease my son, asking 'Why don't you have a daddy?' There's no one with whom to share the kids' growing up. It's always Mommy, Mommy. . . . Our household is lopsided, not balanced." She feels she would like to marry again. "But the problem is finding someone I like enough and love enough, someone who would have a good mutual relationship with the children. . . ."

Marianne's ability to help her child grieve even in the midst of her own grief is testimony to the remarkable resources that mothers can muster to comfort their young. But Marianne had her own needs, too. The most helpful person to her during those first years after John's death was her own father, who lived in the neighborhood and came over twice a day to feed the baby and to give her other aid and consolation. "My mother-in-law was helpful in the beginning, but it was my father who really came through. Everyone needs help in times like that," she says. Early on, she joined the local chapter of Parents Without Partners. Being able to share experiences and counsel with others in similar circumstances was helpful to some extent, she says. But she feels a real turning point in her recovery came when she consulted her physician. She complained of exhaustion and other symptoms that seemed to be building up. He was able to assure her that she had no serious illness, that she was experiencing physical manifestations of bereavement's emotional turmoil. He advised her to find a part-time job and get out of the house part of every day. She did so, and this was instrumental in her recovery, she feels. Eventually, she has become active socially, knowing that "you can't sit around the house all the time." She is a member of a bridge club that meets once a week; she can enjoy herself dating and going places. "Now I can laugh again. I can stand on my own feet, and I feel all right," she says. Marianne knows she can't be mother *and* father to her children, but she feels her own recovery has helped her to become closer to her children and to be more effective as a single parent. You have to have a sense of humor, she adds, particularly in facing the frustrations of widowhood and rearing of children alone.

Marianne's case history is instructive in some ways for other widows with young children. First, she was open to the support that came from her own family in the form of her father's help. That sort of supportive—yet not overbearing—aid from one's family in the darkest hours can be a great resource. Depending on life circumstances, individual personalities, and family characteristics, it may or may not be available. But if it is, a young widow is well advised to be open to it and make use of it. Second, we see that Marianne was a solicitous mother, but she also was attentive to her own needs. This brought a renewal not only of herself as a woman but also a renewal of herself as a mother. A young widowed mother's own recovery is as important to her children as it is to herself. She must work through her own grief if she is to help her children work effectively through theirs. Third, there is the way in which Marianne definitely and finally told her son that his father had died, that he would not be returning to them. It is critically important that the young widow does not avoid facing reality with children. With the sudden death of a father, virtually half of a youngster's emotional security has disappeared. Relying on euphemisms or on other partial or total denials of death can only confuse them and further damage their emotional security. Fourth, Marianne managed to be fairly open about her emotions with her children. This is important because no parent has ever successfully hidden emotional conflicts from children for very long. If you are devastated and lonely, be honest about these feelings. If you are, it will help the children to be open about their own feelings.

> Physical contact is essential in life but during this time even more so. The comfort of a parent's arms has long been the haven against the world for children and those arms are also needed in grief. Stay close by, but do not smother them. Do not expect them to be *your* haven. Reversion to bed-wetting, temper tantrums, displays of hostility and destructive behavior may occur. They call for your undivided and loving attention, not harsh discipline nor the thoughtless demands of people who do not share their grief. . . .[1]

The challenges faced by the widowed mother of adolescents are somewhat different from those involved in rearing younger children, as the case of Alice demonstrates:

Alice's husband died, leaving her with one college-aged daughter, who was supportive of her on an adult level, and a fourteen-year-old son, Bill, who had been very close to his father and suffered greatly at his death. Not long after, Bill, formerly an A-student, began to lose interest in school, started receiving mediocre to failing grades, and was reported by his teachers to be a discipline problem. Simultaneously, there was growing conflict between Bill and his mother. "I've been close to both my children," Alice says, "but at times he was so surly and rebellious that I was hard to put to know how to handle him. God knows I did my best to discipline him, but that's difficult for a mother alone. Perhaps if I hadn't had to work full time . . . I don't know. We not only had fights about his behavior, we even had ugly confrontations about mine. He didn't approve of my dating when I started, and that was two years after his father died. That has changed, but he's still very critical of the men I go out with. Bill is basically a good person, and I'm proud of him in many ways. Losing his father has meant a rough growing-up for him. Even now I'd say he's nineteen going on fifteen. . . ."

The case of Bill and his mother illustrates ways in which the expected teenage turmoils can be exacerbated by the loss of a parent. In this age range, the youngster has one foot in childhood and one in adulthood. He or she is really neither. Hence, there is a natural identity crisis in the struggle to grow. Anxiety, the chief characteristic, is compounded by a rebelliousness against parents as the youngster strives to achieve mature independence to live in the world as an adult.

Younger children might seem to be more affected by sudden bereavement than are older ones, but this is not necessarily so. Teenagers, depending on the point of their development and on their individual personalities, can be more deeply hurt than small children. Often they find it more difficult to grieve naturally. This can be particularly true of boys because our culture mandates— unrealistically and destructively—that tears or other expressions of emotional hurt are not "manly." The only son is often told at his father's funeral, "You're the man of the house now." This might come at a time in the man-child's development when he is incapable of taking on such burdens. There are many ways in which a daughter also can repress her own feelings and suppress her own grief in her resolve to be a strong support to her mother. Our cultural environment seems to make natural grieving as difficult for the young as it does for adults. Some teenagers seem to repress nothing and collapse into prostrating grief. Or still others may manifest alternate periods of grieving and repression.

Even though widowed parents of teenagers might well be counseled to develop that golden virtue, patience, and to wait out their youngsters' "stages" of adolescent turmoil, such passivity is not the total answer. There are some important steps they can take.

First—and it's difficult sometimes—try to understand that the anxieties, immaturities, and overreactions of teenagers are natural. These are likely to be intensified and complicated by the loss of a parent, and that is natural too. Do not fear that unaccustomed disrespect or sullen aloofness or disobedience automatically means they are becoming bad characters for life. They need all the security you can provide them in the form of standards, loving discipline, and understanding. Try to be open to them and to empathize with them. Be available to them when they need to talk, but respect their privacy too. All this might be far easier said than done in the depths of your own grief. But finding the strength to go out of yourself in parenting can be an important positive step in your own thrust toward recovery. You also may be surprised that such an approach will help your son or daughter grow toward emotional maturity faster than you could have imagined.

Second, if circumstances are such that you feel you can't cope alone, by all means seek outside help. The source might be within your own family, perhaps an understanding uncle or aunt who is interested and might be able to help sort out the issues and offer companionship for you and/or your teenager. Or the help might be from your clergyman or from a professional family counselor. Preadolescent and adolescent boys need an adult male influence in their lives with whom they can identify. Such organizations as Big Brothers of America and its many chapters across the United States serve well. The one man-one boy relationship that this program provides has helped many a fatherless boy to grow. Widows might well investigate this for their sons or the newly emerging Big Sisters groups for their daughters.

Third, in their growth process, teenagers are trying their wings in a number of ways. They are seeking adult roles and in their own way trying to act them out. It is very important for their development and their self-esteem that they make some accomplishments for which they receive recognition. A parent can help a great deal. Without overtly leading them, directing them, or attempting to force them into pursuits *you* choose, you can support and encourage them in their chosen endeavors toward new avenues of accomplishment. A natural way to do this is by complimenting them and expressing your confidence in them frequently. Honest praise from you—whether it is for academic success or a well-cooked meal, a good performance in a basketball game or the mature way a complex problem has been thought out—can go a long way in reinforcing mature qualities and adult achievements.

Fourth—and we're repeating this for emphasis—continue looking into your own self and toward the needs of your own recovery. For as in the case of small children, the widowed parent's own renewal will directly and indirectly help the healthy growth of her teenaged son or daughter.

MIDDLE-AGED AND OLDER WIDOWS AND THEIR FAMILIES

We have made some important points regarding younger widowed mothers. But the inescapable demographic reality is that the average age of widowhood in the United States is fifty-six. This requires us to focus particularly on that age level. The family situations of middle-aged and older widows are generally very different than those of younger women, although no less significant in terms of the questions they pose about family relationships. As a prelude to this, let us take a general look at the American family and some important research findings about it.

Many of the great changes in the family in the last century are well known to most of us. Technological innovation and economic change, and the mass mobility spawned by them, have a profound impact on the basic unit of society. No longer do we have the simple, essentially agrarian economy of the nineteenth century. In those days, it was common for several generations and even branches of families to live in close proximity, if not under the same roof. Many multigenerational, or extended, families were united in agricultural or commercial enterprises. Farms and businesses were passed from father to son. Nowadays, it is rare if most, let alone all, of the extended family members live even near one another in a single city. The predominant arrangement today is what social scientists call the nuclear family. This means separate, two-generation units—parents and their growing children—living independently, and often far away, from other kin. The demographics reveal that these nuclear families are highly mobile. Great corporate employers regularly relocate their mid- to higher-level management personnel, which results in many family uprootings over the space of a few years. It is not uncommon for today's children to have attended six or eight schools from California to New York before high school graduation. There is even a relatively high rate of moving within cities or greater metropolitan areas because of upward mobility or changes in need or life-style. Years ago, many children grew to maturity in the same home, which in some cases became theirs eventually. Today, that is rare, as indicated by the high turnover rates in suburban neighborhoods. Nuclearization and mobility are bound to have had an impact on individual family members in various ways and indeed on the family at large as a social institution.

Some years ago, sociologists recognized the changes, and they correctly identified the emergence of the nuclear family. However, some, emphasizing the nuclear family's independence, concluded that the nuclear units essentially are isolated from forebears and other kin. They felt that the changes signaled a virtual end to relationships with members of the extended family. They felt that the trend was eroding—if not eradicating—close ties between adult offspring and their aging parents, between children and their grandparents, and among adult brothers and sisters and more distant kin, including aunts, uncles, and cousins.

Recent research, however, has indicated that this is not the case. Sociologist Marvin B. Sussman has described what he calls an "extended kin family network."[2] He says, "The network is a pervasive system and includes member nuclear units interlocked within a structure of social relationships and mutual aid. . . . The evidence also refutes the notion that nuclear family units are isolated and dependent almost entirely for their maintenance and continuity upon the activities of other institutions and social systems. . . ."

Research by Dr. Felix Baredo of Washington State University underscores this. His studies confirm that a "viable kin network" exists, that parents are not isolated from their adult offspring, and that such family ties are important.[3]

Baredo reports these findings from his study of an aging population sample:

• Seventy percent of the respondents said they had contact with their sons and daughters at least weekly.

• More than 87 percent were satisfied with their opportunities to be with their families and relatives.

• Widows exhibited the highest frequency of interaction, with more than three-quarters of them seeing their children weekly or more often (affirming, Baredo notes, his observation that widows were more likely to be living with their children than were married couples or widowers).

• The respondents also had contact with relatives other than their own children, but much less frequently.

• Widowers, not widows or married persons, were most likely to express dissatisfaction with their rate of kin contact.

Baredo indicates that these family relationships mean more than simply frequent contact. They also constitute a "network of kin assistance." This means that the generations help each other in many important ways, such as help with work, a place to live, gifts, companionship, advice, transportation, and, in some cases, money. More than 80 percent of the aging parents reported receiving some form of help from their adult offspring. Every type of help was reported most often by widows. Companionship was the kind of help mentioned most frequently by individuals in the total sample. Two-thirds of the parents received gifts and one-third were given help with transportation. Only 13 percent reported receiving money. These forms of aid were reciprocal. All but 5 percent of the aging parents reported giving some form of help to their sons and daughters. Almost half had given aid in the form of gifts, and nearly 60 percent said they helped their children in every way possible.

From our brief look at the Sussman research, we can say at least that the nuclearization of families does not in itself mean isolation from other kin, including younger families and their widowed parents. Going one step farther, Baredo finds that aging parents indeed maintain close relationships with their adult offspring, and widows particularly seem to have close ties. To some degree, these conclusions seem to be entries in the plus column for families as resources for the widow. But the findings do not tell the whole story for everyone because not all families are the same.

As has been recognized:

> Every family has a history that expresses a particular family theme. That theme will be played out on all occasions, be they joyous or sad. Sometimes it is a theme of interdependence and strong cohesion. Other families have stressed independence and individual growth. Some families have existed only by scapegoating an individual member. Other families are characterized by polarities with the men of the family opposed to the women of the family or a father-daughter alliance versus a mother-son alliance. Some family members are sensitive and responsive; others are withdrawn and indifferent. To depend then, on the family for comfort, support and comradeship is often futile and frustrating. Where the family has always been cohesive and close, it follows that the widowed should expect to have more contact. But families are not cut in the same pattern. . . .[4]

With these points in mind, let us explore some of the major issues involved in a widowed mother's relationship with her adult offspring.

LIVING ARRANGEMENTS

Such a major break in the life cycle as the loss of a mate requires a reevaluation of many aspects of one's life. The question of where and how one shall live is a significant one. Often when grown sons or daughters sense the depths of loneliness and desolation their newly bereaved mother is suffering, they want to reach out to help in any and every way they can. They might feel that part of the solution would be continuous contact and a sharing of the grief work burdens, so they invite their widowed mother to live with them and their family. Just how good an idea is this generally?

Elaine's experience gives us part of an answer:

Elaine had always been a devoted mother and her family a close-knit one, so it was not surprising to her when her eldest daughter and her daughter's husband invited her to live with them and her two grandchildren shortly after her husband died. Margo and Bill had a large house, with a guest room that would give Elaine privacy when she wanted it. They all discussed the proposition in advance and were certain that they had eliminated any potential conflicts and problems. During the first few months, the arrangement seemed to be working well, from outward appearances. All were doing their best to be considerate and there were no problems, or so it seemed. "But after a while, I got uneasy inside about living there. I don't feel there's a really deep generation gap between me and my children, but more than once I found myself biting my lip to avoid saying something about the way Margo disciplined or didn't discipline the children. I gave all the help I could cooking on Margo's busy days, but it's hard for two women to function in the same kitchen for very long. I also felt we were cramping each other's style in some ways such as when Margo and Bill entertained friends. And you know? I seldom really had any peace and quiet, with two growing youngsters and that damned dog running through the house all day. I began to sense that Margo and Bill were becoming uneasy, too. Yet neither I nor they said anything."

Eventually, Bill's employer offered him a promotion, contingent on his moving to another city two hundred miles distant. Elaine seized on this as an opportunity to move out on her own gracefully and with considerable face-saving all around. Congratulating Bill on the promotion, she urged him to take it. "I explained that I couldn't move with them because I didn't want to leave this town where all my friends are. I also told them I had been seriously considering taking an apartment anyway, which I had. We all cried together that night. They were tears of mutual relief as much as tears of love." Since that time, Elaine and her family have visited several times a year back and forth and have kept in contact by telephone and letter. "We seem to enjoy each other now more than before, and if anything, we're closer than ever," Elaine says.

Although the prospect of moving in with one's adult offspring might appear to be an inviting one, a solution to problems of loneliness, it may not be so, as Elaine discovered. She was sensitive to the situation, and so were her children. They resolved it in mutual respect and with positive results. And, apparently, were financially able to do so. Some who try this arrangement are not so fortunate. It appears, however, that the majority of older parents themselves reject in advance the idea of moving in with their children, and for good reasons.

A study of older parents moving into a California retirement community discovered these attitudes:[5]

• The retired parents wanted to maintain closeness with their adult offspring. This means visiting and warm feelings, but it does not mean any physical arrangement in which two families live together. Only 14 percent would approve of married offspring having parents move in with them if they need help. In general terms, only 2 percent would approve of older parents living with their sons' or daughters' families.

• The sample seemed to be solidly independent. They do not wish to let their needs interfere with any economic opportunity that may be offered to their offspring. "Having trained their children to be achievers, they have accepted the consequences of that process."

• The actual behavior of the respondents confirms their attitudes about generations living together. "Only 17 persons (among 411 surveyed) have ever lived with their children but 14 of the 17 describe their experience as a temporary one during a transitional

YOU AND YOUR FAMILY | 139

period in their lives. Furthermore, when they were asked under what circumstances they would ever consider moving in with their children, the majority replied that under *no* circumstances would they ever consent to such a move."

The findings of a research project into the family relationships of retired parents on the West Coast were almost identical with those of a study conducted previously on the East Coast by two Cornell University sociologists.[6] It is true that both research samples included older parents who were married, divorced, and widowed. However, other research involving only widows reveals the same attitude trends.

Lopata found among the widows she surveyed that few live with married children and their families. She reports that this can be accounted for by a number of significant factors. First, social trends have combined to make the mother and her adult offspring mutually independent of each other. The widow desires and values this personal independence and sense of freedom. She does not wish to give up running her own household and become a peripheral member of another one. In her own home, she can retain control and determine her own comings and goings and work patterns. Second, she tends to anticipate conflicts in social roles if she were to move in with a married offspring:

> [The problems] are very specific but can be summarized as involving conflict over authority and the flow of household activity, impingement on the right of others to live their lives without advice or criticism, and concern over the mother's efforts to do as she pleases. The desire for independence and for freedom from conflict and tension is sufficient to offset loneliness and the difficulty of living alone. Those who actually live with their married children often define this setup as a last resort. . . .[7]

The weight of evidence seems to indicate that separate living is best for most widows, who themselves prefer this and for good, sound reasons. This is not to say that in no case could living with adult offspring work out. But for the majority, there are too many real and potential problems involved. If you will consider these findings and look into yourself carefully, reflecting on your family relationships and your own needs and aspirations, you likely will conclude that independent living is best, despite loneliness and other problems. You, like many older parents of adult offspring, might aspire to what sociologists have called "intimacy at a distance." Some achieve this and others do not. In fact, the majority of American widows do not, according to Lopata.[8] But intimacy at a distance is not necessarily all-or-nothing, and there are ways that some widows can facilitate warm, growing relationships with their families.

ADVICE AND HOW TO LIVE WITH IT

The lament of a song popular a few years back, "Everybody's Talkin' at Me," characterizes the situation in which many widows find themselves during the weeks and months following bereavement. Some widows are deluged with advice on what she "should" do, when and how she should do it, and what she should do after that. The greater part of this free wisdom usually comes from family members, and in many cases, it is well-intentioned, a genuine expression of love and caring. Regardless, such advice often turns out to be more of a burden than a help, as Anne's experience suggests:

Anne's married son and daughter were saddened not only by their own loss of their father but particularly so by the suffering of their mother, who seemed stunned, confused, and unable to make any plans for her own future. They discussed the options open to them and presented a united front of detailed suggestions on what she should and should not do. She had never driven, they pointed out to her, so she had better sell the car. She also should put "that big old house" on the market and move into one of those nice garden apartments near the daughter's home. Their advice on these and other matters seemed only to add to Anne's confusion in the midst of her grief. She recalls that she appreciated their concern at first and acknowledged to them that they had made some good points. But she was uneasy about making all those decisions right then. "This house is part of my life," she told them, "and it'd break my heart to leave it and the good neighbors I have." But the son and daughter persisted and were joined by their uncle, Anne's own brother, in trying to persuade their mother. Strain soon began to show in their relationship with Anne, who became increasingly uncomfortable about what amounted to their pressuring of her. "Finally," she recalls, "I refinanced the house in order to make the necessary repairs on it, and rented out two rooms to college students to help with expenses. And I took driving lessons and got my first license at age sixty-three. I'm glad I didn't follow my kids' advice because my home remains important to me, and a whole new world opened up when I became able to drive myself around town and on trips. At one point, we all had some angry words, but our relationship has weathered the conflicts. They still don't completely understand me. I think they view me as something of an eccentric. Even so, I do feel they respect me for standing on my own feet."

Anne's story is not unusual, although not all family advisors are so persistent. The point is that Anne was able to seek her own counsel and weigh her own needs and wants against the arguments advanced by her family. The outcome for some widows in similar situations has not always been so positive.

Helena Lopata has made some important observations about advice to widows. Too much of the wrong kind of advice, she writes, is a common and significant cause of strain in the relationship between a widow and her loved ones.[9]

There are several common disadvantages, Lopata observes, connected with advice to widows from family members. For one thing, relatives are usually ill-informed about possible alternatives the widow has open to her in solving problems; if advice is necessary, it should be sought from appropriate professionals. Second, extensive advice carries the risk of producing a dependency on the part of the widow, instead of helping her develop competence and self-confidence in facing her own needs and challenges. Self-confidence is very important for her future; yet it is not fostered by an attitude that says everyone else in the family, not the widow herself, knows what is best. Third, because family members' advice comes from *their* perspectives, not from the widow's, it tends to ignore *her* personality, *her* real needs and desires.

Fourth, familial advice often is contradictory, coming as it does from several sources.[10]

So if in the first year or so, "everybody's talkin' at you," try to be patient and realize the caring spirit in which the advice is probably being offered. But do not be in a hurry to follow any advice, particularly if it involves important decisions concerning your future. There might be immediate financial and/or legal tasks to be handled. If so, consult with a professional instead of a relative. During your grief, you might feel so confused and stunned that you wonder if you can ever function again. You *will* be able to in the future, even if not now. Do not let anyone rush you, for time is one of your best resources if you use it well. We join with Lopata and other authorities, including lawyers and psychiatrists, who suggest that widows should not make any decisions involving significant changes in life during the first year or so. This is important not only because it is difficult to plan intelligently in the midst of grief's burdens but also because *you* will have changed as you emerge from grief into a new life as a single person. Hasty decisions made in the past, when the widow was a very different person, do not serve her well for the future, as some women have learned from bitter experience.

Looking at the longer range, it is worthwhile to note that advice-giving within families is a two-way street. Some widows become compulsive advice-givers to their sons and daughters, and this is commonly as full of pitfalls as the reverse situation. The family might well take it as an infringement on their right to live their own lives as mature adults.[11] Hence, resentments develop and relationships can become strained, if they do not deteriorate completely.

A common problem area occurs if the widow becomes an advisor-critic of her sons' or daughters' child-rearing practices, for many widows still identify with the role of mother. Grandmothers are sometimes befuddled and chagrined by the approaches to parenthood that their adult offspring take. These women, now in their fifties, sixties, or seventies, reared their children in a vastly different time and social environment—under different "ground rules." The space age seems eons away from the depression or World War II. In just the last few decades, social change has altered the status of children and mutual relationships between them and their parents. Keeping these facts in mind helps one to maintain a more balanced perspective. Yet you have a good deal of timeless wisdom and experience to share. Often, adult offspring seek this out from their older parents. By all means, respond and take advantage of the many opportunities that will manifest themselves—if the relationship is close—for mutual sharing of ideas and feelings. In many cases, all this can be done by both parties in mutually constructive, enriching ways. And it can be done without anyone taking the stance of a persistent advisor.

YOU AND YOUR GRANDCHILDREN

Some widowed grandmothers, such as Marie, enjoy warm, close, relationships with their grandchildren:

A year after the death of her husband, Marie's daughter found it necessary to take a part-time job to supplement the family income. She asked Marie to come over to tend the house and take care of the children weekdays between 10 and 4 while she was away at work. Because Marie had been close to Stephanie, four, and Mark eleven, and because she felt herself at loose ends, she agreed to give it a try. Marie's daughter buys groceries for her in exchange, and no heavy housework is expected. "It has worked very well," Marie reports. "I help some around the house, but I feel I'm making a real contribution as far as the kids are concerned. It's important, you know, for someone to be there when Mark gets home from school, and I'd much rather take care of Stephanie than have her under someone else's care in a strange environment. They're good children, and if anything, I enjoy them as much as or more than I did my own. Now I don't have the twenty-four-hour-a-day worry and responsibility. There's never a dull moment, but that keeps you young. Every afternoon, I go home to my own place two miles away and have all the privacy and freedom I want."

Marie's experiences exemplify the mutually rewarding relationship a widowed grandmother can have with the special youngsters in her life. It also demonstrates what sociologist Barbara P. Payne of Georgia State University calls a potentially promising new role for some widowed grandmothers.[12] Arrangements such as this, she suggests, have none of the disadvantages of the widow living with her adult offspring and their families; yet it does meet mutual needs on many levels and perpetuates meaningful family bonds.

The model, however, is not for everyone, as Louise attests:

> I reared four children of my own years ago and that part of my life is over. I love my grandchildren and I'm happy to see them and my own children, but I'm not about to become a regular babysitter at this point. For one thing, I'm too busy with my other interests. . . .

Margaret has a somewhat different perspective.

> I would like to spend more time with my grandchildren, but I have the feeling that my daughter and son-in-law are not comfortable about it. At any rate, they don't seem to encourage more contact. They have different ideas than I have about raising kids, you know. There's kind of a generation gap there.

These individuals suggest that there is no one single answer or "ideal arrangement" regarding a widow's relationship with her grandchildren. This is established even more by a study of older in-movers to a retirement community which disclosed very mixed attitudes about contact with their adult offspring and grandchildren.

> One-third of this group [of retired parents] wanted to "always" get together for festive occasions. Sixty percent had some reservations about such constant interaction, and four percent rejected the idea completely. . . . Only 21 percent give an unqualified approval to activities which always include children. Fifty-five percent give only qualified assent to this proposition. Twenty-one percent disagree completely. . . . The response to these questions implies that a large group of respondents do not want to see too much of their children's families. . . .[13]

Lopata's findings amplify this and suggest some reasons for the wide range in the types of relations widows have with their grandchildren. More widows than not reported having a feeling of closeness to one or more of their grandchildren. Interestingly, half said they feel closer to some grandchildren than others, giving four main reasons: frequent contact, no interference from the middle generation, special circumstances involving the grandchild, or special attentiveness shown the grandmother by the child. Yet a significant number of Lopata's widowed grandmothers (slightly more than 43 percent) said they did not feel particularly close to one or more of their grandchildren. A frequent explanation for this was that they were separated by geographical distance. Lopata suggests, however, that there are other factors involved because some widowed grandmothers manage to see and feel close to their grandchildren even if they do not live near them. A likely factor is the behavior of the middle generation. If the widowed grandmother's own adult offspring interferes for whatever reason (common ones are tensions and disagreements about child-rearing practices), close relations between grandmother and grandchild are diminished or prevented.[14]

Lopata says that "grandmothers and grandchildren are not so frequently close and free of problems as idealized in the literature," and concludes that:

> Relations with grandchildren are of significance to older widows only if the social distance between the generations is cut down by frequent contacts without interference from the middle generation and if these contacts are conducted in a manner building trust and mutual respect. . . .[15]

PARENTS, IN-LAWS, BROTHERS, SISTERS

For widows with adult offspring and perhaps grandchildren, the role of mother is more important than any other familial role except that of wife, Lopata points out.[16] So it seems logical to conclude that a great many widowed mothers have closer ties with their children and grandchildren than with other family members, who may or may not fit significantly into their lives. Generally speaking, we can say that individual personalities, family styles, and case-by-case circumstances account for a wide variation in older widows' relations with other kin, as they do with offspring. Lopata makes these points: the older widow is not highly oriented toward the role of daughter, even if she has close feelings for her mother and father and even if they are great sources of comfort for her.[17] Many widows maintain only minimal contact with their late husbands' relatives or cease it altogether soon after the funeral.[18] Widows' relationships with siblings vary widely in closeness. At one end of the spectrum, some widows have no contact with them at all. Geographical distance seems to account for this in some cases. At the other, some widows are very close to sisters, for instance, who function as understanding sources of support and companionship from the day of their husbands' death, through grief, and beyond. Some widows find that bereavement is the occasion of renewing contact, perhaps close ties, between themselves and siblings. In such cases, Lopata observes, "the family bond is better able to weather interruption of contact than friendship, and crises bring the family together."[19]

OF UNDERSTANDING AND BEYOND

We have discussed individual cases and research findings regarding widows' family relations with the hope that this knowledge will help you to resolve the issues in your own life. One can't help being struck by the wide range of differences in widows' family situations. Going back to our original questions about how viable a source of support families are for widows and what widows can expect from future family relationships, it is obvious that there is no one single answer. If the foregoing has helped you to understand this and some of the complexities involved, it has been worthwhile. Further, knowing that you need not and should not attempt to force yourself or others into preconceived familial molds is wisdom from the start.

Another important observation is the need to keep family relations—regardless of their closeness—in perspective. We have stressed that a widow's recovery and renewal ultimately depend on herself and her own efforts. Thus, any overdependence on family members can become a crutch that in the end will not serve well. Further, a permanent solution to a widow's loneliness and social needs is precarious if one depends *solely* on family. You are an individual with a life apart from, as well as within, your family. With that said, let's take a closer look at your life as a family member.

In some cases, there is great potential for the enhancement of family bonds, which can add real substance to the lives of all involved. A death in the family sometimes provides adults the opportunity to resolve long-standing tensions or conflicts. Or a relationship that already was close becomes even more meaningful and whole as new dimensions are added. In such cases, at least part of such improvements are within your control. If such a prospect is likely in your family situation, how can you help to realize it?

Your first key is that big word: understanding. A widow can be further saddened when she feels that family members simply don't understand what she is going through. This can almost be expected, considering our lack of understanding of death and grief. But understanding, like the relationship itself, is a two-way street. In time, when you are able, you also must be understanding if your family relations are to prosper. This begins with your own grief work and identity reconstruction, which ideally yield a new measure of self-awareness. We have discussed in earlier chapters your need to understand the dynamics of grief and what happens to you in bereavement, so we need not reiterate it here. The only point to emphasize is that the better you understand yourself, the better you will be able to relate to others. Obviously, this can apply significantly to family relations. The quality of understanding also should focus on grief as a social process. Bereavement has affected your family as well, although not perhaps so deeply. Were they not grieving, too, in their way? How did your deep suffering affect them? Surely in the depths of grief, you were not yourself and could not be expected to give as much of yourself as you could under normal circumstances. The upheavals of grief were not confined to your troubled soul alone.

Finally, you must understand your family members as they are. Hopefully, like you, they are changing and growing, and this must be taken into consideration. Taking understanding a step further, analyze your own expectations about family bonds and the behavior of loved ones. In terms of the personalities and circumstances, are your expectations realistic? Answers to these questions come easier when you reach for that elusive quality of empathy—the ability to walk in the other person's shoes. Advice such as the following is well-taken:

> Do not be impatient with the older son or daughter who is already establishing a career or home, if they seem preoccupied with their own concerns. The bereaved parent may feel that these children now in their maturity should assume more of the burden caused when the mate died. They are, after all, his children and your children. You may feel that they ought to do more than come to the funeral and then check weekly to see how you are doing. Remember that they are in the establishing phase of their careers and of their families. They are as immensely involved with this as you are with your problems. If you need them, tell them. They will probably respond. But it is unrealistic to expect them to change their commitments to their expanding life goals to accommodate your needs. If they seek you for a weekend or a holiday by all means go and share their family and their life. They may be asking you to awaken memories, and share their less intense but more extended grief or their guilt.[20]

Another area of family relating that is most important is communication. This, like understanding, might seem too obvious to mention, but because effective communication is so often neglected in families, it is worthwhile to make some brief points. Nothing could be more important, for it literally is the pathway by which one reaches out to another. Family members often designate certain subjects as "things we don't talk about" because they have been the sources of disagreement in the past. If politics or religion, for instance, are traditionally avoided in your conversations, that is one thing. But if the same approach is applied across-the-board to virtually all matters, including feelings and mutual expectations, there is little prospect for close, meaningful relating. It is true that there is much unspoken content in close relationships, but there is no substitution for open discussion, either. If you develop the talent for frankly and honestly expressing your feelings in a tactful considerate way, potentially stifling or painful misunderstandings will be prevented. If you do this with your loved ones, and you strive to become an attentive listener, it might likewise stimulate open expression on their part. The result can be a new depth of sharing that can improve the quality and depth of your bonds. The prevailing style of some families is that members are uncommunicative, and that might be difficult to overcome. In others, potential for improvement is greater.

Another consideration in this area of family relations has to do with the personal qualities and the growth that hopefully are characterizing your recovery and identity reconstruction. We have suggested that you can take the pathway toward self-actualization that Maslow pointed out. We have suggested that you can cultivate the creative attitude that you can "become a person" in Rogers' terminology, and that you can cultivate personal freedom and maximize its benefits. The personal qualities implicit in such growth patterns include openness, flexibility, a readiness to grow, self-acceptance, courage, and the ability to listen to one's self and others. Such growth qualities eradicate defensiveness and rigidity, which must be seen as impediments to relationships with others. In short, if you are firmly embarked on the path of personal growth and self-esteem, it also means that you can bring a fuller, richer self to family relations. These qualities, coupled with genuine, caring understanding and enhanced by attentive communication, can stimulate the same sort of behavior in others. Behavioral scientists have shown that consideration begets consideration, compromise begets compromise, respect begets respect, and so on. This "circular behavior"[21] constitutes a genuinely creative approach to family and social relationships.

Be aware that we really are speaking of the qualities of love, that most precious of emotional and spiritual experiences. No one has ever defined love, so transcendent is its character. Yet the Apostle Paul eloquently described its spiritual depth in a letter to the Christian faithful of Corinth nearly two thousand years ago. Love, he wrote:

> . . . is patient, is kind; love does not envy, is not pretentious, is not puffed up, is not ambitious, is not self-seeking, is not provoked; thinks no evil, does not rejoice over wickedness, but rejoices with the truth; bears with all things, hopes all things, endures all things. . . .[22]

Paul's eloquent words offer us a model to work toward, an ideal to pursue. But it must not be reserved for others only. Healthy, mature self-love of the same rich character is required if we are to be able to give the same to others.

You remember the moving, articulate words of writer Alan Paton, who describes his emergence from grief into a new consciousness that included heightened mutual love of family: "'Some zest is returning to me, some immense gratefulness for those who love me, some strong wish to love them also. . . .'"[23] That is the way it happens for some widows.

For others, it does not, either by the widow's own choice or not. Statistically, families in America do not appear to be a great resource for widows. But you are reminded that statistics represent a broad-based "what is," and they do not really speak of "what can be" in individual cases. In sorting out the web of your family relationships, you will be well guided by the timeless wisdom of this familiar prayer: "God grant me the serenity to accept the things I cannot change, courage to change the things I can, and wisdom to know the difference."

CHAPTER NINE

THE GROWTH OF
THE SPIRIT

Spiritual growth does not occur gradually but in leaps and with hesitations. This we have learned from those who told us of their reactions to the ebb and flow of good and ill fortune. We remember one night long ago when we pitched and tossed in a propeller-driven plane through a snowstorm above the Rockies. The man next to us was more driven by inner turmoil than were the snowflakes by the buffeting winds. He turned to us and said:

I'm taking my wife's body home to California. You know, I've been too busy to think much about what I heard in Sunday school. I doubt all that stuff about God's love. If anyone should have gone, it was me. My wife was a saint and the children need her, not me. God knows I want to believe now. If I could just believe that she's up there somewhere listening to us and smiling down at me it would make a difference. . . . I guess I should have thought about this before, but I sure have to, now.

All night long, we listened and learned.

Later, we learned more from a woman wandering along a stream in Colorado who turned on us as we complained that the trout were not finding our flies inviting. She cried out:

So there aren't any fish. There isn't anything anymore.

When we invited her to sit down and talk, she poured out a torrent of anger and fear and misery:

I came up here to see if I could find some comfort in these hills. That's what the Bible says, isn't it? Lift up your eyes unto the hills, from which cometh my strength. . . . But it's all just rocks. . . . (then with sobs) I lost my husband and a little girl in an automobile accident, and nothing makes sense. There isn't any strength for me here or anywhere. Everything I believed is betrayed.

It was a long afternoon. The sunset came. It was a rainbow of color, but she couldn't see it. The birds sang, but she couldn't hear them. But we heard her need for some meaning, and so we listened.

Those plaintive petitions from persons suffering loss are as ancient as the rocks on that mountainside. We remembered, when listening that long ago, that Job lost his sons and his daughters, his herds and his camels, his servants and his health. His body was covered with boils, but his spirit was suffocating for answers. He bitterly complained:

He hath cast me into the mire, and
I am become like dust and ashes.
I cry unto thee, and thou dost not
hear me; I stand up, and thou regardest
me not.
Thou art become cruel to me; with
thy strong hand thou opposest thyself
against me. . . .
Did not I weep for him that was in
trouble? was not my soul grieved for the poor?

When I looked for good; then evil
came upon me: and when I waited for light,
there came darkness. . . .
My harp also is turned to mourning,
and my organ into the voice of them that weep.[1]

Job thrust his fist in God's face in bitterness. He was known as a good man; yet he lost all that he had gathered and loved, and all about him, the wicked prospered. Then his three close friends, Eliphaz, Bildad, and Zophar, came to mourn with him and to comfort him. But they were shocked at his insolence and anger, and they condemned him. Their arguments ran off him like water off oil, and he called them "miserable comforters." He strikes out, saying that "God has made me weary but you, my friends, have made me desolate." Then God Himself comes in the whirlwind to confront Job.

God asks Job who it was that put the hinges on the world and hung stars in the firmament. He finally asks Job where he was when He laid the foundations under the continents.[2] Job is humbled and asks forgiveness, one of the strange reverses that strikes us as so paradoxical in the Bible. Before God leaves, He turns on Job's three friends and condemns them because they have not spoken "the thing that is right." But Job has said the right thing.[3] So the three friends must make a sacrifice if they are to be restored to grace.

Where had they failed? They were cast down because of their arrogance. Job seemed to be approved because he shouted his defiance. His soul was troubled and he would not leave the confrontation until there were some answers. All that he had learned from his elders was denied by his experience. All the platitudes were contradicted. He had the courage to face that awful conflict between what he had so glibly repeated and believed and what he now could not believe. It was not the loss of his thousands of sheep or camels or the boils on his body that plagued him. It was the eternal conflict between justice and injustice in the world. And God said he had done the right thing to fling his anger at Him. He was right to express his desolation when nothing made sense to him.

You recall that God had made a bargain with Satan to test Job. It was significant that when Job thinks himself more righteous even than God that Satan does not claim to have won the battle because, in his blind anger and his insistence on answers, Job was true to an inner self. He had his integrity. He was struggling to grow. The story has meaning for every angry or desolate person in sorrow.

Modern man is not really in search for his soul. He is not remarkable for his spiritual exercises. Most of us have learned a few biblical phrases and a few stereotyped religious sentiments that we repeat like old parrots. Job's friends were repeating old clichés, and Job would have none of it. His spirit was ruptured. He would not give up until he had some answer to the real torment in his soul. If the peaks of experience in life, such as birth, love, and death, are to enrich, there must be confrontation. For century after century, the richness of the land about the Nile comes with the devastating flood that brings nutrients to the land so that plants may grow. In life, too, there must be devastating floods that overwhelm and challenge us, or the spirit does not grow. And even then, it may not grow if we are not responsive.

A cataclysmic loss, such as the death of a mate, often raises what has hitherto seemed an indifferent issue to burning questions. If there is love and compassion at the heart of our universe, why does a child die? If there is any justice at all, why does a mate leave us in the prime of life? Why do the "wicked" prosper while those who go about doing kindness are kicked away by fate? Is life after all a tale told by an idiot, full of sound and fury, signifying nothing? It is easier to idly pass and avoid these eternal problems. They are disturbing. But unless they are faced, wrestled with, and probed, we are the more inert and vulnerable before the "slings and arrows of outrageous fortune." God approved Job and restored him because he battled. There is more to it than that, as we shall see. But God egged Job on. He asked Job for answers. He wanted dialog with him. He was not displeased because Job pried into such elemental issues.

At least one historian, Arnold Toynbee, has accounted for the uneven progress of man by his principle of "challenge and response." Civilizations die when there are no threatening frontiers.

At least one school of sociologists attributes invention and innovation to confrontation with conflict. A few psychologists have pointed out the same process for individual man. Still, history indicates that individual greatness is often the response to challenge. So for all of us, there comes "the moment to decide" whether we follow Job and struggle with ideas and our basic anger or whether we retreat into clichés and somnolence.

THE SEARCH FOR MEANING

Job was desperate to find some meaning to the contradictory and seemingly meaningless things that happened to him. The man who turned to us in the winter storm and the woman pacing along the stream were both searching for some explanation. Perhaps for the first time they were confronting the fact of death both for loved ones and for themselves. The bell tolls not just for the friend or mate but for ourselves. It is a basic psychological insight that our sense of loss at the death of a dear one is so keen because it reawakens those fleeting terrors that have visited us when we have contemplated our own death. And in denying the death of a mate or forgetting it with the aid of drugs or alcohol or clichés, we are enabled to put aside the final question of the significance of our own death. But no one is in tune with life if death has not been confronted.

The danger point arrives when the paroxysms of grief seem less intense and we begin to feel the pull of new roles and new experiences, for then it is so convenient to push aside the questions we have been asking about mortality, justice, and explanation. We should suppose that the benediction from God to Job came partially because he was not content to "adjust" and relax. His friends kept prompting him to forget his anger, his doubts, and his quest. But Job would not abandon it until he found some explication of his doubts. What did Job learn? Seemingly, he accepted the insights God offered that there was a reasonableness about the universe. It had a beginning. It was full of wonder. Where there were such wonders and order, there must be an Orderer, a Creator who stood eons of time and megatons of energy above frail human beings. Job became humble and said that now he could not only *hear* but for the first time he could *see*. We suppose that his seeing is meant that he achieved a new perspective that answered his doubts. So grand was the design, so overwhelming the work of God that Job could accept his loss as part of that design. Whatever he made of the new evidence that God supplied, it comforted him and humbled him. We are not party, unfortunately, to Job's subjective struggle and the way he found peace. We only know that he thought, he searched, and he discovered some answer for himself.

The answers that seemed to quiet the vicissitudes of Job's spiritual pilgrimage have helped many. To feel and sing "How Great Thou Art" enables many to accept fate. We must honestly add that it does not comfort the authors very much. But we live in a different age and have long ago noted the rational analysis of that argument. And we are glad that the answers to the spiritual quest of yesterday no longer appeases us today. If it did, there would be no further questions, only clichés. Every man must make his own pilgrimage and question and hone and improve yesterday's answers.

Nor do we feel that in this childhood of man's years there can be a final answer. In a pluralistic society, there will be many stances. Some of them will reject the theistic position entirely. There are many courageous men and women who, tutored by science, see themselves only as part of a purposeless and mechanistic universe. But they have a steady and consistent world view. They could repeat Luther's words with sincerity: "Here stand I . . . I can do no other." They know what they believe, and they find comfort in the integrity of that belief. When we speak of the growth of the spirit due to loss, we are not limiting ourselves to evaluating any creedal or dogmatic position. We are suggesting that every man must come to terms with his own finitude and the fact of death. Consider the case of Bart.

Bart was a skeptical soul. He had a rational mind and seemingly could confound any of the bright minds of his small town, including the judge and the local minister. He repeated throughout his life, "Give me proof." He meant it. Through the years, he gradually adopted a kindly, understanding, and agnostic philosophy.

When in his seventies he was about to die, his son, thinking that perhaps his father would now repent and lay his bets on heaven, called in the minister to pray for him. Bart was only semiconscious, but he knew what he was hearing. He had enough strength before he died to raise up in his bed, look the minister in the eye, and say: "Go to hell."

We think God would have respected Bart for that as He did Job. He had his own integrity and strength in confronting life and death. He was not about to affirm a belief that he had denied his whole lifetime. Whatever we think of Bart's agnosticism, for him, it was always tested, confronted, and a source of strength. On the other hand, the judge, an equally intelligent man, looked at the same phenomenon and found proof that there was reason and promise in life. He died with full faith that a life invested like his would be rewarded by an understanding and merciful God. But both Bart and the judge "knew that in which they believed." It had been no superficial quest that had brought them their certainty. Both had grown in wisdom and serenity because of their quest.

We have one final point to make about this search for the meaning of life. This questioning spirit, this search for certainty can be constructive if it is not haphazard, but for many of us, the spiritual quest has a very low priority. We are born a Jew, or a Catholic, or a Protestant, and it is too troublesome to allow our doubts to enrich our lives. So we go like the lowing cattle to our final bed. But each significant loss threatens us and makes our security less secure and our evasions more firm. In the end, we do not really have a profound belief with which to face our own demise. One of the fulfilling aspects of tragic losses is the incentive to rethink the meaning of life and death. To probe and think and question until at the end we can wrap our robe about ourselves and lie down to pleasant sleep in the security of some convictions forged in the fires of loss.

There is evidence that many of us feel a spiritual sense of loneliness. Like Job, we have lost whatever anchor we had to hold us against the tidal waves of fate. In an era of rapidly changing cosmic views, shifting scientific truths, and uncertain political and social philosophies, it is not surprising that many have come to question the old certainties of childhood. In this mood, they join the millions who faithfully purchase the doubtful guides of the astrologer, or who seek to pinion their faith on the manifestations of Psi, mental telepathy, or prescience. So we confront extreme loss with frail reeds and little faith to support us. But all this can make the quest for truth the more exciting if we choose to confront the ultimate meanings that life may hold.

THE ANSWERS FROM THE PAST

Religion has had something to say about those ultimate answers. But when we say religion, we mean the way humanity's experiences have been institutionalized and preserved. The religious community has developed common symbols and time-tempered beliefs to bring solace to untold generations who have faced the gales of nature and the tempests of change.

The most hopeful answer that has been given to those who lose a loved one is that the loss is at most temporary. The Creator would not have molded the heavens and the earth and given man dominion only to abandon him. The rational Greek philosophers . . . before the Christians . . . had their own intimations of immortality. Listen to Socrates:

> *It must be so;—Plato, thou reason'st well—*
> *Else whence this pleasing hope, this fond desire,*
> *This longing after immortality?*
> *Or whence this secret dread, and inward horror*
> *Of falling into nought? Why shrinks the Soul*
> *Back on herself, and startles at destruction?*
> *'Tis the Divinity that stirs within us;*
> *'Tis Heaven itself that points out a hereafter*
> *And intimates eternity to man. . . .*
> *Here will I hold. If there's a power above us,*
> *(And that there is, all Nature cries aloud*
> *Through all her works) He must delight in virtue*
> *And that which He delights in must be happy. . . .*
> *The Soul, secured in her existence, smiles*
> *At the drawn dagger, and defies its point.*

The stars shall fade away, the Sun himself
Grow dim with age, and Nature sink in years;
But Thou shalt flourish in immortal youth,
Unhurt amidst the war of elements,
The wreck of matter and the crash of worlds.

Both the Old and the New Testaments echoed this feeling of the worth of the human spirit and the conviction that it would not perish in the dust. Generation after generation learned to say in faith and reverence:

The Lord is my shepherd,
I shall not want

. . . .

Yea, though I pass through the valley
of the shadow of death,
I will fear no evil:
For Thou art with me. . . .[4]

Jesus, following the tradition of the Psalmist, said it even more directly:

Let not your heart be troubled:
Ye believe in God, believe also in me.
In my Father's house are many mansions:
If it were not so, I would have told you.
I go to prepare a place for you.[5]

The long lines of the bereft that stretch from the caves of antiquity to the main streets of our cities have heard those words of the shepherd, and they have had their troubles quieted. The poets have said it another way. Longfellow put it:

Life is real! Life is earnest!
And the grave is not its goal;
Dust thou art, to dust returneth,
Was not spoken of the soul.[6]

And Tennyson's words have been spoken or sung at memorial services for a hundred years:

For tho' from out our bourne of time and place
The flood may bear me far,
I hope to see my Pilot face to face
When I have crossed the bar.[7]

God was a ruler of Love, and He would not permit His beloved sheep to suffer or to die. Even if ninety-nine were safe, He would wander into the night to care for the lost lamb. In past centuries, that conviction compelled the humble peasants to crawl with bleeding knees across the rough stones of Chartres to kneel finally before the image of Jesus and Mary. For in that hope was an eternity of sunshine and joy. A decade ago, we watched as the present generation went on knees to clasp the feet of Mary and Jesus and wet them with tears of gratitude in the same cathedral. Life was hard in the sixteenth century, and it is still hard today. Still, all of the sacrifice means nothing compared to the exaltation that one will have in the final day of reconciliation.

This is the answer of faith to human destiny. It answered the spiritual needs of ancient man, it answered the questing philosophers of Greece and Rome, and it answered these who, having been won by the spirit of Jesus, gave their lives to Him. How important is that faith today? Does it have promise in a day of science and sophistication? We sought the answers to these questions by studying the responses of our three rural and urban populations. The result of our inquiry is found in Table 4, where we see that about one-third of our respondents still found their greatest comfort in their religion, either Jewish or Christian.[8]

Our man in the airplane and our woman by the stream could not quite accept this answer. They had not cultivated the acceptance of their intimations. In our studies of religion and loss, we have discovered that religion is meaningful to those individuals who have worked at their faith; who have tested it; who have forged it in the fires of doubt, argument, and rebellion. Job may seem an obstinate, and even cantankerous person, but when Job emerged from his conflict he knew what he believed. Any belief that enables us to stand as Job stood is not casually

TABLE 4
RELIGION AS A COMFORT WHEN THINKING OF DEATH

Which of the following comforts you most as you think of death?	PASADENA (N = 189)		LAGUNA HILLS (N = 183)		MOUNTAIN STATES (N = 115)	
My religion	62	32.8%	58	31.7%	43	37.4%
Love from those around me	49	25.9%	51	27.9%	29	25.2%
Memories of a full life	78	41.3%	74	40.4%	43	37.4%

achieved. Grief helps us grow if we accept the challenge to our shallow beliefs and make them solid—or change them.

DEATH AS PART OF THE LIFE CYCLE

There is another aspect of our religious heritage that tempers frustration. This is accepting death as a part of life. In the Old Testament, almost every story finishes with the words "he was gathered to his fathers." The Book of Job concludes "So Job died, being old and full of days." The story of David concludes: "And he died in a good old age, full of days, riches and honour." Death was accepted as a normal part of the life cycle. There is a season for all things, a time to be born, a time to grow, and a time to die. Our neurotic denial of death prevents us from seeing the great rhythms of life. It is hard to look at the sun or death because we have not learned how to look. A great old friend died last year at the age of ninety-one. She once told us:

When I was younger and had little children, I was a victim of tuberculosis. Then I fought to live. I wanted to raise my own children; they needed me. I sat in the sunshine. I willed to live. They are all grown now and have their own children. I am old

now and worn out. It is the right time for me to go. I have been
most fortunate and I am grateful, but my time has come.

If we can see death as she did, as part of and as a consequence of
life, it loses some of its sting. It becomes less fearful and a more
significant part of life itself.

It may well be that the morbid fixation of the church and the
poets on the fires of hell has made it difficult to think kindly of
death. Dante's *Inferno* is a case in point. It is difficult to reconcile
a creative or loving God with the sadistic portrayal of eternal
punishment. We once heard a priest at a funeral of a beautiful
girl speak on the text: "The wages of sin are death." Then death
gets overburdened with terror. Instead of being the final great
event in life, death becomes haunted by fear. It seems a small
tribute to think of Him as less humane than a human being. Nor
do we like to picture ourselves as so spineless that we must be
hounded and coerced by fear into good works. That seems bar-
baric.

Some persons are more fortunate than others. The farmer
and his wife, who deal every year with the miracle of the seed
and the aging and death of their animals, may be closer to the life
cycle. The man who can range the beach and ponder the crawl-
ing crab, the minute fish, and the empty nautilus shell is close to
the rhythm of the seasons of life. Each day he touched the birth
and death of living things. But the city dweller is not so exposed.
His urban style of life denies him any relationship to the inevitable cycle of being. When his grandparents die they are only seen
in a "slumber room." He lives in the midst of a conspiracy to deny
the normal range of living beings. He is alienated from what is
natural, and he is afraid.

We wonder if the ecological movement is motivated entirely
by a desire to preserve the clarity of our heavens and the purity
of our water. It may well be that there is an archaic, primitive,
and compelling need for the urban dweller to re-establish his
contact with nature's life cycle. In his autobiography, Charles
Darwin said that his life had been impoverished because he had
been alienated from the world of poetry. In a more profound
sense, most of us are impoverished because we have lost some

sense of the eternal rhythms of nature: the birth and death of beings, the greening and graying of grass. Perhaps death may sting us enough that we can escape from the concrete prisons in which we live and venture out into the land. Only then will we understand the comfort of the poet who said in the Psalms: "I will lift up mine eyes unto the hills, from whence cometh my help."[9]

RELIGIOUS VALUES AND OUR NEEDS

The widow and the widower are both confronted with the question of guilt. We have already described their many guilt reactions. They curse the departed and then feel guilty. They condemn themselves with "if I had only—" and feel remorseful. They even feel guilty if they find themselves wondering if there is another person who might bring them joy. The capacity of human beings for self-immolation is unlimited and destructive. Through the experience of the ages, the church long ago understood man's need to be guilty; and his greater need for forgiveness. If you are a widow or a widower, you have probably not escaped self-incrimination for all the things you did or did not do.

Some of the most persistent religious rituals have been aimed at relieving guilt. The most obvious of these is the Catholic confessional, where persons under the burden of crippling guilt can find absolution. Our prayers and benedictions constantly reiterate the plight of finite man seeking some restitution in spite of his failures. The Lord's Prayer says: "And forgive us our debts, as we forgive our debtors." The emphasis upon the mercy of God is ubiquitous. In the words of a familiar prayer: "Oh, Father, forgive this our sin, and lay it not to our charge," and again "pardon and deliver us from our trespasses."

Any relationship with a loved one is close, tenuous, and limited because we are all fragile. It is possible in the best of all marriages to find things that were faulty or incomplete. In the sorrow of separation, it is all too easy to concentrate on those negative memories. We all need help to gain perspective and thus to come to honor what was. But before we can do that, we need a sense of forgiveness for our errors. Prayer, meditation, and God's forgiveness help us gain that perspective. If we ask for forgiveness, we are often granted a new balance that enables us to see the good as well as our failures. This is essential for our good mental health throughout all of life, but it is crucial during grief work. It may be achieved by prayer, meditation, professional counseling, or reading the Scriptures, but it must be done. Sorrow is a tribute to our closeness to someone, but it also distorts.

Even Jesus in his extremity on the cross felt forsaken and alone. His cry "My God, my God, why hast Thou forsaken me" may sound sacrilegious, but it was not. It was his humanity, his suffering that prompted that cry. And at one time or another in life, all of us, even though we feel guilty about it, may utter the same cry. In a sense, our utter desolation joins us with Jesus and every other person who has felt betrayed by life. It is honest then to say how we feel, but it is not sane to stay at that point. We need through sincere probing, through prayer or meditation to rediscover our philosophy of life. A sense of proportion helps relieve us of guilt so that we can go on with a better view of what we have contributed to the person who has been lost.

At that point, we do not need a sedative so much as we need a searching mood. We cannot drown our guilts in alcohol because the next morning they will come back to us in the form of a headache. What we really need is a sense that we are human, frail, and incomplete; that we have tried; but that often our efforts were ineffective. This is the common lot of our fellowman. We remember that we once said to a woman who held herself entirely responsible for her husband's suicide:

> So you want to make him a nothing. Did he not have a will of his own . . . ? If you were that responsible for his life, he was your child and not your husband. There is no way that you caused that suicide.

She listened. There are decisions by others in life over which we have, but should not have, control. We often influence them poorly, and for that, we ask forgiveness; but no man or woman is responsible totally for the decisions or health of another.

All this sounds morbid enough. But under the constraints of

grief, men and women exaggerate responsibilities, but this will rarely bear the test of reason. It is wise to help our friends bear these exaggerated burdens and finally put them in perspective.

What is worse is that guilt and self-recrimination eclipse the real meaning of life and death; they cloud what we ought to see and feel. Can you be exultant that he lived? Do you know that when he was conceived the chances were that any one of 20 or 30 million sperm might have united with the egg? That someway he or she was chosen out of all those almost infinite possibilities? He lived! He was brought into being against insurmountable odds, and he lived! But *he might not have been at all*! And even after he was conceived, he might not have survived because only about a hundred embryos out of one hundred and thirty manage to make it to birth. But he lived. Then in infancy and childhood, he survived the ravages of development and came finally through tempestuous adolescence to manhood and was united with you. But we are so numb with grief that we do not remember that the chances for any person to live are beyond mathematical calculation, but he was chosen, and he lived, and he had life . . . with you. He breathed and laughed and walked in the sunlight, and he loved you. Certainly, he was with you for a shorter period than you would have wished, but aren't you glad that he was elected to have life? There is a possibility that long grief is an insult to life because it denies us the potential of the celebration of *just being*. When one thinks about the possibility that that person might never have been, that he or she might never have shared our lives, we may then replace grief with gratitude.

It is true that your union left some things undone. We have never known a marriage where that was not the case. But beyond that, there were some moments of high ecstasy in each other's arms; there were times when you watched the moon hand in hand and when you both delighted over "Stardust" or the "Moonlight Sonata." You faced the failures of your financial plans and the joy of achievement together—sometimes if not always. And that union might not have been. He might have lived a hundred miles from you, and you might have gone through life passing as "ships in the night." But you met, you loved, you quarreled, you had resentments and fulfillments . . . in other words, you lived and you loved as humans live and love. And it might not have been. Is it possible that your grief is a little egocentric and your sorrow self-centered because you have not thought about the gift God gave you to meet and be together. You are now alone. But even your tears in aloneness are a tribute to the one you loved. Those tears are jewels of praise for him. The tears will pass, but in the years to come, you will more and more transpose your song of sadness to one of exultation . . . that somehow you had life with him, and it was meaningful.

You may not accept this now, but in the months ahead, it will be possible for you to change memories of sadness to joys. Forever more, these memories will be a mantle of remembrance. They will make each moment richer. You may, and we hope you will, find other arms to comfort you. But they will be more tender because you have already loved. You may find excitement with another, but it will be different. You will find that what you think is lost is not lost but is always there, adding depth to your present.

Each generation has its special phrase, and if we were to pick one out that is most significant for our time, it would be that we have become aware that we may "raise our consciousnesses." That means that we become much more sensitized to ourselves and to others. This is the gift of grieving. If it serves its purpose, we come to cherish life and its great moments, its high peaks and even its difficulties. All those exaltations and achievements with our lost mate add to our spiritual appreciation of every human encounter.

RELIGIOUS INSTITUTIONS AND OUR NEEDS

Most of the research that has been done on the church and its contribution to widows and widowers has not been in terms of the spiritual encounters we have described. This does not mean that those studies do not have much to offer. They have looked at the way in which the church offers social opportunities to widows and widowers, and we should pay attention to those possibilities.

Without repeating charts and graphs, we can summarize that research. It indicates that for many widows and some widowers (who turn less frequently to the church after bereavement) there is a possibility of meaningful contact. A woman who has had children or who has worked with children may find in Sunday school teaching a rewarding avocation. A woman who needs social contact may find new friends in the Ladies' Aid or the Quilting Circle or the Altar Guild. Beyond that, she may gain a sense of usefulness that is essential to every human being. Older persons tend to become more religious and yet have less contact with the church. This seeming contradiction is partially explained by problems of transportation. And many churches are now arranging car pools or transportation guides that are assisting isolated persons in attending their functions.

The modern church has a great many social and community functions. Some of them, such as Shepherd's Center is Kansas City, focus particularly on older persons or on widows and widowers. When you come to the place in your convalescence from grief, where you want to have human contact and be useful, you may want to explore the fellowship of the church or of that particular church in your community that is "going about doing good."

CONCLUSION

The Bible records that after Job had gone through his trials and had confronted God in his misery, all of his herds and his family were restored to him. We are not sure, because the story is obviously allegorical, whether this means that they were actually restored or only in his mind. We feel that what happened was that Job forgave God for all his losses, that he "came to himself," put things in perspective, and started to live creatively again. We assume that all that was in the past became part of his consciousness (his memories, if you will) and that he lived richly with himself until he was old and died. There are many ways to have things. They may be material, or they may be in memory. But in either case, they are very real. If you have lost a husband or a wife, he or she will not be restored to you in the flesh but can come to be a part of your life, a benediction of joy, a companion for the rest of your journey.

CHAPTER TEN

TO SLEEP ALONE OR . . .

The status of widows has been difficult in most societies. In the traditional Chinese family, a widow was not supposed to remarry; in fact, her husband's family could block any new union. Furthermore, she was not allowed to take any of her property into a second marriage. There were both social and economic sanctions against remarriage for the widow. But the widower was free to do what he pleased.

If one looks at the statistics of widows and widowers who remarry, it is not surprising that the interval between the death of a mate and remarriage is twice as long for the bereft woman as it is for the man. The long tradition of male supremacy has given the male all the prerogatives of initiating new relationships, but if a woman behaves in similar fashion, she is regarded as forward and unseemly. She is in a double bind because she must wait for some male to make an overture, and she is burdened with the judgment that she is "older." Aging lines on a man's face give him "character," but, for the woman, the loss of her skin tone is a major disability. Still, during the age interval of thirty-five to fifty-four, 50 percent of widowers who remarry pick widows and 40 percent choose divorced women. However, over age sixty-five, over 80 percent of widowers choose widows. Over all, for all widowers, some 60 percent of their new brides are widows. But for widows over sixty-five, only 45 percent of their new mates are widowers; 37 percent come from the ranks of divorced men. The basic problem is the overwhelming plurality of widows over widowers. There are some 251,000 new widowers each year and nearly 600,000 widows. Even if all the widowers and all the divorced men married only widows, there would still be 7 or 8 million single women in this country. We shall look first at the problems of those who are fortunate enough to remarry and then at the sexual and emotional situations of those who do not.

REMARRIAGE

The possibilities of remarriage in this kind of market depend upon the vivacity, the radiant health, and the personality of the widow. It is a highly competitive market and it is not for the ill-equipped or the fainthearted. But, as we have said consistently in this book, the widow can be what she wants to be. If she is dull and sorrowful, she is not attractive. If she does not exercise or watch her figure, she will not have the bounce and vitality that draws men to her. While we would not depreciate Susan Sontag's insights about the difficult position assigned by society to older women, we can counter her pessimism somewhat by other examples. There are many older women who manage to have captivating and dynamic appeal in their sixties and seventies. There are some crucial factors in the transformation of the widow from a grieving, sad person to a positive and expectant individual.

The timing of a new courtship and marriage is thus very critical. There is no more important factor in wise marriage choice than motivation. If a woman begins her relationship with eligible males too soon, before the grief period is over, she will ruin her chances by her demeanor. What is it that is moving us to seek out and win a specific person? In the early months of widowhood, loneliness is overwhelming. It tends to make one desperate. One may then move into a relationship only as an escape from an intolerable life situation. Any companionship will do, regardless of its promise or perils. The perils are rationalized away because we so desperately need someone close by. This is a type of compulsive mate choice that is not really a choice at all. It is a surrender to our emotions.

In months to come, we may contemplate a new love not to answer loneliness, which may have been partially conquered, but because we have grave fears of our loss of attractiveness or our loss of ability to attract others. These fears may condition the widow to cherish any gesture of affection, no matter how gauche or inappropriate the other person may be. A marriage consummated to prove that we are still attractive is apt to be full of suffering. Years of misery might be avoided if we wait until most of our readjustment process is finished and we have some balance in our feelings about ourselves and our needs. Every person should always ask herself over and over why she is developing a relationship. It is surprising how often the motivation is inadequate and even self-destructive.

There are further psychological problems. We may have been so hurt by the death of our cherished partner that we shrink from a repetition of that loss. Thus, we unconsciously pick out someone as far different as possible from the mate who left us. A case illustrates this self-defeating reaction:

> Henry was a forty-two-year-old man married to Alpha. Alpha was an artist sensitive both to beauty and to people. Their marriage was one of those that could be described as idyllic, and there are not so many of these. Henry literally adored Alpha, and that adoration grew during their sixteen years of marriage. He fought his time schedule so that he could shower her with attentions and companionship, and she reciprocated by nurturing every facet of Henry's life. Their joy in sharing their occupational interests, their joy in exploring nature, their sexual responsiveness—all grew through the marriage. They were so engrossed in each other and lived so much for each other that children seemed a threat, so they had none. One day, Alpha went on a painting trip in the mountains. As she was coming around a curve, a truck that had

lost its brakes slammed into her car at ninety miles an hour, and Alpha was killed instantly. Henry went into shock. He had great difficulty in continuing his work or escaping a deep depression, which he conquered only through long psychotherapy. His friends and his therapist thought that he should remarry, which he did after two years of loneliness. But he chose a woman who was the exact opposite of Alpha, a brilliant mathematical chemist who lived by syllogisms. She was as cold as Alpha was warm. Her career came first. The marriage was stormy. It took Henry a long time to understand why he had married a person who met none of his needs and who was so different from his first mate. He finally came to see that unconsciously he had to marry someone so different that she would not leave him, or if she did, would not hurt him again.

Sometimes the motivation is just the opposite. Widows or widowers may feel that to ensure the kind of marriage they had had previously they have to find the psychological and physical twin of their lost mate. In most cases, no marriage occurs because no one can measure up to the already idealized figure of the dead person. Unless such persons modify their techniques of comparing the potential husbands with the old ones there is no chance of marriage. As Genevieve told us:

> No . . . I won't marry. I've looked around, and the men I meet just don't measure up to Bill. Why should I settle for a mediocre person when I had the best. I'd rather stay single.

Genevieve made a wise decision, at least for the moment. She would drive even a superior man crazy as she constantly compared him with her earlier husband. We thought, too, that there were some overtones of guilt in her analysis of her future. What she was feeling was a reluctance to violate her marriage bonds with Bill, even though he had been dead for three years. She felt that she had to be true to him. She simply was not ready for a new marriage, and whatever her rationale for that decision, it was a wise one.

All relationships should have their uniqueness. An idealized picture of a past mate and a determination to make a new partner fit that picture is a procrustean bed. You recall Procustes, a giant who made travelers fit his beds. If they were too long, he sawed off their legs, and if they were too short, he stretched them. Obsession with the past mate is similar to that. It has some insecurity about it, too, as though we did not trust ourselves to new experiences and new adventures. In fact, it would be sad if Genevieve found a person just like "good old Bill." Her adjustment might be easier, but there would be little creativity or uniqueness. We understand Genevieve and tried to help her because after twenty years it is not easy to reach out and play new roles with a new partner. But one must, because all human beings differ.

We do not want to sound too negative. If the bereaved person has taken enough time to put her past marriage into perspective and if she does not need to talk all the time about "Bill," but can concentrate on responding to another person, she is ready for romance. When these precautions are observed, second marriages prove to be satisfactory. In fact, Dr. Jessie Bernard, in her splendid study, *Remarriage*, and William Goode, in his study of divorce, both found that second marriages had as good adjustment as, and in some cases better than, the first. For example, Goode studied 425 Detroit-area remarriages. Eighty-seven percent of the women in Goode's sample claimed their second marriages were more successful than their first. Of course those were divorced women, but the same possibility applies to the widowed. Most studies indicate that second marriages are good.

They may be good for the couple, but not everyone regards them as made in heaven. Friends of the deceased may regard the marriage as a betrayal of the memory of the friend they loved. They may give small but sure clues to their disapproval. They may not cease to give invitations, but their displeasure is evident. This has to be endured with as much grace as possible. In time, those negative reactions can be overcome.

There is another problem when there is a chance for remarriage. There are often problems with children of one mate or the other. They may resent, for personal or economic reasons, a second marriage. (Given the divorce rate in our society, the chances of divorce and remarriage for younger people are quite high, but they somehow feel that widowed parents ought to be "true" to the departed. Thoughts of remarriage fall somewhere between a violation of the ten commandments and high treason.) We recently attended two marriages of widows and widowers. In one case, the children did not come at all. What unconscious motivations beset children who oppose the remarriage of their parents can only be discovered through psychotherapy, but they are often obstacles to the joy of a couple who have lost previous mates, who find much in common, and who are in love. If such a marriage takes place, it should be only after considerable premarital companionship. We are not suggesting that they should live together for a time, although that is not uncommon. We are concerned that they test out their temperamental, emotional, and social compatibility and not marry simply because they are lonely. The grief work should be well over so that the marriage is not a quickie replacement for a lost loved one. If that happens, the marriage is damaged early by insidious comparisons of the new mate with the old one.

A very honest evaluation should be made of the economic resources of both parties, what they intend to do with them, and what each will contribute to the marriage. Premarital agreements are fairly common in remarriages, and these help to eliminate much internecine warfare among families later on.

If children are made party to those agreements, their resentment will often be overcome. This opportunity to go over the premarital agreement also will give them an opportunity to discuss their emotional feelings. If everything is talked over honestly *before* the marriage, many later difficulties can be avoided. In cases where the children are adamant against a remarriage, the use of a good family therapist is recommended. We have recently gone through such a case:

> Gretchen and Harry, in their early sixties, had been close friends for twenty-six years. When their mates died, they naturally gravitated to each other and found much comfort in their companionship. They announced to their friends and families that they would soon be married. But that announcement resulted in a tempest of denunciation and condemnation. Harry's three married

daughters made an appointment to see him. They flatly stated that they would not accept Gretchen as a mother. Harry very quietly told them that regardless of their feelings, he was going to marry Gretchen, and they could like it or not. But the girls were not appeased. They next visited Gretchen and much to her chagrin told her that they thought she was interfering in the family, that she was after Dad's money, that they did not like her and would have nothing to do with her if she married their father. Gretchen was humiliated and unhappy. She told Harry that if she was going to break up his family, then perhaps they should not get married. But Harry was adamant. They had much to offer each other, and he was not going to give her up. The matter reached a stalemate until Harry and Gretchen visited a family therapist who advised a few sessions in which all the children and Gretchen and Harry come together to state their points of view honestly. The therapist felt that perhaps some agreement could be reached. The first session was very stormy because the daughters were again quite snide to Gretchen, which prompted her two boys to turn on them. But they all agreed to come for another session. This session explored other feelings: the needs and loneliness of older persons. Emotions calmed down a bit. The third session was devoted to very specific fears and feelings, and it turned out that the three daughters were themselves quite guilty because they had in some sense abandoned their mother after their own marriages. This guilt made them very sensitive to the "memory of mother." When they realized what they were doing to their father, they began to relent. A fourth session was devoted to planning how the new marriage would relate to the others.

When we turn our attention to the first years of a remarriage, we find that there are a number of common problems. Housing is an area that needs a good deal of attention. One basic suggestion is that they do not try to live in the home they had occupied with another mate. There are too many memories associated with that house, constant reminders of yesterday that can add to the ever-present problems of adjusting to any new marriage. It is discomforting to many women to sleep in the same bed that was warmed by her predecessor. If economics dictate staying there, some new furniture and decorations may ease the problem. There is also the difficulty that with decreasing energy the old house may be too large to keep up. A smaller house or an apartment may be more in keeping with this decreased level of energy. There is also some problem of location. When one is young, a longer trip to church, to the doctor, or to the bank is no great threat, but as one gets older, distances become more formidable, and one sometimes gives up participation rather than make the effort.

Many remarried people do not live alone. There is the ghost of the dead mate, who can be a very active third member. A recent bitter divorcee is an example. She said:

> It was as if Helen [the former wife] was there all the time. Jim constantly reminded me how she seasoned the veal, watched the checkbook, and served him. He must have felt very guilty in marrying me because he constantly praised her. Everything we did reminded him of some occasion when he had done the same thing with her. I just couldn't compete with her.

Different ways of handling the financial role have proved to be a great source of friction. In some families, there has been a companionship role in which major fiscal decisions were always made together, but in others, the husband made them unilaterally. If there is any secrecy about money, this implies a lack of trust and faith. One widower who had just remarried said frankly to us, "Well, I was just trying her out to see how good she was handling my money." But she didn't like to be on trial. A somewhat carefully drawn budget with agreement as to its limits can do much to limit financial conflict. The budget can be relaxed later. But if a couple can produce a budget that reflects both of their priorities and needs, some adherence to it is a useful way to avoid money problems in the early months of marriage. This kind of careful planning in terms of finances, recreation, and social participation can relieve anxiety and promote cooperation.

A second marriage generally can bring rich sexual experience to an experienced couple. But here, too, there needs to be much discussion. It is not easy to leave the arms of one man and adjust right away to another. For many, the change is exciting, but to some, it is disturbing. By the time of the second marriage, both the man and woman ought to know a great deal about their erotic responses, and these should be communicated to the other. If they can share their needs in both verbal and nonverbal ways, they can move without too much difficulty to rewarding physical sharing. Of course, in later years, both a male and a female must cope with various physical decrements. But few of these offer serious impairment to good sexual response. Widows and widowers who have concluded their grief work, who are reasonably healthy, and who have normal sexual attitudes can anticipate a sexual mutuality that will bless their relationship. If they have any problems, they should talk with a doctor or a qualified sex counselor.

Counselors who have made a life work of dealing with both widowers and widows all recommend second marriage. We have also indicated that studies show that these remarriages have a good as and sometimes a better adjustment than first unions. But such marriages should not be hurried. Past relationships must not interfere; family cooperation is essential; and there must be much talk, planning, and mutuality.

THE SINGLE PERSON

There are a great many reasons why persons once married will not contemplate a second marriage. In some cases, the first experience was so dismaying or so frustrating that they cannot bring themselves to try again. In some other cases, the first relationship was so magical, so rewarding that they prefer a rich memory to a dubious future. On the other hand, this is often an idealization that has nothing to do with the reality of their past.

More significant is the discovery that about one-third of our widows choose singleness over remarriage. Even those who judge their marriages to have been very happy find the independence of singleness a preferable state.

Finally, we have to confront the inescapable fact that the statistical plurality of older single women means that millions will not be able to find a second mate even if they want to remarry. The older the widow, the less her chance of finding a mate because the disproportion grows with the passing of the years. It is therefore critically important to see what style of life can be significant for single persons. We are not talking here just about sexual intimacy. A great many widows are celibate. This is a time-honored stance for single persons. A great many individuals, such as priests, nuns, scientists, and explorers, have opted for celibacy. They have sublimated their sexual energy in their service of humanity, their pursuit of truth, or their desire to master great physical achievements. Society is richer for that sublimation. Celibacy in the later years is a perfectly acceptable life-style.

Nuns find profound values in their service to children, the ill, the aged. There are millions of other volunteers who are enriching their lives and the lives of others. The satisfaction of service is superb. It involves much socialization—much human closeness.

COMMUNAL LIVING

A commune is a group of persons who elect to live together in various degrees of intimacy. In some cases, couples join communes to assure a larger family group, but they remain faithful to each other. Other communes are established by lonely individuals to achieve intimacy. Such communes are characterized by sexual freedom among members, as well as by high idealism. Severe problems of jealousy often develop in such intimate groups that they threaten group solidarity. Still, many communes develop a familylike relationship that buffers isolation.

One retirement community, Knox Village near Kansas City, is experimenting with a plan where eight single older persons share a common living area. This is an economic arrangement, but it offers both privacy and social opportunity.

Communal living has been termed retribalization. The goal of recreating kinship patterns is often a strong motivation. In the urban community, the anonymity and isolation of apartment and hotel living drives many to experiment.

THERAPY GROUPS

The experience of closeness that contradicts urban isolation may well be one of the serendipitous outcomes of the thousands of groups existing in our country. In these groups, trust develops so that one dares to voice anxieties and face the frozen fears. In so doing, one moves toward openness and the possibilities of a more intimate tie not only with the therapy group but with others. We know of many groups that provided such fellowship and decided to continue as social groups once the therapeutic goal was achieved. A widow who is a member of such a group may still sleep alone, but she certainly does not walk alone. Her friends in the group support her spiritually and supply her with sociability. Psychologist Carl Rogers has said that the growth of such groups is one of the great innovations of our society.

CROSS-AGE SEXUAL RELATIONSHIPS

Maggie Kuhn is one of the boldest innovators in setting models for the sex life of older women. She worked her entire life in the Presbyterian Church, but when she retired, she became a militant in the cause of older persons and founded the Gray Panthers. The Gray Panthers are now organized in fifty urban areas to change society's attitude toward older people and to change laws that are discriminatory. Maggie Kuhn also believes that social conventions destroy the possibility of much sexual joy for older persons. When she was asked if she had a boyfriend, she replied:

> Of course I have a boyfriend and he is younger than I am. Many of my older friends have younger men as lovers. I see nothing any more wrong with older people shacking up than young people. Many old men marry young girls. Older women have a lot to offer younger men. Not just sex, but a truly supportive, meaningful relationship. Young people think folks after 60 don't have sex any more. This is pure nonsense.

POLYGAMOUS RELATIONSHIPS

Apart from monogamous marriage, the most seriously discussed alternative to sleeping alone is the possibility of altering marital conventions to return to the Old Testament tradition where one man had several wives. This has been part of the heritage of a strong religious group in this country: the Mormons. Both Joseph Smith and Brigham Young had many wives. The practice was abandoned, not because it didn't work but rather because of the pressure of other religious groups.

Not all widows agree with Bernard Shaw, who said that his female friends told him that they would rather have a part of a creative man than all of a mediocre man. Shaw belonged to a very sophisticated circle, and widows in his acquaintance might have felt that way. But many widows in the authors' discussion groups are still advocating monogamy. One put it very forcefully:

> I never shared my husband with another woman. If I'd ever found out he slept with someone else, I would have left without even packing. And if I marry again, I'd want my man all for me.

But not all widows feel so strongly that a man has to be exclusively theirs. One of them said:

> I don't know that that kind of plural marriage would be so much different from the marriage I and many of my friends had. I knew my husband had girl friends, but he always came home to me, and he always loved me. I guess the only difference would be that it would be legal and above board.

Still other widows wished that society would hurry up and change. They said it was so strange and lonely not to have a man around the house that they would settle for almost any arrangement.

AFFAIRS

Older persons are very candid, and some widows have said, as Maggie Kuhn did, that they were having affairs, some of them with married men. A case study shows their rationale for this type of adjustment:

> Mary said that she had been a very happily married woman and that her sexual needs didn't suddenly wither away when her hus-

band died. She had no wish to remarry, and she was not seeking a part-time partner. It just seemed to happen. She was on a committee in her retirement home when she met Tom. The committee had a long session that went beyond the lunch hour, so Tom asked Mary to have lunch. She was very attracted to him but not to his wedding band. She asked him about his family at lunch, and he told her he had been half-married for the last twenty years. He had sought help from marriage counselors and psychiatrists, but his wife would not go with him, either at his request or at the request of her doctor. She was a complaining, hostile, hypochondriac. When Mary asked why Tom stayed with his wife, he said quite simply that he was the only living thing on the face of the earth she had, and he felt he had to stay. He also added that he had managed to take care of his wife and still find some tenderness during the last twenty years. They talked then about Mary's past, and Tom seemed genuinely happy that she had been so fortunate in her marriage. Mary said that she was not quite sure why she said what she did, but when Tom asked her if they could have lunch again, she said yes and that she would make it. She liked his honesty, was physically attracted to him, and needed male companionship. They have had an intimate relationship for five years. Tom's wife has been bedridden during the last year. Mary is not sure that if his wife dies she will marry Tom, but she loves him.

Mary went on to say that she did not resent Tom's staying with his wife. In fact, she rather admired him for that. She felt her union with him was a very special thing because aspects of his personality were shared uniquely with hers. She was quite forthright in discussing their sexual attraction and satisfaction.

But not all affairs are sexual. In a study that one of our students conducted, we were somewhat surprised to learn that almost one-third of long-term affairs had no sexual component. In some cases, they revolved around common professional or aesthetic interests. Interviews with this group elicited great affirmations of affection for the other person but reiteration of the statement that no sex was involved. One man said:

> Somehow that isn't necessary with Madge—ours is a more mental thing—beyond that, she's got a good physical thing going with her

husband, and so have I with my wife. But I can't talk with my wife as I can with Madge.

In other cases, the celibate relationship was the result of an almost therapeutic dependence of one on the other. It almost seemed they had such emotional needs for understanding that they were afraid a sexual relationship would destroy their satisfaction in this area. Still others had gone to bed, but it was so miserable that they simply decided to save their relationship by staying away from physical intimacy. One droll woman, in describing how much this nonsexual affair meant in the emotional economy of her life, summed it up by saying:

I learned from this experience that man does not live by sex alone.

It is probable that the great virtue of close kinship patterns of the close extended family and perhaps of small communes is that there are enough intimates about so that different basic needs are met by many different people. In the nuclear marriage, it is expecting a bit much that one mate could meet all of the emotional, temperamental, physical, aesthetic, and intellectual needs of the other; particularly when most studies indicate that many couples grow apart rather than closer after twenty years of marriage. In this sense, if a man or a woman engages in either a sexual or a nonsexual affair, it may enable the marriage to endure.

These affairs may be society's first rehearsal of a polygamy to come. It has been said that the cohabitation of college students are far more moral than many marriages because of the concern the young man and woman have for each other. The same thing can be said of many of the affairs of older persons we have studied. They are far from the "shacking up" that Maggie Kuhn talked about (she probably used this term for dramatic effect) but are pervaded by deep desires that their partners should not be hurt but should be nourished.

But affairs are not easy for older persons, who were generally reared in a nonpermissive society where sex was linked with sin and where the piece of paper was the prerequisite to any sexual contact. So any major experiment by seniors is often exceedingly covert and productive of an anxiety which almost destroys free sharing.

There is a further refinement to the conditions under which affairs take place. Many older men and women have said to the authors in many different ways that a long-time loyalty is essential to any relationship. Almost all of them reject promiscuity, one-night stands, group sex, and orgies. Morton Hunt, in his *Playboy* study, also found that whether one discussed marriage, cohabitation or affairs both men and women wanted continuity and emotional security as the basic condition for sexual sharing. Physical expression was not enough. This may be one of the commandments of the new sexual morality. It may be more permissive in some ways but basically more demanding in others.

SAME SEX RELATIONSHIPS

Same-sex relationships involve a spread similar to that which we have noted in affairs. A great many male-male and female-female relationships have no physical components. On the other hand, there are homosexual unions that are as erotic as the most intense heterosexual love affairs. Between these extremes are many unions of warmth and touching and tenderness that never reach the stage of sexual consummation.

Nevertheless, wherever same-sex couples may be, as far as sexual loving is concerned, there is the opportunity for long-term companionship and emotional support between them. All human beings need someone to care for, to be especially attentive to, and to touch. Many same-sex relationships supply that closeness.

Many urban communities have carefully policed large hotels and apartment houses for women that plan social activities and excursions. These serve to establish one-sex social networks that compensate for lack of male companionship. Many close friendships result.

RETIREMENT COMMUNITIES

One of the increasingly popular moves for lonely single women is to move into a retirement high rise or a retirement community. Most of these communities have a far more promising sex ratio than the community at large, thus giving more opportunities for heterosexual contacts. It is true that in such retirement communities as Leisure World in California, Sun City in Arizona, or Knox Village in Kansas many of the men are married. Still, one can mingle with both sexes in the swimming pool and at the myriad community club activities. Widows are not so apt to feel left out in these communities. There are real opportunities for a full life.

One widow from Sun City commented to me about this aspect:

> When I lived in my old home, all my old married friends found me an embarrassment. They didn't know what to do with me at their parties. They would say, bring a date, but I had no one to bring, and if I had, they would have really scrutinized him. Here in Sun City, my status is accepted, and I mingle as I please. Besides that, the nice couple next to me have adopted me. They always invite me for parties and the holidays if my family isn't around. And I notice that they also invite single men. They really want me to find a steady partner. I'm much happier here.

CONCLUSION

If the widow wants to remarry or find a new boyfriend, she has to exert some effort like moving to a retirement community; joining and working in a church, a political party, or a service group like the Red Cross; and frequenting the swimming pool and social hall. She has to be attractive in appearance, friendly, and appreciative.

One must create opportunities but, more important, must be sure that one does not close them off by negativism, personal aggression, or egocentricity. Still, as this chapter has outlined, there are a great many potential types of intimacy. Life is impoverished if we do not develop them.

CHAPTER ELEVEN

NOT BY BREAD
ALONE, BUT . . .

The problems you encounter as a widow are not solely psychological and social. You do not live by bread alone, but you don't live without it, either. For a number of reasons—which seem to feed on themselves like compounding interest—management of finances often is one of the most devastating problems faced by widows. The suddenness of the new responsibilities can be as chilling as a frigid wind off an Arctic ice floe. The emotions generated can swelter and stifle like wave after wave of tropical heat.

A GENERAL PERSPECTIVE

Life does not treat every person in equal fashion. This chapter tries to deal helpfully with the typical economic problems that widows of any age or ethnic background may encounter. At the same time, it must be recognized that there are many widows whose problems have a different dimension. The general situation is seen in a special analysis made in 1967 by the U.S. Census Bureau, which reported:

> *Marital Status and Sex:* Because married couples with one or both members aged 65 and over were roughly three times as likely as the non-married aged to have some income from employment, as a group they had a much higher income level. Thus, in 1967, the median income of married couples at $3,370 was about two and one-half times the median for the unmarried.
>
> The 7.4 million women without husbands were the least likely to work and the most disadvantaged. Their median income was less than three-fourths of the median for men. One-third of them reported less than $1,000 in money income for the year and only 11% reported $3,000 or more. In contrast 5% of the married couples reported more than $10,000, 27% more than $5,000. One-third of the couples, however, were concentrated in the $1,500–$3,000 income range.

Why is this true? The report explained:

> An important factor contributing to these differences is that retirement benefits tend to be smaller for women than for men: both because women characteristically earn less than men during their working life (most retirement benefits are earnings-related) and because many women depend on survivors benefits usually set at some fraction of the deceased husband's benefit . . . $82\frac{1}{2}$ percent for aged widows under the OASDHI program.

Besides the older widow, there is another large disadvantaged group, called the "displaced homemaker." Tish Sommers, one of the founders of the N.O.W. Task Force on Older Women, has proposed remedial legislation for this group entitled the Equal Opportunity for Displaced Homemakers Act. She tells us that there are now more than one million women under age 60, without minor children, and either widowed or divorced. This group, because of their long service in the home, are unskilled and inexperienced, and consequently have little success in the job market. They are too young to receive Social Security payments, and many receive very little insurance or pension monies. The proposed bill would provide training, jobs and job placement, and health care to alleviate the double bind these women experience. Age and sex discrimination sometimes work against the widow in these circumstances.

A third group of widows who are often in severe financial straits is composed of widows who belong to minority groups. They have the lowest financial status in the country. They are often isolated and lack proper medical care or social contacts. Because of their isolation, they are only encountered when met for a moment in the park or in the emergency wards of hospitals.

These groups have grave economic problems that cannot be met by adequate budgeting procedures because there is almost nothing to budget. Their problem will be solved only by legislation and by a quickening of the nation's conscience. One day we may realize that these lonely and underprivileged persons have contributed as much to the nation as have others, but as yet there is little awareness of their plight and they have few advocates. Most of them will not read this book, but those who do might well be moved by learning that there are others who have a concern for these . . . the truly neglected in our society.

FINANCIAL DECISION-MAKING

Thankfully, the worst of these financial difficulties—the acute phase, if you will—usually are temporary, like the other debilitating reactions and emotions and shocks of bereavement.

There is hope, regardless of the severity of the initial problems. This is proved in the lives of many widows who sort out and come to terms with their financial problems, make the necessary adjustments, and learn to manage their resources. They learn how to make decisions that are right for them and how to provide for themselves. It is the aim of this chapter to put the issues in perspective so as to help you work through the early economic decisions and responsibilities. Hopefully, this perspective will help you to avoid or at least minimize common pitfalls and reduce some of the pain and confusion of the difficult early days. This can help you to build a foundation for your future.

Each case is different; yet there are common denominators.

Some widows, like Yvonne, find that the confrontation with finances is not especially difficult. She recalls the early days of her bereavement:

> When Fred died suddenly, I was sick and heartbroken—just lost in so many ways. But taking charge of money wasn't one of them. Fred had been very provident about preparing for the unexpected and had left our affairs in good order. As I look back, I cherish that as a real act of love. With the insurance and the investments we had made over the years, he left me reasonably well off. Not wealthy by any means, but with enough wherewithal to get along quite well by scaling my living standard down somewhat and budgeting. I'd been a businesswoman for years, and we shared management of our finances. So I was up on what the situation was and had the background to take over for myself. God knows I went through hell when he died, but money worries weren't a part of that. I get the feeling from talking with other widows that few of them are as fortunate.

So true. Relatively few widows find their situations as easy as Yvonne's. Many of them are unaware of their finances at the time of their husbands' death. They are inexperienced in handling money matters. They find themselves with limited means. These and other circumstances are thrust on them amidst the staggering morass of widowhood's shocks and losses and grief, and they are weak and vulnerable. Fears easily grow and multiply out of false or incomplete assumptions and distorted emotions. It is not difficult to see the ways in which many women have suffered.

LACK OF PREPARATION

In our culture, death is still a taboo subject. We don't like to think about the unthinkable or mention the unmentionable. Consequently, few husbands—or wives for that matter—give adequate thought to how she will manage if and when she is among the three out of four wives who become widows. Careful planning and preparation that could and should be made are neglected. Relatively few wives are trained in financial or legal responsibilities that would be theirs alone if their husbands were to die. Few couples discuss disposition of insurance payments, planning for future income sources, and other aspects.

Recognizing the need for this in society, the editors of *U.S. News & World Report* recently published a book entitled *Teach Your Wife How to Be a Widow*. Directed to husbands, the thrust of the book is exactly what the title indicates. There is no question that such a book and the preparatory measures it advocates have been sorely needed. If you as a widow are facing or have experienced financial woes for lack of preparation, you certainly are not alone. Quoted in the book are findings of a recent study by the Life Insurance Agency Management Association and the Life Underwriter Training Council. These groups surveyed nearly 1,800 widows living in large metropolitan areas whose husbands had died before age sixty-five. It was found that:

• Almost half the widows experienced difficulty in handling money matters because their husbands always had taken care of family finances.

• Fewer than 20 percent had discussed with their husbands what should be done with life insurance proceeds if he were to die.

• Widows who were life insurance beneficiaries received an average of $9,150. Only 8 percent realized as much as $25,000 from life insurance.[1]

Such research findings are revealing and eye-opening. Their full significance cannot be appreciated, however, without considering the stunning impact on the lives of those concerned. In stark contrast to the story of Yvonne, Peggy recalls the difficult early days of her bereavement:

> As I look back on our marriage now, I can see the mistakes we made. We lived well and enjoyed ourselves, almost as if tomorrow would never come. But it did come—when Brad was killed in a car accident. He always had taken care of the finances; my job was being homemaker and mother. When he died, I didn't even know how to balance a checkbook. There was no will, and at first, I was completely in the dark as to what my situation was. I did realize that the income stopped when he died. That was terrifying. It turned out that there was an insurance policy that would pay

me a few thousand dollars, and there was the equity in the house. And there were also a lot of unpaid bills. I was scared stiff about losing what I did have because, if I did, then I'd have nothing. My only hope was to get some kind of job, but who would want to hire a fifty-six-year-old woman who hadn't worked in the business world for nearly thirty years? I felt worthless. I lay awake night after night thinking and turning my worries over and over again in my mind. It was a vicious circle. I was nearly crazy with worries, and they seemed to paralyze me into inaction because there didn't seem to be any solution to anything. After a while, my anxieties got to the point that they were beginning to tear down my health. My doctor insisted that I needed some outside help and referred me to a psychologist friend of his. That was a real turning point because he was able to show me how emotionally charged money can be. He helped me to sort out my emotions and to understand why I felt the way I did. Then I turned to a former business associate of Brad's for advice about the specifics of my finances. Little by little, I started to gain some faith in myself, a realization that I could learn to manage and work it out. Life goes on, you know. I brushed up on my office skills and finally got a good job. Things are better now. I still worry about money sometimes—more than I really should, I guess. But it's nothing like those awful first few months.

If you were left an unprepared widow in difficult financial straits, it may be precious little consolation that so many others have experienced the same problems. Obviously, there is no way to go back to correct the mistakes and oversights of the past. But you can come to terms with the situation as it is. In suggesting positive ways to go about this, we will take a deeper look at various aspects of Peggy's case history that are common to widows. In so doing, we will examine psychological meanings of money, hopefully clearing up some distortions and debunk some myths.

MONEY AND ITS EMOTIONAL TRAPS

Before we discuss more specifics about widows' financial situations, let's take a brief look at the social and psychological aspects of money in a general way. There are pervasive spoken and unspoken assumptions and feelings about money and material goods in our culture. Many of these are neither sane nor rational. There is no question that money is necessary for our physical needs, but it tends to take on more importance than it really has. It becomes enmeshed in our personal value systems, and the subject can be emotionally explosive.

We live in a highly materialistic era. In the minds of some people, money might not be god, but it surely is king. Not all are so materialistic, but many are influenced by false social meanings that money has taken on. For instance, some feel that financial assets and material possessions are the overriding determiner of "success." It is common to view persons who have accumulated a great deal of money as "successful," even though they really might be emotional and spiritual wrecks, unloved and unloving. Others who may be far more accomplished in a full human sense, but who have only moderate means, are not so uncommonly seen as "successful," or potent, or wise, or worthy of emulation.

Persons who use money as a decisive criterion in the way they view others also are likely to do the same for themselves. All too often one's own concept of self and personal worth is limited by the degree of his or her own material achievement. "If I'm so smart, why is it I'm not rich?"

The ways that some people look at money are no stranger than the ways they use it. Some of them measure expressions of love in material worth, as in determining the value and meaning of a gift by its price tag. Others try to use money as a substitute for love. Some misguided persons attempt to buy friendship and love, while others use it to buy isolation. Sometimes the latter try to buy their own peace of mind and conscience—as with the rich who congregate among themselves to raise funds for the anonymous poor, with whom they never associate or really empathize.

It can't be forgotten that these distortions and complexities surrounding money came in the context of today. This is an era of practically unprecedented inflation, which gives scant indication of abating. The national economy no longer is expanding at rates it once did. Unemployment is high. More and more people are finding it hard to make ends meet. That certainly doesn't make money's psychological traps any easier to avoid.

Perhaps the most perilous financial trap for a widow has to do with emotional security. For most of us, money is a part of this. Most derive security from a regular income. With bereavement, the widow's husband's paychecks stop, and her financial circumstances are suddenly reduced. This diminishes her emotional security, as do the many other losses of bereavement. When a person's security is in jeopardy, it is difficult to cope with all of life, including the economic. A vicious cycle ensues.

Peggy's is a case in point. Far worse than her limited financial means were her lack of preparedness and experience in handling money, and the overriding uncertainties about her financial situation. Fears of the unknown are the most debilitating ones for most of us, as they were for Peggy. Such feelings as "terrifying," and "scared stiff" are to be expected.

But notice the pattern she slipped into from there: She worried about what she didn't have, and she worried about losing what she did have. She even went a step farther, convincing herself that when her equity in the house and her insurance money were gone, she'd have nothing. She understood that she'd have to earn some income, but even that added to her worry, for she felt that she couldn't get a job. "Who would want to hire me?" She convinced herself that there was no way out of her situation, that there was nothing she could do about it. Small wonder that she was paralyzed into inaction and into a vicious cycle of health-threatening anxieties.

But there are solutions, as she later discovered. Psychological counseling helped her to sort out her destructive fears and other feelings. Peggy amplifies:

My counselor helped me to see what I was doing to myself. I came to realize that I could do something about the situation. For one thing, I realized that I need not lose what I had. And even if I did, that wouldn't mean I had nothing. After all, he pointed out, I'm a person, a human being, reasonably intelligent and in good health, with the abilities to learn and change and grow. With this realization came some hope. I realize that with positive action, taking control of the situation, I probably could land a job. It was all very complex. I didn't realize it at the time, but I was ashamed of myself for my feelings and for being so incompetent. Counseling helped me to see that feelings are feelings and being ashamed of them can only make things worse. I also overcame a feeling of worthlessness that was building. I came to realize that gauging my own worth in terms of a bank balance is destructive and unrealistic. As I worked through all this, I became more comfortable with myself as I developed more confidence.

Fear, anxiety, worry, shame, and a loss of self-esteem are not the only emotional traps that widows fall into on the money issue. Anger—sometimes unbridled rage—is another one. Lynn Caine wrote of her reactions in her book *Widow*:

> Money matters. It really does. It is right up there with love and security and identity. After Martin died, I used to wake up with my teeth clenched thinking, 'You son of a bitch! . . . You didn't love us enough to provide for our future. And now we're all alone. No husband. No father. No money.[2]

Caine writes in retrospect that much of her rage at her dead husband and at the world was really directed to herself. She was able to resolve her anger with the help of a psychologist who encouraged her to discuss it, to get it out into the open. The therapist also showed her that she need not be ashamed of it.[3] This is important. Because anger—if it is deep and pervasive and never resolved—can produce another potentially destructive, debilitating emotion: guilt. Guilt can poison the well of our emotions and inhibit recovery at any point in the process, as we've seen in earlier chapters.

Caine thinks that a big step forward in her resolution of financial and other problems came when her counselor suggested that she had the choice of looking at the debit or credit side of her life. She came to see the reality and the importance of her blessings—all that she had going for her in life. These included two healthy children, a good job, good friends, and being attractive and healthy. "This matter-of-fact summing up pulled me out of my self-pity. It was another giant step into life on the other side of grief. . . ."[4] This wise counselor pointed out that most other people are suffering from financial insecurity, too. That simple reminder further helped to jolt her out of her self-pity.[5]

Reducing the distortions and arriving at a sound perspective requires that we come to terms with what money is all about— what it really means in life—what it really means to you. Caine summed up her own view in these words:

> Money can't compensate two children for the loss of a father. Money can't reach out in the night and caress you. Money can't come home at night with a briefcase, a twinkle and a hug. But money can give you ease. And piece of mind.[6]

In short, money is not a substitute for a person, nor is it a substitute for love. But we need it to survive. Can money buy happiness? No. But it can buy freedom from having to worry about money constantly. What is money? It is a medium of exchange that we need to underwrite our physical needs and a few frills, too! This means aspiring to and working toward a decent living and a reasonable contingency for the future and for emergencies. Ease and peace of mind and freedom from worry about money do not require vast wealth. When the clouds of confusion begin to clear away, many widows find that they can live well enough on modest means.

Another issue you must face in your confusion with finances is the aspect of change. For most widows, bereavement means some changes in the standard of living. It is more difficult for some than others, as Julie indicates:

> One of the hardest things for me after my husband died was realizing I would have to do without some of the things we'd really come to enjoy and appreciate. Jack and I had worked so hard for what we had and were just beginning to enjoy the fruits of our labor. We enjoyed good restaurants, good clothes, evenings out, and lots of travel. After he died, I realized I had to forgo many of these pleasures and had to sell some of our things. Now I'm on a strict budget that doesn't allow for many frills. But, you adjust.

FIRST STEPS

The loss of a mate makes you responsible for many financial matters. That responsibility will be less burdensome and you will be more at ease by proceeding in an orderly manner. Most decisions can be postponed, but certain things have to be done immediately.

By the time you read this book, you have already made all funeral arrangements and that difficult period is past. If not, remember:

• If there is a will, or if the wishes of your mate have been shared with you, follow them as best you can.

• After explaining your wishes, entrust the details to a relative or friend.

• Be reasonable about funeral costs. Your mate would want this. There are many options, including cremation and a memorial service without the casket present, or the more traditional service.

You must notify some people or agencies about the death of your mate, such as (1) your bank, for joint accounts are closed at the time of death. Request that your bank release the funds. You should also establish a new account to handle funds received after the death. (2) Your insurance companies. If the funds are not already committed to a financial plan, request only partial payment. Leave decisions about major investments for a later time. (3) Social Security, veteran's benefits, pensions, or association programs. The death benefits that are due should be applied for promptly. (4) Probate court. Wills must be filed within ten days or, if there is no will, this fact must be disclosed. Probate procedures may be a complex matter, depending upon the size of the estate. The advice of a wise friend or a family lawyer is invaluable. If you can be appointed administrator of the estate, this arrangement often saves money. You should know that the court generally does not permit probate to be concluded in less than a year although this will vary from state to state. In any case, some resources may well be tied up for at least that long.

If you become the administrator, you or your attorney must perform the following duties:

File the will immediately.

Petition for appointment as administrator of the estate.

Inventory all assets.

List all costs of administration and claims against the estate, such as medical and funeral costs, all taxes for the past and current year.

File state inheritance and federal estate tax forms, with payment of taxes due.

Petition for approval of specific bequests.

Have trust agreements, if any, reviewed and your administration approved.

Determine widow's and children's allowances, and petition for approval to pay them.

Collect all money owed the deceased or estate, and pay all bills as due.

Pay legacies as promptly as possible.

To do all this, you must keep financial records. You are personally liable for estate resources and must account for them. You must keep a record of every bill you pay and all monies you receive, so you must:

Save all records showing financial data.

Keep a diary of all cash income and expenses.

Your bank, lawyer, or accountant can help you in this effort.

LATER "PAPER" WORK

There are a number of legal obligations that are mandated to you by law. There is no way to avoid them. While you do not have to face these the day after the funeral, they must be accomplished soon, and you will want to finish them as soon as possible in order to get a perspective about your assets and liabilities.

A. FEDERAL AND STATE INCOME TAXES

If you and your mate have filed and paid your taxes by last April 15, you are current. However, your spouse may have been making quarterly payments, which come due January 15, April 15, June 15, and September 15. You may either pay the next installment, or, if you figure your income is going to mean lower taxes, file a new return in lieu of your payment, but talk with your accountant about the taxes you are going to have to pay next April 15. You will need to budget for this.

Your accountant or your lawyer will probably ask you to make some notable changes in your life. One of them will be to record all of your trips, giving mileage as well as expenses. You must keep track of every bill you pay. Some of these will be deductible items on your income taxes, but unless you can prove them by a daily record or receipts, you may have trouble. If you have not done this previously, this may prove difficult at first, but when you realize it is a way to save many dollars, you can stick to it until it becomes routine. It is a safe assumption that many persons pay too high a tax because they have not kept precise records. This is the first way you can begin to maximize your money. We will have many more suggestions.

B. INHERITANCE AND ESTATE TAXES

You will have to file Internal Revenue Service (IRS) Form 706 within nine months of the death of your mate if your estate totals more than $60,000. But even if your estate totals more than this, there are some exemptions.

TABLE 5
HOW TO CALCULATE THE FEDERAL ESTATE TAX

Total Estate	$_____
Less $60,000 exemption	$_____
Less certain other specified deductions	
(funeral expenses, claims against the	
estate, charitable bequests, bequests to	
mate under Marital Deduction Laws,	
losses in business)	$_____
TOTAL	$_____

The tax is then determined from the following abbreviated table.

TABLE 6
FEDERAL ESTATE TAX RATES

(1) NET ESTATE	(2) TOTAL TAX	(3) NET ESTATE IN EXCESS OF (1)	(4) RATE OF TAX on (3)
$60,000	NONE	$5,000	3%
$70,000	$500	$10,000	11%
$100,000	$4,800	$10,000	22%
$120,000	$9,500	$40,000	28%
$310,000	$69,000	$250,000	32%
$11,060,000	$233,200	$250,000	35%

STATE INHERITANCE TAXES

This tax (or a state death tax) is placed on beneficiaries of an estate. The amount of the tax depends on (1) the value of that part of the estate given to the beneficiary and (2) the relationship of the beneficiary to the one who died. In community property states, it is possible that no tax will be levied. However, in California and other states, it is possible that a California estate tax (known as a "pick-up tax") may be levied. Other relatives, if receiving a bequest, will be taxed in direct proportion to their lineal distance from the deceased. In other words, the more distant the relationship, the higher the tax.

But charitable bequests—if they are found to be valid—and life insurance are exempt from this tax.

FEDERAL GIFT TAX

One is taxed on all gifts made by the deceased during that person's lifetime, *but* there are very important exceptions. One can give up to $3,000 a year to any number of persons during one's lifetime—providing that the yearly gifts do not exceed $3,000 per person. In addition, a person can, after exhausting the annual $3,000 exemption, make a large gift of $30,000 anytime during his or her life.

When these exemptions are exhausted, the federal gift tax on other gifts is indicated in this chart:

TABLE 7
FEDERAL GIFT TAX RATES

(1) NET GIFT	(2) TOTAL TAX	(3) NET GIFT IN EXCESS OF (1)	(4) RATE OF TAX ON (3)
0	0	$5,000	2¼%
$5,000	$112.50	$5,000	5¼%
$10,000	$375.00	$10,000	8¼%
$20,000	$1,200.00	$10,000	10½%
$50,000	$5,250.00	$10,000	16½%
$100,000	$15,225.00	$150,000	22½%

Much of this discussion will not make any sense at all to the average widow or widower. It has taken us years to understand it. This only reinforces our admonition that it is critically important for the lay person to study all this in detail and then, early on, seek the advice of a competent tax consultant or lawyer who specializes in estates.

FEDERAL AND STATE INCOME TAXES

We said before that these have to be paid. Sometimes a widow does not know how current her husband is in his payments on his income taxes. His accountant or lawyer can generally inform the widow about this. If not, a search through his checks will help. Finally, a letter or a call to the regional IRS and state income tax center will clear it up.

THE PROBATE QUESTION

A probate simply means a legal procedure in which a court distributes the proceeds from an estate. Probate is valuable because it protects the heirs and supervises the administration of the estate. The disadvantages are that the administration costs and the fees for attorneys and executor gobble up a great deal of money. Further, it advertises to the public all the financial transactions of the estate, and it takes a long time, during which the assets are not available to the heirs. During a period of two digit inflation, this may involve considerable loss. You may have to go through this, but you can arrange your estate so that your heirs won't.

Probate can be avoided by living trusts, life insurance, joint tenancy of property and other assets, token trusts, and lifetime gifts. How to use any of these is a complex matter, and the widow will do well to study the ramifications of each method and then ask her attorney to assist in working out the way her estate will be handled.

THE WILL

At the same time she is arranging for the manner in which her estate is to be distributed, she must write and file a will. If you are totally successful in putting all of your assets in joint tenancy or a living trust or life insurance, the will may not be probated. It becomes an outline of your wishes for heirs and friends.

The will ought to specify the type of funeral and burial that you wish. A great deal of money can be saved if you clearly indicate the type of casket and place of burial, or cremation and disposal of ashes. It helps those already burdened by grief if you can indicate the type of memorial service with some indication of the verses, poems, hymns, and music you wish. Copies of such requests ought to be part of the will and then shared with the family, minister, and undertaker.

In recent years, there has been a remarkable growth of funeral societies. These are cooperative associations that arrange for minimum-cost burials or cremations. They help plan for your journey's end so that when you die one phone call initiates all of your arrangements. This is a great gift to your loved ones.

There are numerous ways you can make the end of your life

a contribution to other lives. You may wish to donate your heart, kidneys, eyes to others; or your body to a medical school. But this must be all prearranged because even hours are important in transplants. A phone call to a medical school will give you details.

While this chapter is being written, the front pages of all major newspapers are devoted to the legal contest between a mother and father of a girl who seems to have no possibility of ever being a functioning human being, even with a machine breathing for her, and the doctors who are reluctant for medical and legal reasons to "pull the plug." There is a simple document called "The Living Will," which indicates that no extreme or heroic measures will be used to prolong existence if death is inevitable. This document is signed by the person; witnessed and filed with the will; and copies given to a minister, lawyer, doctor, and the family. While such a part of the will may not have legal standing, it carries great moral weight.

SHARING ONE'S WISHES

As family counselors, we have presided over a great many bitter, hostile, and destructive family battles over estates. A carefully and well thought out plan for the distribution of an estate helps avoid this. An even better way to avoid problems is to call the heirs together and read them the will. Then if any member feels neglected, the matter can be discussed and settled. At this time, wishes about the funeral, gifts of body organs, the "Living Will," and all other matters like this should be thoroughly discussed.

YOUR FINANCIAL STANDING

Once your taxes and debts have been paid, you are in a position to look carefully at your financial situation and to make some basic decisions about how to manage your money. What you have learned about probate will have a significant bearing on how you plan to manage your money.

The first and most basic inventory you have to make is of your total worth and present total income. The following chart is a simple way of analyzing your financial position:

TABLE 8
FINANCIAL INVENTORY—INCOME

ASSETS	MONTHLY INCOME	YEARLY INCOME
Social Security		
Pensions:		
a. _____		
b. _____		
Cash		
Savings Accounts		
Property (rents and royalties)		
Business Investments		
Stocks and Bonds		
Insurance (trusts; endowments)		
Salary		
Personal Property		
Other:		
_____		
_____		
_____		

The next step in your financial planning is to list your expenditures so that you can begin to measure your financial situation accurately. To do this, a simple chart such as the one on page 202 is recommended.

You are now in a position to look at your needs and your resources to meet those needs. As a result, you may wish to consult your accountant or an investment counselor to help you plan for the rest of your life.

❊ ❊ ❊

TABLE 9
FINANCIAL INVENTORY—EXPENDITURES

EXPENSES	MONTHLY	YEARLY
1. Food	_____	_____
2. Clothing	_____	_____
3. Housing		
a) payments	_____	_____
b) rent	_____	_____
c) taxes	_____	_____
4. Insurance		
a) life	_____	_____
b) medical	_____	_____
c) automobile	_____	_____
d) other	_____	_____
5. Taxes		
a) income taxes	_____	_____
b) personal property	_____	_____
c) automobile	_____	_____
d) other	_____	_____
6. Dental	_____	_____
7. Transportation		
a) auto upkeep	_____	_____
b) bus, plane	_____	_____
c) other	_____	_____
8. Recreation	_____	_____
9. Gifts	_____	_____
10. Utilities		
a) gas	_____	_____
b) electricity	_____	_____
c) water	_____	_____
11. Household	_____	_____
12. Benevolence		
a) church	_____	_____
b) community	_____	_____
c) other	_____	_____
13. Personal allowance	_____	_____
14. Other	_____	_____
15. Reserve for life goals	_____	_____

In formulating a financial plan, you really have to balance three different demands on your monthly income:

LIFE GOALS	YEARLY RESERVE FUND	MONTHLY EXPENSES
Through stocks, bonds, insurance, savings, pre-paid funeral expenses, life-care purchase of home, car in three years, etc.	To meet excess demands coming in other months, such as income tax in April, Christmas in December, etc.	Budget for current expenses and bills

This plan gives inner security because you have anticipated future demands as well as having met the higher costs of some months. Such careful planning will also take inflation and your shrinking dollar into account.

FACING INFLATION

There are a good many ways in which you can compensate for inflationary losses while at the same time balancing your budget and safeguarding your financial future:

1. *Housing:* Should you sell your home or invest the money and move to an apartment or life-care retirement center?

2. *Investments:* Can your investment counselor help you evaluate your stocks and bonds—to assure security and a higher return?

3. *Savings:* Are you getting the best return possible? Should some money be put in five-year deposits to earn more?

4. *Automobiles:* If you have two, why? Should you trade in an older car for a smaller one that costs half as much to run?

5. *Purchases:* Do you wait for clothing sales, paint sales—buy vegetables and meats when prices are low?

6. *Medical:* Do you have medical and hospital group insurance to minimize medical bills?

7. *Personal Property:* Are you clinging to a lifetime accumulation that you don't use and that could be turned into money? (Such as antiques, guns, stamp collections, jewelry?)

8. *Gardening and Canning:* A garden of both flowers and vegetables saves a great deal of money. It is also a healthy hobby.

9. *Eating Out:* Restaurants are part of our recreation, but cutting down on meals out saves a surprising amount. Take your lunch.

10. *Develop Some Creative Hobbies:* Gifts that are made by the giver are always appreciated, and you may in time sell some of your creations.

11. *Consolidate Your Trips:* Two of the largest items in our budget are the automobile and gasoline. Cut down on trips, walk more, and use a car pool when possible.

EMPLOYMENT

The solution of your immediate financial and legal affairs discussed in the previous sections may mean going to work. To provide financial security—or to reap the rich rewards that can flow from meaningful use of time—you may want to explore full or part-time employment.

For men or women who are employed at the time a spouse dies, return to work—to a job and routines they know and people with whom they are familiar—can be a real antidote to the disruption that might otherwise result. In addition to the financial advantages, employment may reduce or delay the impact of being widowed.

Widows need to be very clear about the alternatives. One can, for example, elect not to work at all and live on whatever income is available. Her inventory shows she does not need more income. Or she may have a pattern of life so rewarding that work has little appeal. On the other hand, some widows have good incomes but few contacts. They may elect to enlarge their social life and to meet some psychological needs by doing volunteer work with institutions that serve the community. This experience can be very rewarding. There are still other widows who receive Social Security benefits but need part-time work to ensure a better economic base or to do things that otherwise could not be afforded. For such a person, part-time work may provide the security or extras that satisfy her. Recipients of Social Security survivors' benefits can earn up to $2,675 per year without reducing those benefits.

Many will not have adequate income or Social Security benefits. Regular work is the only way to provide even a modest living. The pressing necessity to produce a weekly income may force aside all other considerations.

When you have made some basic decisions as to your work plan, there are certain steps to be taken in terms of either volunteer or paid work. These are:

• Use the free services in counseling, testing, retraining, and placement offered by your state's Training and Employment Service. You will find this center listed under state government agencies.

• Prepare a resume—an accurate summary of your personal and work history.

• Make an inventory of job possibilities. Help will come in making that inventory from the Training and Employment Service, from Mature Temps endorsed by AIM (Action for Independent Maturity) and the American Association of Retired Persons, from any number of nonprofit employment agencies, and from your personal friends and the business associates of your departed mate.

• Send your resume with a letter requesting an appointment to the most attractive firms or institutions on your inventory.

FRAUD

The American Association of Retired Persons is presenting on national television one of the most effective comments we have seen in a long time. It shows a woman withdrawing money from a bank. She has done this for months, but now she is withdrawing all of it. The comment ends with the terse announcement that by tomorrow that money will be gone. She is being bilked by a con man. There are hundreds of men and women involved in subtle games whose purpose is simply sophisticated robbery.

One scheme is the "pigeon drop." A stranger picks up a purse and engages the victim in conversation. The victim is promised half the money but has to put up some money to show good faith. After the victim produces some cash, the stranger takes it, gives over the purse, and on one pretext or another disappears. The purse is empty.

Another scheme offers you fabulous returns for part-time work. But the returns go to the promoter, not you. You pay a fee for an expensive kit or materials, or even a franchise, and you cannot get your money back.

Many frauds are perpetrated by con men who impersonate bank or government personnel. They demand money back on payments for Social Security, medicare, or any other account. They are rough individuals and threaten the unsuspecting victims. Of course, the very appearance of such a person at your doorstep should start the alarms ringing. Never deal with anyone without calling the bank, the IRS, the Social Security office. They will be long gone by the time you finish the call.

There has been a rash of fradulent transactions recently where the caller asks for a donation to a church, medical facility, or youth organization. Even if they have what looks like a valid permit from the city, it is wise to check before you give your money. It may well be used for an airplane ticket to Acapulco!

Equally deceptive are the medical quacks who will offer a quick cure for anything—at a price. They may be food supplements; miracle drops; cures through magnetism, electricity, and so on; and they are not proven. Medical ethics prohibits advertising so that anything advertised as a cure certainly is not advocated by doctors. Talk any treatment over with your doctor, he'll give you good advice.

There are also gangs of fradulent repairmen who promise to resurface your driveway or repaint your roof. They may say that they are in your area and just happen to have material left over so they will do your job for half-price. If you agree, they will do the job with shoddy materials and in a fast, shoddy way. When the material crumbles and cracks and you call them, you will find the phone number is phony! You have no recourse. If you hire someone, insist on seeing his contractor's license, his ad in the phone book, and a reference to someone for whom he has worked. Be sure he is properly insured.

A word should also be said about making your home secure

against burglaries. A few bars for windows and double locks on doors is enough to discourage most criminals. A small investment of this kind gives much protection. The police departments in most cities have crime prevention departments that will be glad to inspect your house or apartment and help you plan. It is ironic that many persons are very careful about finances but not at all wise in safeguarding their belongings.

RECORD KEEPING

Order in life is a great boon to inner security. It is a great service to yourself and your family if you keep all essential papers in one safe place, such as a safety deposit box or in a fireproof home safe. The items that should be included are birth certificates, marriage certificates, divorce decrees, wills, stocks and bonds, insurance policies, mortgages, pension plan certificates, auto ownership slips, Social Security records, safety deposit box locations, bank records of checking and savings accounts, titles to home and other property, income tax records. Your family should know where these items are located.

VOLUNTEER WORK

Every individual can make a difference. Even if you do not need a paycheck, you will want to be useful and productive.

Our citizens' experiences, talents, and creativity represent our greatest national resource. If these resources could be brought to bear in greater force, constructive social change would be hastened and human needs would be met more fully. Volunteerism, a concrete and important answer to this challenge, is only beginning to tap our vast human resources. It is growing. Never before have there been so many positive and important opportunities in volunteer work. The challenges are diverse. The personal rewards can far outstrip a paycheck of any amount.

As a mature woman, you undoubtedly have much to contribute that would be most valuable in any number of volunteer pursuits. As a widow, you might have that precious commodity that so many persons lack—time. If you helped make a good marriage in the past, you necessarily have the habits of giving and sharing. Many of the advantages of paid employment come with volunteer work, and there are some that are unique to volunteerism itself. As we have mentioned previously, helping others to share their burdens and suffering can help us to bear our own. If you enter volunteer work on a regular basis, there is a routine that might be very helpful as you work through your own recovery and renewal. There are abundant opportunities to meet stimulating persons and to make new friends. There is the likelihood of developing new lines of interest in life.

Whether or not you get involved as a volunteer depends on a number of circumstances, such as your time, motivation, and energy. If you do not need full-time paid employment, investigating volunteer opportunities in your area might be the beginning of a new lease on life for you. A good first step, which we suggested in relation to the job market, is to analyze your interests and your talents. Do you like lots of personal contact with children? If so, there is a multiplicity of possibilities—ranging from serving as a classroom aide at your local grammar school to work with exceptional children. Are you an organizer? Why not explore work with fund drives for major charities? Do you have a rapport with the aged? There are many opportunities to bring some light into their lives either in an institutional setting or in their own homes. Are you a "natural" at cheering up sick persons? Hospitals and other health-care facilities in most cities have formal volunteer programs that constantly seek help. Are you inclined to work for political change? Your party can use your help in a number of important ways. What are some of your particular talents? Can you write well? If so, you'll have no trouble putting this to work on a volunteer basis, for there is continuing need for good communication of goals by every public and private organization. Can you type? Are you good at cooking and meal planning? handcrafts? music? All these skills and many more are needed. If you are interested in volunteer work, you probably don't have to look farther than your own local community—or even neighborhood—to find a stimulating challenge. Other good sources are the daily newspapers; churches, which are expanding social action programs; private institutions; and public and governmental agencies at the local, state, and federal levels.

In this brief look at volunteerism, we've only scratched the surface. It is beyond our scope here to give many details. Yet we note the advantages, for many widows have found new fulfillment and self-actualization by applying their talents on a volunteer basis, and if volunteerism fits into your desires and capabilities, you can, too.

JOB TRAINING AND THE JOYS OF CONTINUING EDUCATION

Preparing to enter the job market after years of being a homemaker might necessitate education of one kind or another to brush up on old business skills or to learn new ones. Many opportunities for such training are available in every community. One source, for instance, is evening adult school conducted by local school districts. The adult school bulletin of one relatively small school district picked at random lists several job-related courses—available at a total tuition cost of six dollars for a trimester period, whether you enroll in one or more classes. They include bookkeeping, accounting, business machines/job training, business preparation and typing, employment and advancement, medical office procedures, medical terminology, office machines and business communications, pbx switchboard operation, shorthand workshop, stenoscript, and beginning and advanced typing. Every metropolitan area has several business, trade, and vocational schools that offer training in specialized work skills. These range from secretarial to semiprofessional or paraprofessional fields. Such schools are profit-making ventures that charge higher rates of tuition but also advertise counseling and placement as part of their service to students.

If you are embarked on professional or semiprofessional career plans that require more advanced and involved education, there are many opportunities as well. Investigate the possibilities at junior colleges, colleges, and universities in your area. Programs at these institutions are available part time or full time, day and night, credit or noncredit, degree-oriented or non-degree-oriented, extension or regular session. Counselors are available to help you firm up your plans and your program after you have made a few preliminary decisions.

For many, returning to school will not necessarily be oriented to job or career prospects. Looking at random again at the same adult school brochure, we find that there is a plethora of classes that can be most helpful for the various practical concerns of living, financial and otherwise. Also offered at the total six dollar tuition fee, they include: apartment house management, auto maintenance, home maintenance and repair, problems of retirement—how to avoid them, solving everyday legal problems, drivers' training, diet, budgets, personal defense for women, and physical education.

Continuing education at the local level is not limited to courses that are "practical" either. Also included is instruction in leisure and hobby activities that enrich your life and open new vistas for you. Another glance at that same adult school brochure indicates a wide range of fine arts, crafts, and music offerings. You can enroll in classes that will enhance your sewing skills in a number of categories, teach you gourmet cooking, or offer instruction in such diverse pursuits as photography, basic gardening, and continuing growth and communications for senior citizens.

Finally, another word about continuing education is appropriate because it has to do with your future, although perhaps not directly related to finances or job. Many a widow has started work for a college degree years before, perhaps before she was married, and never completed it for one or the other reasons related to her responsibilities as wife and mother. Some of these same women, either as wives or after widowhood, have sent their own children through college and have wished—silently perhaps —that they could have completed their own educations. Others may have no college units to their credit but have had a suppressed desire to enter higher education. Perhaps you completed your baccalaureate long ago but have aspired to graduate education. If you fall into one of those categories, consider it now, if you can. Why not? Certainly, you should not automatically reject the idea because of your age. More and more older people are entering or reentering colleges and universities as undergraduates after periods of fifty years or more. Persons in their seventies and eighties are finding that they work well at their new study challenges and fit in well with other students young enough to be their great-grandchildren. Gerontologists have noted this and foresee an increasing "graying of the universities" in the years to come. Do not let age—or other concerns of dubious validity— deter you from higher education. Even if you must work, various sorts of programs are available at different institutions, and we encourage you to explore them. If you hunger for the challenges and the enrichment available in the humanities, the social sciences, or the sciences available in higher education, nothing can quite take their place for you. Herein lies a path to personal growth that is rarely surpassed for those so inclined.

A FINAL WORD

We have covered a good deal of ground in this chapter. We ended by indicating that education for your own personal development is most important . . . an indication that you do not live by bread alone. Yet the major thrust has stressed that you do not live without it either, and this implies rising to the challenges of being a financial manager and breadwinner. The two basic threads might seem to be entirely separate concerns that ought to be discussed as if they really were divorced from one another. But they are not. If anything, a rereading of and careful thought about this chapter will show how intricately intertwined material and psychological or spiritual concerns really are. It is such with the many issues of life, widowed or not. Here is another lesson from which all of us can benefit. No set of concerns should be neglected in favor of another. Personal growth and fulfillment ideally come in several areas—each of which helps the other— within the rich tapestry of all that you are as a human being.

CHAPTER TWELVE

LIFE CAN BE
FULFILLING

In dedicating his best-selling novel, *East of Eden,* author John Steinbeck likened the work to a box. ". . . Nearly everything I have is in it, and it is not full. Pain and excitement are in it, and feeling good or bad and evil thoughts and good thoughts—the pleasure of design and some despair and the indescribable joy of creation. . . . And still the box is not full."[1] So it is with this book. *This* box is not full, either. It does not pretend nor does it aspire to be one neat package containing all the personal answers to all the problems of every widow. No one book could be so, for there is always the "something else" unique to each personality. Still there is much in it. Presented herein are some important universal truths and concerns about widowhood and beyond that can help you. So if you will, do not regard the box as half-empty; see it as half-full. And go on to fill it according to the dictates of your splendidly unique self.

Science and art are in this half-full box. The findings and

212

facts and conclusions have a certain chemistry to them. Not as specific ingredients of a desired compound but rather as catalysts that hopefully will stimulate a positive reaction among the components that already are present within you. There is no strict, grand design, no step-by-step formula to be superimposed upon you from without. Instead, we have presented helps for you to synthesize your own formula. Rather than being artists painting a picture to show you, we are offering support as you create your own vivid, personalized painting. Rather than being musicians playing our song to you, we are urging you to listen to the music of your own soul.

Accomplishing these purposes depends on using the contents of this half-full box. Hopefully, you will find that most if not all of the chapters contain real meaning for you in one way or another. Discovering these meanings in the most efficacious manner—and putting them to use—requires that you meditate. Ask yourself how and to what extent specific ideas apply to you. Read, think, discuss with others, and refer again to the material when you, as a changing, growing person, can look at it in different lights. This book definitely is not to be read once and then set aside. Read and reread, whether you were bereaved two months or twenty years ago. The book's potentials as a catalyst are not limited to one so-called stage of widowed aloneness, any more than they are to any specific age, social status, or personality "type." The work of *individualizing* the contents of this half-full box—and adding to them—can be done by your own concentration and creativity.

In books such as this, it is common practice for authors to devote the last chapter to a summary of the material. We, however, will not give a standard, capsulized overview for two reasons. The first lies in the difficulty of doing justice to the complex material in any thumbnail sketch or minirepetition. The second reason flows from our recommendations above about how the book should be used. If it is to be an effective guide for you, the material should be read in its fully developed form. That, not a summary, is the in-depth source for creative meditation.

In this last chapter, we will make some points that flow from and complement all that has gone before and furnish some additional perspectives for you on your road to recovery and renewal.

These points are designed to reinforce three basic themes that are stated or implied throughout this book: the need for realism, the need for action, and the certainty that there is hope. You must be realistic about the weight of problems that have been imposed on you with widowhood. Without that sense, you will be unable to be realistic about the solutions that you surely can bring to bear. Action—personal resolutions that only you can make—is the only way that recovery and renewal will be accomplished. Then hope will come, for hope is as surely written within you as it is in the pages of this book. You have only to discover it for yourself.

BEREAVEMENT AND LOSS REVISITED

You need to be realistic about the process and progress of bereavement as they occur in you. In her book, Lynn Caine gives us a helpful retrospective:

> If only someone whom I respected had sat me down after Martin died and said, "Now Lynn, bereavement is like a wound. It's like being very, very badly hurt. But you are healthy. You are strong. You will recover. But recovery will be slow. You will grieve and that is painful. And your grief will have many stages, but all of them will be healing. Little by little, you will be whole again. And you will be a stronger person. Just as a broken bone knits and becomes stronger than before, so will you. . . ."[2]

Such counsel for a widow is good and true. We hope that the overall message of this book and the sources of help we have recommended will convey this important understanding to you.

Early on, we discussed some of the losses of bereavement. When a woman is widowed, she not only loses a companion, a friend, a lover, a person around whom she organizes her work; she also loses much of her previous identity if indeed she had found a good part of that in her husband, being Mrs. John Doe instead of Mary Doe. She loses status. She loses roles, the parts she plays with others in life. These losses usually come suddenly with no preparation or anticipation whatever. You must be realistic about the stunning impact that such a volume of significant losses inevitably must have.

You need to be equally realistic about an immutable psychological truth concerning loss: *there must be compensation.* If you are to regain your equilibrium, if you are to recover and renew yourself, there must be a replacement of what has been lost. Obviously, you can't bring your mate back to life. Rushing into another marriage on any terms is out of the question. What can be done in time, though, is to replace lost roles with new ones; previous status with new status, lost friends with new ones, a lost identity with a new identity—other than "widow." Thus, Ellen, a very perceptive woman, recalls:

> Before my husband died, I was somebody, you know? I was needed by him in a lot of ways. But when he died, I suddenly felt like a nobody. I wasn't a wife any longer, with all the things that go along with it. Eventually, I carved out a new place for myself in the world. Now my career means everything to me. I'm somebody again, with important things to do. . . .

In her own words, Ellen is saying that she has replaced the status and roles she lost. A new career was at least part of the way she accomplished it. A career per se is not the answer for all widows. There are many paths to take that can ensure a restoration of what has been lost. The important thing is that it take place, in whatever ways are right for you as an individual. Ultimately, the restoration will come from no other source than yourself and the actions you take.

UNDERSTANDING FROM OTHERS

You also need to be realistic about yourself as a social being. We all need a certain amount of understanding from others; an extreme lack of this can produce an isolated, alienated individual. When a woman is widowed, circumstances often deny her a deep sense of understanding from others. There is plenty of evidence— much of it spoken in retrospect by widows themselves—that few people really understand. Pat, a professor of social work highly attuned to human behavior, recalls reading over the many condolence cards she received:

I read the messages without looking at the signatures, and by that, I could tell which of the cards had come from friends and associates who themselves had experienced deep loss, whether by widowhood, or losing a child, or whatever. The ones who had suffered indicated in their words that they really understood what I was going through. Their messages were the most comforting. I went back to look at who the senders were, and I was right about every one.

More than a few widows find themselves in this situation. Close relatives and friends are loving and caring and want to help, but in the final analysis, they really don't understand the widow's reactions nor do they fathom what she is going through. No matter how close they are, they might see only the tip of her suffering and grief.

Eleanor remembers that her cousin, with whom she had been close throughout her life, repeatedly tried to comfort her. "She kept telling me that she understood, and how she knew the loneliness must be terrible, and on and on. I'd listen to what she said, and I appreciated her concern. But as she talked, I could see she really didn't have any idea of what was going on inside me. I felt like screaming, *'That isn't the half of it! You don't know what the hell you're talking about!'* . . . but I didn't. Even though she didn't understand, she really did care. And I needed that, too. . . ."

Eleanor presents us with a dilemma faced by many widows, and at least a partial solution. On the one hand, if you depend *solely* on persons who don't understand, you may feel isolated and stifled in communicating your deep feelings. Yet as Eeanor concluded, you need the support of those close to you even if they do not fully understand your problems. In their way, albeit imperfectly, they can help by being listeners and confidantes, even though they might not be experts by their own experiences. You might find among your friends and relatives a wide spectrum of attitudes and capabilities. On the one end, there may be an older widow who has known her own deep suffering and who can offer you the solace of understanding in a remarkably complete way. At the other end, there may be persons who are so uncomfortable in the face of death and so limited in their empathy that they have little or nothing in the way of emotional support to give.

Both Pat's and Eleanor's reminiscences point out the possibilities inherent in widow-to-widow communication and the need to be realistic about that, too. More and more widows' groups—a development of the last few years—are being formed under various auspices around the country. Researchers have reported good results in individual widows who have been able to participate effectively in them, particularly those who are able to discuss their feelings openly.[3] But recall from our ealier chapter on grief work that there are widows' groups—and then there are widows' groups. Some might be better than others for you. Or perhaps a formalized widows' group is not an answer for you. Lynn Caine wrote that it was not for her.[4] She further feels that widow-to-widow interaction can be dangerous to some extent if it encourages women to make widowhood a career or an identity in itself.[5] She warns of an "addictive," "seductive underground of widows" that might be such a comfortable port that it can discourage one from getting out into the world again and building a new life.[6] Still the evidence is persuasive that widow-to-widow communication and groups can be helpful. And it is a two-way street. Not only might you be helped by other widows, you might be able to return the deed for others who will walk the difficult path of bereavement after you. Other widows might then profit from the potential of your suffering. The act of giving also can help you in your own recovery and renewal. We help ourselves by helping others.

GROWING OLDER

The poet bids his mate, "Come, grow old with me. . . ." With bereavement, that possibility is once and for all erased. The prospect of growing old alone can be as frightening as it is sad for the newly bereaved woman, whether she is thirty-five or sixty-five. It is especially important that we address this in view of the average age of widowhood in America, which is fifty-six. That is a time of life when many couples are beginning to enjoy the fruits of their labors and are dreaming and making plans for their future after the husband's retirement. Suddenly, dreams of togetherness cease, and specific plans must be forgotten. The widow sees only uncertainty and bleak prospects for her mature years. Being alone and growing older seem like double jeopardy.

It is not difficult to understand how such a dismal outlook can develop. Ours is a youth-oriented culture that devalues old age in a number of ways, some subtle and others not so subtle. The mass merchandisers pummel us with advertising aimed at the so-called youth market. Once we're much beyond the Pepsi generation, we lose our effervescence and ought to be becomingly quiet, content with taking our iron tonic once a day. The mass media contribute to negative stereotypes of aging by portraying older people unrealistically, cruelly, condescendingly, or not at all. Forced retirement often pushes people out of jobs at the very peak of their experience and productivity. Our society seems to ooze an attitude that says to be young is to be beautiful, potent, worthwhile, and "with it"; while to be older is to be "over the hill," wherever that is. As a popular song asks, "Is that all there is?"

Definitely not. We've heard what society continually murmurs about aging. Now let's listen for a moment to those who ought to know best what aging is all about—today's elderly. A recent poll taken by Louis Harris for the National Council on Aging is most revealing. It was found that the general public's expectations about growing old were strikingly more pessimistic than actual life experiences reported by old people themselves. For example, about half the general public expect that poor health and crime to be very serious problems for the elderly. But only about 25 percent of the older respondents report those concerns. About two-thirds of the general public expect older people to sit around watching television, but only 36 percent of the elderly say they do so. Public expectations are more negative than the actual experiences of older people on all these items: not enough money to live on, loneliness, not enough medical care, not enough education, not enough to do to keep busy, not enough friends, not enough job opportunities, poor housing, not enough clothing.[7]

The same sort of findings emerged a few years ago from the

largest survey of its kind ever taken of senior citizens. Responses of some 70,000 members of the American Association of Retired Persons debunked the myths that the elderly generally are depressed, dissatisfied, and alienated. To the contrary, results indicated that they are well adjusted and positive in their responses to life.

• About 90 percent said that they are pleased with their relationships with family and friends.

• Eighty-nine percent are satisfied with their housing arrangements and their environment.

• More than 80 percent of all income-level groups reported that they are happy with their independence and freedom from responsibility.[8]

The truth is that negative anticipation of old age is often based more on myth than it is on facts. In a news interview a few years ago, Dr. Vern L. Bengtson, a sociologist at the University of Southern California's Andrus Gerontology Center, listed a number of myths about aging that have been discredited by research. Among them were the following:

• IQ declines and people lose the ability to learn as they grow older. Research based on extensive testing of older subjects denies this. In fact, some aspects of intellectual function actually increase.

• Old age means institutionalization sooner or later. Wrong. Only about 5 percent of those over sixty-five are in nursing homes or extended-care facilities.

• People always become more conservative as they grow old. This has been disproved by Bengtson's own research into generational continuities and differences in three-generation families.

• Sexual interest ceases in the later years. Several studies have documented what older people know: That this simply is not so.

Bengtson said the tendency has been to base perceptions of aging on myths such as these.

This is unfortunate, particularly considering that with more than 20 million persons over 65 in this country, we literally have a population explosion of older people who are happy, active and in good health. The negative stereotypes of the elderly which have fostered these myths certainly do not fit the characteristics of the new type of older person in today's society. Demographic data show that those who are now entering later life are healthier, more mobile, more able to be active, better off economically and better educated than any past older generation. Retirement and old age actually offer freedom and significant opportunities compared to the demands of the middle years. But our society has paid little attention to this.[9]

Furthermore, gerontologists and others have become aware of a new spirit of self-indentity and a class consciousness among older people. With the number of older people in the United States approaching or exceeding the entire population of Canada, there is a growing "Nation of the Retired" within our own country, as Dr. James E. Birren, director of the Andrus Gerontology Center, pointed out. Recalling his experiences as a delegate at the 1971 White House Conference on Aging, he finds that many elderly are articulate about their needs and problems and are working for their own cause at local and state levels.[10] This is in addition to the growing efforts of retired persons' national associations.

Again, there is the need to be realistic. The problems of the elderly are real, complex, and difficult. In many ways, the older generation—like widows themselves—have been one of the most neglected minorities of our society. They have tended to be misunderstood and ignored by the younger majority—scandalously and shamefully so. Make no mistake. Many older widows indeed have suffered double jeopardy because of their age and aloneness, perhaps with financial problems and a lack of experience and skills for the job market. These are the so-called displaced homemakers whom we mentioned in an earlier chapter. What then should be a reasonable outlook for an older widow in the face of these undeniable problems?

Being realistic also requires us to see that there is hope. In fact, there are plenty of reasons for it. The first lies in our oft-repeated conviction throughout this book: Regardless of how severe our problems are, each of us has remarkable human capacities to deal with them. A second reason for optimism lies in the surveys of older persons themselves and the findings of researchers about what being old really means—and does not mean. Clearly, despite the problems, the mature years can be one of the most challenging and fulfilling periods of the life cycle. Third, there are many stirrings in society that portend change in attitudes about aging. There is a heightened interest and attention that can bring positive results. For example, gerontology— the study of aging from many professional viewpoints—is only slightly more than a generation old itself, and it is growing at rates unimagined by the handful of scientists who pioneered it in the 1940s. The research, education, and social action that are growing out of gerontology are positive. Fourth, progress is being made slowly but surely within the "establishment," politically, for instance. At this writing, there are two pieces of pending federal legislation that would aid the displaced homemakers. All these signs are hopeful. There is an even more specific cultural trend that furnishes real hope for women of any age, especially those who have been widowed. The trend speaks to the long- and close-range future of younger and middle-aged widows and to the present and future of older ones. Let us look at it in more detail.

OLDER WOMEN'S CONSCIOUSNESS

No doubt born out of the women's liberation movement, there indeed is a growing "older women's consciousness." Several leading women journalists have recognized the spirit and the impetus of this in the last few years and have written about it. One such syndicated column of a few years ago by Sharon Curtin of the *Washington Post* captured the essence of the trend:

> The women's movement, through a process of education and continuing struggle, is beginning to change the way women view themselves and each other. It seems possible that even though the physical process of aging is irreversible, older women need not accept the picture of themselves as useless, unattractive, dependent and devoid of intelligent thought. As we grow in understanding of ourselves as women, we begin to change our view of all the stages of life. . . .

... As women change as individuals, they are beginning to move for changes in the larger society. The actions of women in groups such as Older Women's Liberation and the Gray Panthers are beginning to weaken the discriminatory social and economic structure that oppresses all old people....[11]

In the same column, Curtin presented some case histories to illustrate her contentions. The first involved her own mother:

My mother is 60 years old. A few years ago she decided to find a job. Although she would probably deny that she is in any way influenced by the women's movement, her ability to move out of the role of "housewife" is certainly an example of the impetus of the movement on women who are neither politically active nor particularly liberated....

Another involved a friend:

One woman refusing to accept the judgment that "you're too old for this" passes on the strength of her action to us all. For example, I know a woman, 68 years old, who wanted to "better herself" by becoming a nurse. She was refused admission to her local community college on the grounds she was too old. They did not feel she was too stupid or too weak or too unhealthy to do the academic and clinical work required; they just felt she was too old to enter a new profession, and that education was better reserved for the young. She wrote letters to local politicians, contacted the state Human Rights Commission, got recommendations from local people she had cared for in an informal capacity, had a complete physical checkup to make sure she could do the work. She was finally admitted to the nursing school and has completed her first semester at the top of her class....

Summing up, Curtin concludes that:

... There are millions of women like my friend and my mother, older women who are beginning to demand a chance to contribute more to their communities and to demand the recognition and respect they deserve for the jobs they have always done....[12]

Syndicated columnist Georgie Anne Geyer also has written penetratingly about the issues of an emerging female ethic and women's consciousness. Not long ago, she wrote a philosophical yet lighthearted column on the occasion of her fortieth birthday. She said she felt "absolutely great" and decided it was cause for celebration:

> . . . Maybe it does mean something that many of us women today do not see ourselves as merchandise from the bargain counter that wears out by 40, only to be replaced by new merchandise that will wear out in turn. Perhaps it does mean something that we can now see our lives building and enriching with age, just as most men have throughout history. . . .
>
> . . . As for future birthdays, I am already planning ahead. And I already have my heroine. Mrs. Elma Tchumy of Fremont, Ohio, a retired kindergarten teacher, recently gave herself a 70th birthday party to which she invited only 253 men—everyone from her garbage men to her doctor to her former pupils. "I've always had this crazy notion," she said, as she jumped, fully-clothed, out of an artificial cake.
>
> Once it gets to you, it's like a cat that gets hooked on catnip.[13]

Not being grim is one of the most beautiful aspects of older women's consciousness. In its acceptance of self, there is freedom to confront all the sides of life—the sad, the funny; the stifling, the amusing; the tragic, the joyful—with a fullness of pride and poise. Implied in this is the wonderful freedom to take yourself seriously, but not too seriously. This is important to you as a widow. You don't have to jump out of a cake, but there does come a time in your progress that you need to regain a certain lightheartedness. In the depths of grief, many widows have thought they would never laugh or smile again. Yet like the dawn's early light, little rays peek through the windows of your soul. Eventually, the sunshine becomes full and warm. Be receptive to it and appreciate it as you can. Learn to chuckle again at the genuinely amusing things in the world. Above all, cultivate that fullness of older women's consciousness that enables you to smile and laugh at the whimsies and paradoxes of yourself.

Behavioral scientists have confirmed what most of us know almost instinctively—that laughter can be very healthy. Psychiatrist Martin Grotjahn has written:

> . . . Everything done with laughter helps us to be human. Laughter is a way of human communication which is essentially and exclusively human. It can be used to express an unending variety of emotions. It is based on guilt-free release of aggression, and any release makes us perhaps a little better and more capable of understanding one another, ourselves and life. What is learned in laughter is learned well. Laughter gives freedom and freedom gives laughter. He who understands the comic begins to understand humanity and the struggle for freedom and happiness.[14]*

Elaine Cumming of the New York State Department of Mental Health wrote of older widows:

> . . . Our own study showed that between the ages of 65 and 80, widowed women who have reasonable health and sufficient income can have a lot of fun. In fact, there is something about a gaggle of widows in a restaurant that suggests a group of teen-age girls. . . .[15]

We agree that widows in this age group can and indeed do have fun. But not necessarily in "gaggles," nor by comporting themselves like aging Girl Scouts. It is true that there are those who really fail to come to terms with their own aging by denying they're older and insisting they're "forever young." These women are just too, too merry. But not the majority of women who are becoming imbued with the burgeoning older women's consciousness. If there is anything that this new consciousness tells us, it is that stereotypes are out because they're invalid and destructive. Many older women, in coming to terms with exactly what they are, find much in themselves to value and celebrate. With this comes a genuine lightheartedness. They are finding that they themselves—not the gorgeous young things who've just stepped from a beauty contest—are the ones who have a depth of richness

* From *Beyond Laughter* by Martin Grotjahn. Copyright 1957. Used with permission of McGraw-Hill Book Company.

and experience that calls for real smiles and optimism. They are inviting society to meet them on their own terms for a change; to accept them and respect them for what they really are.

Forced gaiety is out of the question because it simply is untrue to yourself. Yet as your burdens lighten, you will find much to smile and laugh about. Don't deny yourself these opportunities because to laugh is as much a sign of renewal as crying is a sign of recovery. You owe them to yourself as an individual and as a social being. In another sense, you owe them to others. Jane Gunther, widow of the author John Gunther, had this to say in a magazine article on "How to Survive Widowhood":

> . . . People are needed and liked if they are cheerful. There is something inappropriate about being mournful. The world shuns dismalness. "Never be dreary!" my grandmother once said to me. Know that you are alive, that pleasure is open to you, that new enthusiasms can be found, that there are friendships to be made. Living is a spiritual matter, and you must accept your changed state and regard it as a challenge which you can meet. It is never too late for fresh experience and adventure.[16]*

YOUR PERSONAL APPEARANCE

We have said little about personal appearance previously. It deserves comment because it has much to do with the personal pride implicit in older women's consciousness.

Janet's recollections are interesting:

> Throughout my life, before and after marriage, I had prided myself on a good appearance. I never had a great deal of money to spend on clothes, cosmetics, and hair stylists, so I learned these skills myself. I was proud of the compliments I got from my husband and from others. But after George died, I was so numb and apathetic that I didn't care much about anything—including the way I looked. I got fat and didn't take any pains. One day I took a good hard look at myself in the mirror and got mad, just

* Excerpted from "How to Survive Widowhood," by Jane Gunther, *The Reader's Digest*, June 1975. Copyright 1975 by The Reader's Digest Assn., Inc.

plain mad at myself. I'd really slipped, and there wasn't any reason for it but my own neglect. I made a resolve right then and there that I'd do something about it. I started by putting myself on a diet. I looked through the pattern books for some ideas for dresses I could make. I bought some bright print fabrics to add some color to my life and started to work. Before long, I had the beginnings of a new wardrobe. Then I took the bull by the horns and went to an expensive salon for a beauty consultation—the works. They styled my hair, tinted it, gave me a manicure, even a pedicure. They also gave me a lot of good ideas—things I could do myself that are right for my figure and face. I started to feel like a new woman. As I look back, it's hard to tell whether my renewed interest in my appearance was a sign of recovering from widowhood or whether it was one way of recovering. Whatever, it surely was a lift for me psychologically.

Not all widows "let themselves go" in the apathy of grief. Regardless, many find that a rebirth of attention to their physical appearance indeed has an important psychological lift for them.

Renewal of one's physical appearance does not necessarily involve becoming a fashion plate, nor does it require spending vast sums on posh cosmetics and salons. However, it does mean a concrete refocusing of attention on yourself and the way you appear to others. Personal appearance is not important only if you are entering the job market. It is a matter of personal pride. You again care about yourself physically as well as emotionally.

It is not our purpose here to suggest specific things to do with your appearance. That is up to you and your own good taste and judgment. Rather, we're saying that caring about it is important. There are many things that can be done. Our pervasive youth-oriented culture does a brisk business in dispensing products and techniques designed to take the years off one's appearance. Some women say that dyeing the hair, new cosmetics, "younger" clothes, even cosmetic surgery have given them a new lease of life. With today's plastic surgery techniques, virtually all that sags can be lifted, and wrinkles can be minimized. Yet there is another perspective closely attuned to older women's consciousness. Gray is beautiful, too. There is a heightening interest in cosmetology for older women. New ways are being found to enhance their timeless beauty—without really attempting to make them twenty again. There are many, many beautiful older women who would not ever consider cosmetic surgery. In a newspaper interview, Adela Rogers St. Johns, the pioneering woman journalist and author, offered a refreshing perspective. She recalled being on a television talk show during which another woman participant made a frank suggestion:

> . . . She told me that I should have my face lifted. I said, "I don't think so. You may want to present to the world a blank sheet of paper, proving that you've written nothing on it in the years you've lived. I would much rather they could see on my face that I have lived, loved, and had one hell of a time, bad and good." To me, age is simply not a valid concern. I'd like to be thought of not as an 80-year-old but as a person who enjoys every moment of life. That's the way I really am.[17]*

Enough said. And articulately so by one of the most liberated of them all.

A FINAL WORD

The time has come to close the lid on this half-full box and to hand it to you with the wish that you will fill it for yourself. It is the authors' hope that the insights contained within these pages will help. In doing so, you will come to a bright new day of realizations from amidst loneliness and desolation. There are many parables with which we could illustrate this process. This recent contribution to a national magazine is a graphic one:

> . . . She lived in a region of New Hampshire that was devastated by a hurricane. Her huge pines had been her pride and joy; they had been guarded and loved by her during most of her 87 years. Now they lay in a tangle of utter destruction. I offered exclamations of sorrow and unbelief. She took me by the hand,

* Excerpted and reprinted by permission of the author, Marshall Berges, from a copyrighted article published in the *Los Angeles Times Home Magazine*, February 16, 1975.

and in her straightforward manner, led me to a spot on her lawn facing northwest. "Look," she said in triumph. "There are the Green Mountains. I haven't been able to see them from here in 50 years."[18]

We wish you new and different richness and beauty such as this woman found. Another way of saying our wish is recalling W. H. Auden's definition of poetry's essence: That which comes from the heart and creates order.

We hope that you will become the poet of your own life.

NOTES

CHAPTER 2. THE NUMBING ALONENESS

1. James A. Peterson, *On Being Alone, AIM's Guide for Widowed Persons* (Washington, D.C.: Action for Independent Maturity, American Association of Retired Persons and National Retired Teachers Association, 1974), p. 1.

2. Peter C. Pineo, "Disenchantment in the Later Years of Marriage," *Journal of Marriage and Family* (February 1961). John F. Cuber and Peggy Harroff, *The Significant Americans* (New York: Appleton, Century, Crofts, 1965).

CHAPTER 3. WORKING THROUGH THE SEPARATION

1. Eric Lindemann, "Symptomatology and Management of Acute Grief," *American Journal of Psychiatry* CI (September 1944), pp. 125, 158.

2. Henry J. Heimlick and Austin M. Kutscher, "The Family's Reaction to Terminal Illness," in *Loss and Grief: Psychological Management in Medical Practice*, ed. Bernard Schoenberg *et al.* (New York: Columbia University Press, 1970, pp. 275–279).

3. Carol J. Barrett, "The Development and Evaluation of Three-Group Therapeutic Intervention for Widows" (Ph.D. dissertation, University for Southern California Libraries, Los Angeles, Calif., August 1974).

4. James Thomas Mathieu, "Dying and Death Role—Expectations" (Ph.D. dissertation, University of Southern California Libraries, Los Angeles, Calif., 1972).

5. Marjorie Fiske Lowenthal, *et al. Aging and Mental Disorder in San Francisco* (San Francisco: Jossey-Blass, Inc., 1967).

6. Felix Baredo, "Social Adaptation to Widowhood Among a Rural-Urban Aged Population," Washington State University, College of Agriculture, Bulletin 689 (December 1967).

CHAPTER 4. THE NEW YOU

1. Alan Paton, *For You Departed* (New York: Chas. Scribner's Sons, 1969), p. 156.

2. David K. Switzer, *The Dynamics of Grief* (Nashville and New York: Abingdon Press, 1970), p. 200.

3. Paton, *For You Departed.*

4. Helena Z. Lopata, "Grief Work and Identity Reconstruction" (unpublished paper), p. 6.

5. *Ibid.*, pp. 9–10.

6. *Ibid.*, pp. 12–14.

7. *Ibid.*, p. 16.

8. Lindemann, "Symptomatology and Management of Acute Grief," pp. 141–148.

9. Theodore Isaac Rubin, *The Winner's Notebook* (New York: Trident Press, 1967), p. 83.

10. *Ibid.*, p. 228.

11. Eugene Kennedy, *The Pain of Being Human,* (Chicago: The Thomas More Press, 1972), pp. 44–45.

12. *Ibid.*

13. Paton, *For You Departed*, p. 156.

CHAPTER 5. FINDING A NEW WORLD

1. George Santayana, "O World Thou Choosest Not the Better Part," in *Poems,* (Charles Scribner's Sons, 1923).

2. Helena Z. Lopata, *Widowhood in an American City* (Cam-

bridge, Mass.: Schenkman Publishing Company, Inc., 1973), pp. 75–77.

3. Rollo May, *Man's Search for Himself* (New York: W. W. Norton and Company, 1953), pp. 159–160.

4. *Ibid.*

5. *Ibid.*, p. 164.

6. Carl Rogers, "What it Means to Become a Person," in *The Self: Explorations in Personal Growth*, ed. Clark E. Moustakas (New York: Harper and Row, 1956), pp. 195–211.

7. Abraham H. Maslow, "Self-Actualizing People: A Study of Psychological Health," in *ibid.*, pp. 160–192.

8. Abraham H. Maslow, *The Farther Reaches of Human Nature* (New York: The Viking Press, 1971), pp. 41–53.

9. Abraham H. Maslow, *Toward a Psychology of Being*, 2nd ed. (Princeton, N.J.: Van Nostrand, 1968).

10. Erich Fromm, "The Creative Attitude," in *Creativity and Its Cultivation*, ed. Harold H. Anderson (New York: Harper and Brothers, 1959), p. 44.

11. Abraham H. Maslow, "Creativity in Self-Actualizing People," in *ibid.*, pp. 93–94.

12. *Ibid.*, p. 84.

13. Fromm, "The Creative Attitude," in *ibid.*, pp. 48–54.

14. Maslow, *Farther Reaches of Human Nature*, p. 57.

15. Lynn Caine, "How to Be an Optimist Now," *Vogue* Magazine (January 1975), p. 106.

CHAPTER 6. THE BEST TIME OF THE YEAR

1. Lindemann, "Symptomatology and Management of Acute Grief," pp. 141–148.

2. Peter Marris, *Widows and Their Families*, (London: Routledge and Paul, 1958).

3. Colin Murray Parkes, *Bereavement* (New York: International Universities Press, Inc., 1972), p. 22.

4. N. W. Clerk, *A Grief Observed* (Greenwich, Conn.: The Seabury Press, 1963), p. 8.

5. Daryl Lembke, "Valium: All Is Not Tranquil as Use Grows," *Los Angeles Times* (February 11, 1975), Part I, pp. 1, 12, 13.

6. *Ibid.*

7. Herbert A. deVries, *Vigor Regained* (Englewood Cliffs, N.J.: Prentice-Hall, 1974), pp. 26–28.

8. *Ibid.*, p. 22.

9. *Ibid.*, p. 37.

10. *Ibid.*, p. 26.

11. *Ibid.*, p. 30.

12. Lindemann, "Symptomatology and Management of Acute Grief," *op. cit.*

13. Josef P. Hrachovec, M.D., *Keeping Young and Living Longer: How to Stay Active and Healthy Past 100* (Los Angeles: Sherbourne Press, Inc., 1972), p. 78.

14. *Ibid.*, pp. 82–83.

15. Carol Powers and the editorial staff of the American Association of Retired Persons and the National Retired Teachers Association, *Your Retirement Widowhood Guide* (Long Beach, Calif.: AARP and NRTA), p. 17.

16. DeVries, *Vigor Regained*, p. 71.

17. Josef P. Hrachovec, *Keeping Young and Living Longer*, p. 64.

18. *Ibid.*, p. 89.

19. DeVries, *Vigor Regained*, pp. 68–77.

20. Rose Dosti, "Dietline—It's How You Eat That Really Counts," *Los Angeles Times* (April 11, 1974), Part VI, p. 2.

21. Hrachovec, *Keeping Young and Living Longer*, pp. 69–77.

22. Edmund Jacobson, *Progressive Relaxation* (Chicago: University of Chicago Press, 1938).

23. DeVries, *Vigor Regained*, pp. 55–57.

24. *Ibid.*

CHAPTER 7. A NEW WORLD OF PEOPLE

1. Lopata, "Grief Work and Identity Reconstruction."

2. *Ibid.*

3. Baredo, "Social Adaptation to Widowhood."

4. *Ibid.*

5. *Ibid.*

6. *Ibid.*

7. James A. Peterson, Theodore Hadwen, and Aili Larson, *A Time for Work, A Time For Leisure: A Study of Retirement Community In-Movers*, unpublished paper, University of Southern California, Los Angeles, Calif., 1968.

8. The Sierra Club is a committed group of some 80,000 persons of all ages who are dedicated to the preservation of our natural resources and beauty. This group encourages searching discussion of

environmental issues, the enjoyment of nature, and group advocacy. Many concerned persons have found lifelong friends as well as rewarding activity in this organization. Of course some of the same types of rewards come from participation in such organizations as the Wilderness Society.

9. Parents Without Partners is a national organization of single parents who come together so that their children will have some experiences with adults of the opposite sex from their parent. The organization also stresses social activities for members as well as broadening the social contacts of the children.

CHAPTER 8. YOU AND YOUR FAMILY

1. James A. Peterson, *On Being Alone, AIM's Guide for Widowed Persons* (Washington D.C.: Action for Independent Maturity, 1974), p. 3.

2. Marvin B. Sussman, "Relationships of Adult Children with Their Parents in the United States," in *Social Structure and the Family: Generational Relations*, eds. Ethel Shanas and Gordon F. Streib (Englewood Cliffs, N.J.: Prentice-Hall, Inc. 1965), p. 91.

3. Baredo, "Social Adaptation to Widowhood."

4. Peterson, *A Time for Work, A Time for Leisure*, p. 4.

5. *Ibid.*, pp. 54–56.

6. Gordon F. Streib and Wayne E. Thompson, "The Older Person in a Family Context," in *Handbook of Social Gerontology*, ed. Clark Tibbits (Chicago: University of Chicago Press, 1960).

7. Lopata, *Widowhood in an American City*, p. 147.

8. *Ibid.*

9. *Ibid.*, p. 273.

10. *Ibid.*

11. *Ibid.*, p. 121.

12. Barbara P. Payne (Informal Interview with the Authors), September 1973.

13. Peterson, Hadwen, and Larson, *A Time for Work, A Time for Leisure*, pp. 57–58.

14. Lopata, *Widowhood in an American City*, pp. 169–170.

15. *Ibid.*, p. 175.

16. *Ibid.*, p. 148.

17. *Ibid.*, pp. 174–175.

18. *Ibid.*, p. 91.

19. *Ibid.*, p. 175.

20. Peterson, *On Being Alone*, p. 4.

21. Harold H. Anderson, "Creativity as Personality Develop-ment," in *Creativity and Its Cultivation*, p. 130.

22. St. Paul the Apostle, "A Digression on Charity," I Corinthians 13; verses 4 through 7, in *Catholic Family Edition of the Holy Bible* (New York: John H. Crawley and Company, Inc., 1953), p. 212.

23. Alan Paton, *For You Departed*, p. 156.

CHAPTER 9. THE GROWTH OF THE SPIRIT

1. Job 30: 19–31.

2. Job 38: 4.

3. Job 21:7.

4. Psalm 23: 1–4.

5. John 14: 1.

6. Henry Wadsworth Longfellow, *The Psalm of Life*.

7. Alfred Lord Tennyson, "Crossing the Bar" in *In Memoriam*.

8. James Thomas Mathieu, "Dying and Death Role-Expectations" (Ph.D. dissertation, USC Library, Los Angeles, 1972).

9. Psalm 121: 1.

CHAPTER 10. TO SLEEP ALONE OR . . .

1. Jessie Bernard, *Remarriage* (New York: Dryden Press, 1956).

2. William J. Goode, *After Divorce* (Glencoe, Ill.: The Free Press, 1956).

CHAPTER 11. NOT BY BREAD ALONE, BUT . . .

1. Joseph Newman (directing editor), *Teach Your Wife How to Be a Widow* (Washington, D.C.: Books by U.S. News & World Report, 1973), pp. 22–23.

2. Lynn Caine, *Widow* (New York: William Morrow and Co., 1974) p. 90.

3. *Ibid.*

4. *Ibid.*

5. *Ibid.*

6. *Ibid.*, p. 91.

7. Newman, *Teach Your Wife How to Be a Widow*, p. 191.

8. Peterson, *On Being Alone*, p. 8.

9. Caine, *Widow*, p. 128.

10. Peterson, *On Being Alone*, pp. 8–9.

11. *Ibid.*

12. "A Divorcee Who's Just Begun to Fly," *Los Angeles Times* (May 27, 1975), Part IV, pp. 1 and 8.

13. Peterson, *On Being Alone*, p. 10.

14. Carol Powers and the editorial staff of the American Association of Retired Persons and the National Retired Teachers Association, *Your Retirement Widowhood Guide*, p. 28.

CHAPTER 12. LIFE CAN BE FULFILLING

1. John Steinbeck, *East of Eden* (New York: The Viking Press, 1952), dedication.

2. Caine, *Widow*, p. 68.

3. *Ibid.*, p. 113.

4. *Ibid.*, p. 114.

5. *Ibid.*, pp. 120–121.

6. *Ibid.*

7. "What We Expect and What It's Like," *Psychology Today* (August 1975), pp. 29–30.

8. From a news interview of the senior author, May 1973.

9. From a news interview of Vern L. Bengtson, September, 1973.

10. From a news interview of James E. Birren, January, 1972.

11. Sharon Curtin, "Flexing Selfhood—New Stature for Older Women," *Los Angeles Times* (May 23, 1974), Part IV, p. 1.

12. *Ibid.*

13. Georgie Anne Geyer, "Even at 40—Life Can Be Bountiful," *Los Angeles Times* (June 3, 1975), Part IV, p. 1.

14. Martin Grotjahn, *Beyond Laughter* (New York: McGraw-Hill, Blakiston Division, 1957), p. ix.

15. Elaine Cumming and William E. Henry, *Growing Old: The Process of Disengagement* (New York: Basic Books, 1961).

16. Jane Gunther, "How to Survive Widowhood," *Reader's Digest* (June 1975), p. 186.

17. Marshall Berges, "Home Q and A: Adela Rogers St. Johns," *Los Angeles Times Home Magazine* (February 16, 1975), p. 21.

18. Mrs. John S. Peck, "Life in These United States," *Reader's Digest* (September 1975).

BIBLIOGRAPHY

ADAMS, CHARLOTTE, *Housekeeping After Office Hours*. New York: Harper and Brothers, 1953.

American Institute for Economic Research. *How to Avoid Financial Tangles*. Great Barrington, Mass. 02130. $3.00 per set.

Section A
Elementary Property Problems and Important Financial Relationships, 1973 $1.00

Section B:
Taxes, Gifts, and Help for the Widow, 1973. $1.00

Section C:
The Harvest Years Financial Plan, 1971. $1.00
A thorough, though sometimes technical, text that can help with every aspect of your economic life.

CHAMPAGNE, MARION G. *Facing Life Alone: What Widows and Divorcees Should Know*. Indianapolis: Bobbs Merrill, 1964.

FANNING, JOHN, and GEORGE SULLIVAN. *Work When You Want to Work*. New York: Macmillan Company, Collier Books, 1969.

GIAMMATEI, HELEN, and KATHERINE SLAUGHTER. *Help Your Family Make a Better Move.* Garden City, N.Y.: Doubleday, Dolphin, 1968.

Institute of Life Insurance. *A Discussion of Family Money, How Budgets Work and What They Do. Money in Your Life.* 277 Park Avenue, New York, N.Y. 10017. (Free upon request.)

KUTNER, LUIS. *The Intelligent Woman's Guide to Future Security.* New York: Dodd, Mead, 1970.

MIELKE, ARTHUR W. *Through the Valley.* New York: Association Press, 1976.

Public Affairs Pamphlets. *How to Cope with Crisis.* 1971. 381 Park Avenue South, New York, N.Y. 10016. (25¢)

SCOBEY, JOAN, and LEE MCGRATH. *Creative Careers for Women.* New York, Simon and Schuster, Essandess paperback, 1968.

U. S. Department of Labor. "Job-Finding Techniques for Mature Women" (pamphlet). Women's Bureau. Superintendent of Documents. *Government Printing Office* Washington, D.C. 20401. (30¢)

WINTER, ELMER. *Women at Work—Every Woman's Guide to Successful Employment.* New York: Simon and Schuster 1967.

BASIC BOOKS ON FACING THE FACT OF DEATH

BOWMAN, L. *The American Funeral: A Way of Death.* New York: Paperback Library 1964.

BRIM, O. G., ed. *The Dying Patient.* New York: Russell Sage Foundation 1970.

FEIFEL, H., ed. *The Meaning of Death.* New York: Blakiston Division, McGraw-Hill, 1959.

FULTON, R. L., ed. *Death and Identity.* New York: Wiley, 1965.

GLASER, B.G., and STRAUSS, A. L. *Awareness of Dying.* Chicago: Aldine, 1965.

GORER, G. *Death, Grief, and Mourning.* Garden City, New York: Anchor Books, 1967.

HINTON, J., *Dying.* Baltimore: Penguin Books, 1967.

KASTENBAUM, R. "Time and death in Adolescence." In H. Feifel, *The Meaning of Death,* New York: McGraw-Hill, 1959.

LINDEMANN, E. "Symptomatology and Management of Acute Grief," reprinted in *Death and Identity,* ed. Robert Fulton, page 186.

TOYNBEE, A. *et al. Man's Concern with Death.* New York: McGraw-Hill, 1969.

INDEX

Adams, Franklin Pierce, 83
Andrus Gerontology Center, 48
alcoholism, as related to widows, 89
adjustment to loss as a widow:
  through subjective grief work, 46
  the identity crisis, 55
  adjustment and freedom, 64
  through self-actualization, 70
  through creativity, 77
  through new social contacts, 119
  financial adjustments, 185
Auden, W. H., 227

Baredo, Felix, 47, 112, 113, 185
Barrett, Carol, 36, 37, 39, 46

Bengtson, Vern, 176
Berges, Marshall, 221
bereavement, for widows:
  physical effects, 85
  alcoholism, 88
  drugs, 87
  health, 91–107
  loneliness, 109
Bernard, Jessie, 102
Birren, James, 220
blood pressure, controls, 47

Caine, Lynn, 81, 82, 192
cholesterol levels, and health, 39
church relationships of widows, 77
continuous education and widows, 210

CRUSE (widows' groups in England), 39
Cumming, Elaine, 224
Curtin, Sharon, 210

Dante's "Inferno," 162
Darwin, Charles, 162
dating, for the widow, 123, 124
de Vries, Herbert, and exercise, 93
drugs, use in bereavement, 87

exercise, in relation to widows' health, 92

family and the widow:
    changing structure, 8
    supports for widows, 183
freedom, achieving personal, 64
Fromm, Erich, 77, 78

Geyer, Georgie Anne, 223
Goode, William, 172
Grotjahn, Martin, 224
grief work, 40ff.
Gunther, Jane, 225

Harris, Lois, 218
housing:
    alternatives for widows, 115, 116
    retirement communities, 116

hypertension, in widows, 102, 189

incidence:
    of widows, 7
    of widowers, 7

Jacobson, Edmund, 105
Jesus, philosophy of, 159, 164
job, losses and adjustment, 152–55, 166
job training, for widows, 209
Journey's End Foundation, 48
Journey's End (film), 48

Kennedy, Eugene, 57
Kuhn, Maggie, 178

La Rochefoucauld, François de, 47
Lempke, Daryl, 88
Lindemann, Eric, 32, 56, 85
London, Perry, 101
Lopata, Helena Z., 52, 53, 54, 64, 65, 109, 145
Lowenthal, Marjorie, 42
Luther, Martin, 156

Maris, Peter, 85
Marston, Albert, 101
Maslow, Abraham H., 71, 72, 73, 74, 75, 77, 78
Mathieu, James, 38, 39

May, Rollo, 65, 66, 68
menopause, in relation to widows, 91

nutrition and widows' health, 95

Parents Without Partners, 120
Parks, Colin Murray, 85
Paton, Alan, 49
Paul, the Apostle, 150
Payne, Barbara, 144
Peterson, James A., 17
physical health, and widowhood, 82, 93
probate, for widows, 198

relaxation, for widows, 103
remarriage for widows, 169
Rogers, Carl, 70, 71
role losses of widows:
  loss of mate, 28
  loss of friends, 28
  loss of social status, 28
Roosevelt, Eleanor, 82
Rubin, Theodore Isaac, 56, 57

Santayana, George, 63
Schoenberg, Bernard, 32
sex and widowhood:
  communal living, 177
  polygamy, 178

remarriage, 169
singleness, 176
Shakespeare, William, 55
self-esteem, and widowhood, 60
Shepherd Center (Kansas City), 166
Sierra Club, and recreation, 120
Socrates, philosophy of, 55, 158
Steinbeck, John, 212
Sussman, Marvin, 135

taxes for widows:
  gift tax, 197
  income tax, 195
  inheritance tax, 196
Tennyson, Alfred, Lord, 159
tranquilizers, and tension, 88

volunteer work, and the widow, 207

weight control for the widow, 98
Widowed Persons Service, 120
widows:
  and adolescents, 130–34
  and affairs, 143, 144
  and children, 129
  and families, 133, 134
  and grandchildren, 143, 144
  and living arrangements, 137, 138
  and money, 180
wills and widowhood, 199

ABA/NACS Category: 372, Sociology—Marriage & Family   1897-4 $7.95

WIDOWS AND WIDOWHOOD

A Creative Approach to Being Alone

by James A. Peterson and Michael P. Briley

CONTENTS

1. The Sign on the Mantel
2. The Numbing Aloneness
3. Working Through the Separation
4. The New You
5. Finding a New World
6. The Best Time of the Year
7. A New World of People
8. You and Your Family
9. The Growth of the Spirit
10. To Sleep Alone *Or* . . .
11. Not By Bread Alone, *But* . . .
10. Life Can Be Fulfilling

ABOUT THE AUTHORS

DR. JAMES A. PETERSON is director of liaison services at the Ethel Percy Andrus Gerontology Center, University of Southern California. A past president of the American Association of Family Life and Marriage Counselors, he is the author of *Married Love in the Middle Years*, and co-author of *Love in the Later Years*, both published by Association Press. MICHAEL P. BRILEY specializes in writing on the social and behavioral sciences, the health sciences, and gerontology. He has conducted the column, "What the Doctors Say," in *Modern Maturity* magazine.

Cover design by Jane Sterrett

291 Broadway   ASSOCIATION PRESS   New York, N.Y. 10007

PRINTED
IN
U.S.A.

Date Due